Table of Contents

ACKNOWLEDGEMENTS

I would like to take this opportunity to thank first of all, the Almighty God, from whom originated the revelation embedded in this book. Without Him, this publication would not have been possible. All good and perfect gifts come from God. I would also like to thank Bishop Dominic Newlove Allotey of Living Faith International Church; for all that the Lord has used him to do in my life. Bishop, your powerful messages over the years have been a tremendous blessing to me.

Then also, I would like to thank Bishop E.O. Ansah of Kingdom Life Ministries International, London England, my spiritual father. It all started with you. I remember the day I told you about how the Holy Spirit, through the scriptures, revealed Christ Jesus to me. You demonstrated the heart of a father by encouraging me to know that revelation knowledge is a gift from God. Imagine if you had said otherwise, maybe this book would not have been published. Thank you very much for leaving an indelible mark on my life. I learned so much from you. May God continue to bless and expand your territory.

To my senior Pastor, brother, and confidant, Christie.Y. Smith of Revival Christian Center: I love you dearly, and I thank God for giving my family and me the opportunity to be a part of your family.

I am also saying a big thank you to Henry Ayensu and Elsie Osae Kwapong, for your ministerial support through your monthly publication, Adonai magazine, which is helping to expand the Kingdom of God on earth. Thank you very much, Franklin Kyei, for your prompt and efficient proofreading and editing of this book. I couldn't have done it without you.

To all my friends especially, Valli Manley (you are so special), I am saying thank you for your friendship. To my church family at Living faith International Church, my co-workers at Hospital for Special Surgery, and all my students, past, present, and future: I am saying a big thank you for enriching my life in one way or the other.

Finally, to my lovely wife, best friend, and partner, Becky Ama Tutu; I say thank you very much for your unflinching love and support during those long nights of studies. God bless you. Thanks also to you, my children; for your understanding and co-operation whilst I was engaged in writing this book. May the Almighty God continue to bless everyone mentioned on this page. I pray that you will enjoy reading this book. God bless you all.

Introduction

The kingdom of God is a doctrine, which has been misunderstood by many professed Christians. This doctrine was the sole message of our Lord Jesus Christ when He walked this Earth. He spent most of His ministerial life explaining what the kingdom of God can be likened to. The first sermon Jesus preached as recorded in Mark 1:15 was, " Repent for the kingdom of God is at hand..." He went about the cities and towns preaching and demonstrating the kingdom of God to all who were hungry for righteousness. During one of His ministrations, Jesus made an astounding statement with the claim, "*...the kingdom of God comes not with observation: ...for behold the kingdom of God is within you.*" He emphatically said the kingdom of God is not visible to the naked eye, whereby one can see it, but it is a way of living or lifestyle, which emanates from within the hearts of men. This means the kingdom of God is simply the reign of God in the hearts of those who have accepted Jesus Christ as their Savior, Lord and King.

He also revealed that there are mysteries of the kingdom of God, which have been given to those who have chosen to receive the kingdom in their hearts. The heart of man is, therefore, the seat of the government of the kingdom of God. So the effects and benefits of the kingdom have to come from within. All the blessings; prosperity, success, healing, and deliverance are supposed to come out from within us. When the bible says in Ephesians 1:3 that God has blessed us with all spiritual blessings in heavenly places in Christ Jesus, it was making reference to the kingdom of God within the hearts of those that are born again. These spiritual blessings, according to Dr. Tony Evans of Oak Cliff Bible Fellowship Church in Dallas Texas, are not an offer of cotton candy happiness. Cotton candy is very sweet, but it doesn't last.

When you put it in your mouth, it melts soon after. Its longevity is short-lived. He said the kingdoms of this world offer cotton candy. It is very sweet, but don't expect it to last long. On the other hand, spiritual blessings in the kingdom of God have to do with resources deposited on the inside of men that can over-ride circumstances on the outside. So the manifestation of these spiritual blessings begins in our hearts and then become expressed outwardly. The bible says that *"Christ in you is the hope of glory."* This means that whatever we, as Christians, are hoping for by faith is supposed to be accessed from the inside out. We have to live our Christian life, first of all, from within before it can manifest in our lives.

In life, whatever we see physically originated from the unseen or spiritual realm. Everything you see around you like houses, automobiles, electronic equipment, and others originated from someone's thoughts and imaginations before it was transmuted into reality. The bible says in Hebrews 11:3 that *"by faith we understand that the entire universe was formed at God's command, that WHAT WE NOW SEE DID NOT COME from anything that can be seen."* This scripture confirms that the universe we see was formed and manifested by unseen spiritual forces. Since God created man in His own image, and has endowed him with the same creative ability, man is also supposed to create his environment from the inside to the outside. Many people who have come to the realization of this truth have demonstrated the validity of it.

A lot of people come to mind when I consider the truthfulness of this divine principle. People like Joseph and Daniel in the bible were examples worthy of emulation. One individual of recent memory is, John Augustus Roebling, the man who designed the Brooklyn Bridge; but did not live to see the construction of it. After constructing comparatively smaller suspension bridges in other cities in the U.S.A, Mr. Roebling was given the contract to construct the Brooklyn Bridge. Against all odds and opposition that such a long suspension bridge that spans about 1600 feet across the East River is impossible, Mr. Roebling was resolute and convinced with a deep conviction that it was possible. This was

4

after the collapse of the Tacoma Narrows Bridge, a suspension bridge in Washington. Therefore, there was a lot of skepticism about the construction of such a long one like the Brooklyn Bridge.

However, John Roebling believed and nurtured that belief continually until he finally got the opportunity to demonstrate what he had believed in his heart for so long. Unfortunately, during the early days of the project, whilst conducting surveys for the construction of the bridge, Mr. Roebling had an accident which eventually led to his death. His son, Washington Roebling, had to continue with the project until he also had an accident that paralyzed him from the waist down, and consequently made him homebound. All these unfortunate circumstances did not deter the Roebling family. Emily, Washington's wife, became the one to supervise the project by carrying orders from her husband to the engineers due to Washington's disability.

The lesson and morale behind this story is that, no matter what obstacles one may face, a determined mind can never be stopped from achieving and manifesting his purpose, aspiration, and goal that have been nurtured continually in the fertile ground of the heart. The death of John Roebling and the incapacitation of his son Washington did not prevent the construction of this historic landmark; because the dream and vision of John Roebling in regards to the construction of the Brooklyn Bridge was clearly and vividly defined. Therefore, it was a matter of commitment to the cause of his father coupled with perseverance, which enabled Washington Roebling to carry through the project despite his physical disability.

The bible says in proverbs 18:14 "*The spirit of a man will sustain his infirmity.*" Although he was physically disabled, yet his inner man, the unseen human spirit, was so strong that he relentlessly persevered against all odds until success was achieved. At the time of completion, the Brooklyn Bridge in New York City was the longest suspension bridge in the world. Today, 130 years later, this historical landmark still reminds many of the power and the ability of man to accomplish whatever dream he conceives and nurtures continually in his heart. Many were the oppositions encountered by the engineers of the bridge, but with determination, conviction, and perseverance they achieved the goal, which originated from the inside. You too can achieve whatever dream you nurture and incubate from within.

About two months before this book was published, the Lord gave me an opportunity to witness personally another example of the validity of this truth. A man, whom I have the privilege to work with almost every week, invited me to my homeland of Ghana, as a volunteer at the newly constructed FOCOS Orthopedic Hospital in Accra. This trip changed my life completely and I will forever be grateful and thankful to the Almighty God for the privilege accorded me. Dr. Oheneba Boachie-Adjei is the chief surgeon of scoliosis service at the prestigious Hospital for Special Surgery in New York City. He is also Professor of orthopedic surgery at Weill Cornell Medical College. Moreover, he is the founder and president of the Foundation of Orthopedic and Complex Spine (FOCOS) of U.S.A and Ghana. Born in Kumasi,Ghana, Dr. Boachie-Adjei dreamed of becoming a physician to help others after a chronic abdominal illness almost took his life at an early age. After his recovery, he vowed at that early age to become a physician in the future to help others.

This dream burned in his heart continually and served as a guiding light, which kept him disciplined, committed, and focused until the dream was achieved. Today, more than fifty years after the conception of his dream, Dr.Boachie-Adjei is living the dream that he continually nurtured and held onto all these years. Twenty five years ago, he conceived another dream to build a modern state-of-the-art orthopedic hospital in Ghana to serve the under-privileged people of Africa. In 2012, this dream was also realized, and FOCOS Orthopedic Hospital, the first orthopedic hospital in West Africa, was inaugurated in

Accra, Ghana. During my humanitarian trip to FOCOS Orthopedic Hospital in Accra, Dr.Boachie-Adjei told me that he had nurtured the dream of constructing a well-equipped hospital in Ghana for

6

twenty five years, before it manifested and became a reality. During those nurturing years, he systematically took steps that were calculated and measured, to achieve his ultimate dream; which is the construction of the hospital where he will be able to help others. The buildings of the hospital occupy a 10 acre piece of land with enough space for expansion.

This is the essence and power of the kingdom of God in the hearts of men. There are many people who are not born again, but are practicing the principles of the kingdom with great results. The kingdom of God highlights universal principles, which can be applied by all. Jesus taught in the gospels the dynamics and workings of the kingdom to all, but only a few comprehended the truth. All throughout the bible, man is likened to a tree subjected to the prevailing elements around him. Some trees shed their leaves at certain seasons and others are evergreen. The bible says that the righteous shall flourish like a palm tree. It also says in Psalm 37:35 ***"I have seen the wicked in great power, and spreading himself like a green bay tree."*** According to these scriptures, both the righteous and the wicked are likened to trees. So you may ask, what is the basis for the comparison of man to a tree in the bible? The similarity between men and trees is that the prevailing conditions around them determine and enhance their growth. When a man is born under unfavorable conditions, it influences the quality of lifestyle he may live. Likewise, trees need favorable conditions in order to grow from a seed into a tree through a process known as photosynthesis. In the same vein, a man also needs favorable conditions to be present in order for spiritual photosynthesis to take place.

In our case studies, these men had visions and dreams, which could be likened to seeds nurtured diligently until they grew into full-blown reality. This is the theme of this book. We will take a very close look at the scriptures and uncover the elements involved in spiritual photosynthesis. Our Lord Jesus Christ taught this principle, and it is recorded in the synoptic gospels. I believe, without a shadow of doubt, that you will be tremendously blessed by the time you finish reading this must-read book. The biblical

7

principles taught in this book were applied in the presentation of this work. There are numerous instances that can be cited to support the validity of these principles. Many millionaires and rich men acquired their fortunes through the application of these biblical principles in their lives. Countless others have applied these principles to accomplish great feats. There are also many who can be counted as living testimonies of this divine truth.

The comprehension of these principles does not guarantee instant success, but rather it becomes a valuable knowledge, which will eventually yield great dividends when diligently applied to one's life. As the old adage goes, "Rome was not built in a day." Therefore, these principles would give you the tools to begin a journey, which will be very rewarding if you stick to it and apply it wholeheartedly. The Lord Jesus Christ taught many things in regard to the kingdom of God through parables, which need to be understood in order to grasp the magnitude of the kingdom of God in the lives of believers. These principles become powerful only when they are applied consistently and diligently. You are about to uncover divine truths that have been tried, tested, and proven since the beginning of time. Make a conscious effort to apply them in your life, and you will be tremendously blessed. I highly recommend that you read this book very often in order to imbibe the principles into your life. God bless you, and enjoy this gift to you.

CHAPTER 1

THE PROMISES OF GOD ARE SURE

The bible is a book of promises from God, who has proven time and time again that He is faithful. God, who created the heavens and the earth and declared the end from the beginning, has also given us assurances or promises through the knowledge of His word. These promises are available to us in His word and our knowledge of them empowers us to partake in His divine nature. They also enable us to tap into astounding spiritual principles through faith. What is a promise anyway? A promise is an expressed assurance upon which an expectation is to be based. I am very confident that we are all accustomed to promises in one way or the other.

We are also accustomed to seeing them made and broken. Anyone who has lived for a number of years would never lay claim to having kept every promise ever made. There are many reasons why this is true. Sometimes we forget, or become negligent; and at other times it may be due to circumstances beyond our control. A brokenhearted young lady I once met said to me, "But he promised to marry me", and then all of a sudden he said: "Yes, but I have changed my mind". People do change their minds, and they do break their promises; but God is a faithful promise-keeper, and He changes not.

What can we say about the promises of God? How certain or sure are they? Apostle Paul, in writing about the promises God made to Abraham, shared these words in the letter to the church of the Romans: " *For the promise that he should be heir of the world, was not to Abraham or his seed through the Law, but through the righteousness of faith . . . therefore it is of faith, that it might be by grace; to the end the promise might be sure to all the seed* " (Romans 4:13, 16). This promise to Abraham was first pronounced in Genesis Chapter 12 and it was later repeated in Chapter 22:18, which says: "*And in thy seed shall all the nations of the earth be blessed; because thou hast obeyed my voice* ".

This was a promise to Abraham, which pointed to the coming of our Lord Jesus Christ through whom all nations of the world have been blessed through faith; a promise which was given thousands of years before its manifestation became a blessing to you and me, thus enabling us to partake in it through faith in the Lord Jesus Christ. Anybody who believes in his heart and confesses with his mouth that Jesus is Lord becomes a partaker of this divine promise and its consequential blessing. This, indeed, is a strong evidence that God is a promise-keeper.

Now, a promise is of no more value than the ability of the one who makes it to carry it through, and also the willingness to do so. God did carry through with His promise to Abraham that all nations would be blessed through his seed (Jesus Christ) and as a result, all people throughout the world have been adopted into God's family through Jesus Christ. Moreover, Paul pointed out in Galatians 3:16, that it was through Christ that God intended to fulfill the promise to Abraham. Also in Acts 13:32-33, the bible says: "*And we declare unto you glad tidings how that the promise which was made unto the fathers (Abraham, Isaac and Jacob), God hath fulfilled the same unto us their children, in that he hath raised up Jesus again.*" Indeed, God is a promisekeeper; a fact that is evident throughout the bible.

The study of Jesus' life, whilst He was on earth reveals that He absolutely trusted in the power of the promises of God. When Jesus said: "*I am that bread of life*", John 6:48, "*I am the light of the world* ", John 8:12, "*I am the resurrection and the life.*" John 11:25, He did so fully realizing that He had been empowered with this assertive right by the Father who had promised to raise Him from the grave. He demonstrated absolute trust in the promise of the Father to the point of laying down His life for all humanity. There were hundreds of brethren at one time who bore witness to the fulfillment of this promise, according to I Corinthians 15:3-6.

These brethren, saw Jesus when He resurrected and appeared onto them.

On the other hand, some say that, a promise is a comfort to a fool, but when it comes to the promises of God they are "Yea and Amen." God is not a man that can lie or change His mind. Whatever He says always comes to pass and He is a promisekeeping and faithful God. When God told Abraham in Genesis 15:1 "....*I am thy shield, and thy exceeding great reward"*, He implied that besides all the livestock and possessions that He (God) had blessed Abraham with, He (The Almighty God) would also protect him and all that belonged to him.

Since Abraham was a nomad moving from place to place, he needed protection from evil people who attacked travelers that had thousands of cattle, oxen and sheep. The bible tells us that Abraham lived onto a good old age and the Lord kept His word onto Abraham. Moreover, there are numerous instances in the Bible when God gave His word and then later fulfilled it. He promised Abraham to give onto his descendants the land that flows with milk and honey, and He kept His word.

Since the day that I brought forth my people Israel out of Egypt, I chose no city out of all the tribes of Israel to build an house, that my name might be therein; but I chose David to be over my people Israel. And it was in the heart of David my father to build an house for the name of the LORD God of Israel. And the LORD said unto David my father, Whereas it was in thine heart to build an house unto my name, thou didst well that it was in thine heart. Nevertheless thou shalt not build the house; but thy son that shall come forth out of thy loins, he shall build the house unto my name. And the LORD hath performed his word that he spake, and I am risen up in the room of David my father, and sit on the throne of Israel, as the LORD promised, and have built an house for the name of the LORD God of Israel" (1 kings 8:16-20). This bible passage is highlighting the intention of David to build a house where the name of the Lord would be. King Solomon, the son of King David, built the house for God in Jerusalem and if you go to Israel today, you will see the physical remains of the temple that King Solomon, a descendant of

Abraham, built to honor God. God promised David that his son (Solomon) would build the temple of the Lord God in Jerusalem, and He fulfilled that promise in the days of King Solomon.

Also, the children of Israel that God scattered all over the world have been gathered again to the promise land. Through them, God has blessed all humanity in all areas of our lives with scientific inventions. Men like Sigmund Freud, Albert Einstein and many others who have changed the world we live in with God-sent philosophies were all physical descendants of Abraham. The contributions of the Jewish people to humanity in all walks of life are also indicate that God's promises are sure. Therefore, based on these truths, we can assuredly say that God can be trusted. The bible is a sacred promise book from God, our heavenly Father, and it speaks to us in whatever situation we find ourselves. If we take the time to search the bible, we can find the answers and solutions to all our daily questions and problems. There is a divine word directed specifically to every situation and condition we encounter. Whatever we are feeling, suffering, or hoping for, the Bible has something to say about it. God is the giver of every good and perfect gift.

The bible says that, "*Whatever is good and perfect comes down to us from God our Father, who created all the lights in the heavens. He never changes or casts a shifting shadow. He chose to give birth to us by giving us his true word. And we, out of all creation, became his prized possession*". (James 1:17-18) NLT

Sometimes, it becomes very difficult to trust a promise given by someone, simply because he has a questionable character; but when a trustworthy and faithful individual gives you his word, it brings assurance. Many people have become disappointed and dismayed due to unfulfilled promises. Others have lost fortunes by trusting someone on face value without verifying their integrity base or doing the needed due diligence. A man is known by his words, therefore, if his words cannot be trusted, then he is not reliable. Trust is a virtue that is earned but not given or demanded and as such would only be developed over a period of time. In order for someone to trust you, there must be a proven record of your integrity without blemish. It takes time to build trust in someone or something. Human nature is such that the strong always prey on the weak; that is why so many people find it difficult to trust.

Do you trust or believe everything you are told? Are you considered naïve by others simply because you trust easily? Well, it is proven that people who trust easily are trustworthy and tend to assume the same for others. Unfortunately, many people find it difficult to trust in a God they cannot see. It is therefore, an act of faith to live according to the word of God.

The Bible tells us that God has given onto us ALL THINGS that pertain to life and godliness through our knowledge of Him. These things are given to us through precious promises scattered throughout the bible. There are about three thousand promises that God has given to us through the scriptures in the Old and New testaments. These promises are for the children of God to appropriate in their lives, but many just don't know how. Many are struggling in their walk with God regardless of the bountiful resources that God has placed in the earth for His children. So now the question is, how do we activate these promises of God in our lives? How do we translate these promises from the spiritual realm into the natural realm? How do we apply them to our lives?

The Bible says in the book of Ephesians 1:3 *"Blessed be the God and Father of our Lord Jesus Christ, who has blessed us with all spiritual blessings in heavenly places, in Christ"*. It is evident from this scripture that we have been blessed already in Christ Jesus. It is a done deal. It was accomplished by Jesus on the cross two thousand years ago. These blessings are already embedded in us as a result of the indwelling Christ. Everything that we need in life has already been deposited in us through Christ Jesus but we have to learn how to withdraw it.

This truth can be compared to the electrical power supply to your house. Once you are up to date in your monthly payment to the electricity company, the power supply to your house would be available. However, if you do not plug your electrical equipment and appliances into the already provided power source, the electrical supply would not benefit you. But if you connect your television, computer and refrigerator to the power source, then you can enjoy the benefits of the electricity. So also are the blessings of God to the believer. They are already deposited in Christ Jesus and it is up to us to do the withdrawals from this limitless supply of blessings, riches, prosperity, and power.

The Bible says in the book of 2 Peter 1:2-4 " *Grace and peace be multiplied to you in the knowledge of God and of Jesus our Lord, as His divine power has given to us ALL things that pertain to life and godliness, through the knowledge of Him who called us by glory and virtue, by which (calling,) have been given to us exceedingly great and precious PROMISES, that through these (promises) you may be partakers of the divine nature, having escaped the corruption that is in the world through lust.* ". This scripture is clearly indicating that God wants you to partake in His divine nature, through His promises that are given to you. The blessings of God are all embedded in the promises.

For example, God promised Abraham that all nations of the world are going to be blessed through his seed. God also promised in the days of old that a time is coming when He's going to pour His Spirit upon all flesh and write His words on the tablets of their hearts. The word of God will no longer be written on the tablets of stone, but in our hearts. He also promised that He's going to pour His Spirit upon all flesh to indwell them. In those days, He'll be able to communicate with us individually.

This promise was fulfilled in Acts 2:1-4 *"And when the day of Pentecost was fully come, they were all with one accord in one place, and suddenly there came a sound from heaven as of a rushing mighty wind and it filled the entire house where they were sitting. And there appeared unto them cloven tongues like as of fire and it sat upon each of them. And they were all filled with the Holy Ghost and began to speak in other tongues as the Spirit gave them utterance."* So, the Spirit of God that was given to us on the day of Pentecost also empowers us to partake in God's divine nature whereby we think just like the way God thinks and see things like He sees them. This does not discount the importance of statement in 2 Peter 2: 4 that predicates the experience on *"having escaped the corruption that is in the world*

14

through lust". The Spirit of Christ that lives in us also guides us into all truths. Even though the Holy Spirit indwells us, yet He doesn't impose His will on us; but allows us to exercise our God-given freewill. Therefore, the promises that God has bestowed on us, must be activated by us willingly. These are promises that even though we have the Holy Spirit, we still have to take bold and conscious steps to see them manifest in our life. The outpouring of the Holy Spirit on the day of Pentecost was one of the many promises in the bible to the believer. As a result of it, every believer has been filled with the precious Holy Spirit. It is now our responsibility to apply, activate and utilize these promises in our lives.

"But as it now is, He [Christ] has acquired a [priestly] ministry which is as much superior and more excellent [than the old] as the covenant (the agreement) of which He is the Mediator (the Arbiter, Agent) is superior and more excellent, [because] it is enacted and rests upon more important (sublimer, higher, and nobler) promises. For if that first covenant had been without defect, there would have been no room for another one or an attempt to institute another one.

However, He finds fault with them [showing its inadequacy] when He says, Behold, the days will come, says the Lord, when I will make and ratify a new

covenant or agreement with the house of Israel and with the house of Judah. It will not be like the covenant that I made with their forefathers on the day when I grasped them by the hand to help and relieve them and to lead them out from the land of Egypt, FOR THEY DID NOT ABIDE IN MY AGREEMENT WITH THEM, AND SO I WITHDREW MY FAVOR AND DISREGARD THEM, says the

Lord. For this is the covenant that I will make with the house of Israel after those days, says the Lord: I will imprint my laws upon their minds, even upon their innermost thoughts and understanding, and engrave them upon their hearts; and I will be their God, and they shall be my people. And it will nevermore be necessary for each one to teach his neighbor and his fellow citizen or each one his brother, saying, Know (perceive, have knowledge of, and get acquainted by experience with) the Lord, for all will know me, from the smallest to the greatest of them". (Hebrews8:6-11AMP).

In the preceding scripture, Apostle Paul talks about the new covenant being a better covenant than the old, where God gave the children of Israel a promise that He was taking them to the promise land; a land that flows with milk and honey, but they did not regard it. They did not understand it and, therefore, did not believe it. As a result, they were unable to activate the promise spoken to them. Now, however, God wants believers to have their minds and hearts filled with his word so that they may be able to apply and activate the promises in their lives.

In life, it is always important to learn from your mistakes and also the ones committed by others. The children of Israel heard a promise from God that He was taking them to a promise land: a land that was so rich that it flowed with milk and honey instead of rivers and streams. They doubted the word of God and failed to act upon it. They, as a result, did not benefit from the promise. It is imperative that we learn a valuable lesson from their failure or inability to actualize the promise that God gave to them. Apostle Paul said that we should learn from their mistakes, because the bible is meant for us to know the wrongs that people did in the past so that we do not repeat them or do likewise.

The bible says in 1 Corinthians 10:11 *"Now all these things happened unto them for ensamples: and they are written for our admonition..."* The events that happened to the children of Israel in the wilderness were examples for us to learn from. What they failed to do must be identified so that we do not fall prey to similar situations. It is also said in 2 Timothy 3:16 *"All scripture is given by inspiration of God, and is profitable for doctrine, for reproof, for correction, for instruction in righteousness"* So, what is it that they did that we should not repeat? Let's look at what they didn't do. Hebrews 4:2 says *"For indeed we have had the glad tidings [Gospel of God] proclaimed to us just as truly as they [the Israelites of old did when the good news of deliverance from bondage came to them]; but the message they heard did not benefit them, because it was not mixed with faith (with the leaning of the entire personality on God in absolute trust and confidence in His power, wisdom, and goodness) by those who heard it; neither were they united in faith with the ones [Joshua and Caleb] who heard (did believe)."(AMP).*

The children of Israel did not mix faith with the promise God gave them and as a result could not enter the promise land. The scripture teaches us that mistakes or things of old are examples meant for our admonition, so that we will know how to conduct ourselves when we encounter the word of God. So, it is written, "for unto us was the gospel preached as well as unto them. But, the word preached did not profit them because it was not mixed with faith in them that heard it."

The promises had been preached to us, just like it was preached to them. But, they did not benefit from it because they did not mix them with Faith. Likewise, we will not benefit from the promises if we do not mix them with faith. So, one of the things that you need to do, when you hear the word or promise of God, is to receive it with faith. You have to add faith to it. When God spoke to Abraham, he believed the word of God, and it was imputed onto him as righteousness. The promise of God has to be mixed with faith in order for it to be actualized. Peter also emphasized this truth when he was talking about the promises that God has given us in all things that pertain to life and godliness through our knowledge of Him.

2 Peter 1:2-5 says *"May grace (God's favor) and peace (which is perfect wellbeing, all necessary good, all spiritual prosperity, and freedom from fears and agitating passions and moral conflicts) be multiplied to you in [the full, personal, precise, and correct] knowledge of God and of Jesus our Lord. For His divine power has bestowed upon us all things that [are requisite and suited] to life and godliness, through the [full, personal] knowledge of Him who called us by and to His own glory and excellence (virtue). By means of these He has bestowed on us His precious and exceedingly great promises, so that through them you may escape [by flight] from the moral decay (rottenness and corruption) that is in the world because of covetousness (lust and greed), and*

become sharers (partakers) of the divine nature. For this very reason, ADDING

YOUR DILIGENCE (TO THE DIVINE PROMISES), EMPLOY EVERY EFFORT IN EXERCISING YOUR FAITH to develop virtue (excellence, resolution, Christian energy), and in [exercising] virtue [develop] knowledge (intelligence) AMP" (emphasis mine).

This scripture clearly says, beside all this, add to the promises; faith. That means when you hear the promise of God and it is seen to be relevant to whatever you are going through, you must activate that promise in your life by adding faith to the promise. On the other hand, when you don't apply faith to it, the promise will not materialize in your life because you do not believe in it. Moreover, it is not faith alone that you apply to the promise but there are other elements that you have to add to the word in order to see it manifest in your life. The Bible tells us that the word of God is an incorruptible seed and therefore as a seed, it needs nurturing and the right environment, in order to grow just like any other seed. In the natural realm, a seed doesn't grow in a vacuum. We know in the physical world that, before a seed can grow, there need to be certain conditions prevalent or present in order for the seed to grow.

For example, in order for a seed to grow, there need to be a good and fertile soil; that's first and foremost. Secondly, there needs to be moisture or water in the soil. Thirdly, there needs to be sunlight, and finally, there needs to be a farmer to keep the land from weeds. So, there must be present a good soil, moisture, sunlight and a keeper to till the land in order for a seed to grow. Also, there need to be systematic efforts applied by the farmer to ensure that unwanted vegetation does not prevent the seed from receiving the required nutrients. The Bible tells us that the words that we hear, they are spiritual seeds and the human heart is a spiritual ground where the seeds are sown. The human heart is the ground where the seed of the word of God is planted, nurtured and protected until it dies, germinates and bears fruit for us.

Jesus said *"these words that I speak unto you, they are spirit and they are life"* (John 6:63). The word of God is infused with spiritual power which can only be activated through faith. As a seed, it needs to be planted in a fertile ground of our hearts where gestation or incubation would take place. When the word of God is planted in the fertile ground of our hearts, it brings up more fruits to nourish the whole body. Also, the scripture declares that, we were saved by the incorruptible seed of the word of God. *"Being born again, not of corruptible seed, but of incorruptible, by the word of God, which lives and abides forever* (1 Peter 1:23). So if the word of God is a spiritual seed, then it means that, just as in the physical world a seed needs light, water and a good soil to grow; so also does the spiritual seed need the same light, water and a good soil in the spiritual realm to grow. In order for the spiritual seed, which is the word of God, to manifest in your life, it needs to be in a fertile ground. There need to be water and light. When these elements are present, coupled with good nurturing by man, the spiritual seed would grow and manifest in the natural or in our lives.

Thus then is how we activate the word, which contains the promises, in our lives. God is a promise and covenant keeper. He is also faithful and he watches over His words to perform them. God changes not; He is the same yesterday, today and forever. Therefore, His promises can be trusted and applied in our lives; but in order to do that, we have to know what the light of the word is, what the water of the word is, and what this good soil is; and then how and when we can apply it to our lives. Knowing and applying these principles would empower you and avail you all the good things that God has in store for you. That is why it is written in James 1:25 that whoever becomes a doer of the word shall be blessed in his deed. Remember what Peter said that grace and peace would be multiplied to us through our knowledge of God. The bible says that *"For lack of knowledge (of the promises and principles of God), my people perish"* Hosea 4:6 (Emphasis mine). The bible also says that lack of knowledge of the word of God leads to errancy and bondage – Matthew 22:29, Isaiah 5:13; but the knowledge of the promises of God would multiply onto us grace and peace. The bible says that, *"those that know their God shall*

be strong and do exploits". Knowledge of the promises of God, will also afford you the ability to discern when to apply the promises of God in your life. The most dangerous Christians that are feared by the devil are the ones that know how to deploy the word of God at the right time and place. The strategic application of the word of God is very paramount in every believer's life. Jesus once made a very profound statement about the word of God and how it needs to be received. He was telling his disciples that the word of God is not only a seed, but it is more than just a seed. It needs other things to be added to it in order for it to bear its fruit or to yield to us what it is meant to do.

CHAPTER 2

THE WORD OF GOD AS WATER

The bible says in Isaiah 55:10-11*"For as the rain and snow come down from the heavens, and return not there again, but WATER the earth and make it bring forth and sprout, that it may give seed to the sower and bread to the eater, so shall My word be that goes forth out of My mouth: it shall not return to Me void [without producing any effect, useless], but it shall accomplish that which I please and purpose, and it shall prosper in the thing for which I sent it."*

Did you hear that? This scripture said that just as the rain comes down from above and waters the earth, and causes it to bud and grow, so that it will give seed to the farmer and food to the consumer, likewise, the word of God that proceeds out of His mouth will not return to Him empty but it will cause its' assignment to manifest. This means that the word of God is also water just as it is a seed. The word of God will water your heart or ground and cause the seeds that you have planted in it to grow. The word of God will prepare and condition your heart to bring to pass the scriptures you have planted in it. It also cleanses by removing through washing all impurities out of your way. It hydrates and waters the seed of the word sown in your hearts. It takes the word of God to reinforce our faith, because faith comes by hearing the word continually. This verse also assures us of the validity and reliability of the word of God as a potential energy and force that can achieve all things when applied properly. It is the creative power of God given to man to also create his world.

Jesus came to the world to show us the right way to live, and He did that by living an exemplary life, and also by telling us about how the kingdom of God operates. Some of the tools he used in bringing this message across were illustrations, analogies and parables. Parables are stories that have double meanings. There was always the surface meaning and then the deeper meaning. The deeper meaning of a parable can only be attained either by revelation or diligent study with the help of the Holy Spirit. In these parables, He used natural elements to illustrate spiritual truths; Jesus spoke to

His audience in a way that they could understand by using illustrations and symbols to communicate spiritual truths to them. Most of the time, in order for Him to communicate effectively, He had to use things that they were familiar with as an analogy to create a picture, which demands His audience to use their imagination.

One of those parables that Jesus taught was the parable of the sower. When you analyze critically the parable of the sower, it talks about so many things. Many people have interpreted it in so many ways. There have been numerous expositions about this parable but, I thank God that He deals with each and every one of us on a different level and in a different way. The way God deals with me when I open the scriptures to read is very unique. He leads me to understand scriptures deeply beyond my own ability. God leads me by His own Spirit to scriptures that will open up other scriptures to me and give me a better understanding of what He is saying. As a result, everything eventually ties up together, and then it all fits perfectly like a puzzle. I remember very well the first time I had this experience. I was in Ghana, and I traveled from Kumasi to Accra. Whilst in Accra, I stayed in a hotel; because I just wanted, for some reason, to be alone in the hotel so I didn't even go to my family. What happened at the hotel made me aware of the reason why God wanted me to be there alone. In Ghana, most hotels have bibles in the rooms for their guests. So there was a bible by the side of the bed, and I picked it up to read. Prior to this time, I was a strong Islamic brother who never believed in Jesus as the Son of God; but rather just another prophet. So, out of curiosity, I picked up the bible to read.

Although I was born into a Christian family, I became a Muslim as some point in my life; because I was aggressively searching for the truth. I even studied the bible as a subject at some point in my life, but I only had "head knowledge" of the bible and nothing of the spirit, because the Holy Spirit of God, the author of the bible, was not my teacher. I only read the bible out of curiosity. So, at that time in my life, I didn't believe in Jesus as the Son of God, but rather I believed that we are all children of God; so how could anyone single out Jesus as the only begotten Son of God. This, therefore, is the reason why I didn't believe in Jesus Christ at that time.

Hence, when I picked up the bible to read at the hotel, the first page it opened to was the gospel of John. It went straight to the gospel of John, the Chapter 1, which reads, *"In the beginning was the Word, and the Word was with God, and the Word was God. The same was in the beginning with God. All things were made by him; and without him was not anything made that was made."* This is a scripture that I have read so many times prior to this time, but that very night, something jumped out at me and I understood that scripture with my heart; because it said *"In the beginning was the word and word was with God and the word was God". "without him was not anything made that was made."* I said to myself, "wait a minute, the word was with God and the word was God, and "without him was not anything made that was made"?

Then I went further down the page to verse 14, which says *"and the word became flesh and dwelt among men"*. So, I said, wait a minute. "The word became flesh and dwelt among men; the very word of God that was in the beginning with God became flesh and dwelt among men; all things were created by Him and without Him was not anything made that was made"? Then, right away, by the leading of the Holy Spirit, I opened the bible to the book of Genesis chapter one and looked at it; and, I realized to my amazement that, everything that God created, was just spoken or commanded into existence. And God said "let there be light", and there was light. And God said let the earth bring forth grass and it was so. Then I went through the whole chapter underlining all the phrases "and God said". Right there, something was happening to me. Afterward, I was led by the Holy Spirit to the book of Revelation 19:11-13 where it says *"And I saw heaven opened, and behold a white horse; and he that sat upon him was called Faithful and True, and in righteousness he doth judge and make war. His eyes were as a flame of fire, and on his head were many crowns; and he had a name written, that no man knew, but he himself. And he was clothed with a vesture dipped in blood: and his name is called the WORD OF GOD."* **SO, JESUS IS**

ALSO CALLED THE WORD OF GOD AND HE INCARNATED AND DWELT AMONG MEN. HE WAS WITH GOD IN THE BEGINNING AS THE WORD AND HE WAS THE

AGENT OF CREATION. ALL THINGS WERE CREATED THROUGH THE ETERNAL WORD, WHICH IS JESUS CHRIST. The Holy Spirit systematically diffused my wrong beliefs about Jesus and showed me the Christ through the pages of the bible. As a result of this revelation, I received this truth wholeheartedly and it changed my life from that very moment. This is the absolute truth; Jesus was the incarnated WORD OF GOD that lived on earth.

Right there and then, I got down on my knees by the side of the bed crying like a baby; because it was just as if some scales had fallen off my eyes because I had lived in the dark for so many years without the knowledge of this truth. Jesus Christ had been revealed to me in a very special way by the Holy Spirit. No mortal man taught me about the divinity of Jesus Christ. At that point, I didn't understand some of the basic things. But, thereafter, I realized that Jesus is the main theme of the whole Bible right from the start of Genesis up to the end of Revelation.

He was foreshadowed as the sacrificial lamb of Abraham in the book of Genesis when Abraham was asked to sacrifice his only son. He was symbolized as the Passover lamb in the book of Exodus, and the serpent of brass that was raised in the wilderness in the book of Numbers. He was also symbolized in the book of Leviticus as the scapegoat. Until God opens your eyes to see these truths, you'll think Jesus only appeared in the New Testament; but,

He goes all the way back to the Old Testament and beyond into eternity; and He can be seen in every book of the bible. When he appeared to Moses, He said I AM THAT I AM. He said that He is whatever you need Him to be. If you need healing, He is your Healer, and if you need deliverance, He is your Deliverer.

This is what He meant when He said "*I AM THAT I AM*" He is (I AM) whatever you need Him to be. Then, in the book of John, He said "*before Abraham was, I AM*" And, He also said "*I AM the light of the world... I AM the Good Shepherd... I AM the bread of life...*" Jesus is simply the same I AM THAT I AM that appeared to Moses. The great I AM. What am I talking about? It takes the Spirit of God to unveil Christ to you and to understand, that the power of God is embedded in his word which incarnated to live amongst us as the man Jesus Christ; and this very word has been given onto us to actualize and create our own worlds.

The bible says that in the beginning when God created the heavens and the earth, the first thing that He created was a seed, and the first tangible substance God gave to Adam was the seed, which was symbolic of the word of God. It says in Genesis 1:29 "*And God said, Behold, I have given you every herb bearing SEED, which is upon the face of ALL THE EARTH, and every tree, in the which is the fruit of a tree yielding SEED; to you it shall be for meat.* The seed (word of God) is meant to be our meat (provision and sustenance). The seed literally, is sown to produce food for our physical sustenance, and symbolically, it is the word of God that feeds our spiritual man. This is the reason why Jesus said in the book of Mathew that man shall not live by bread alone (physical food), but also by every word that proceeds from the mouth of God (spiritual food). Man was meant to live by the word of God in order to feed his spiritual body through which he relates to God; and physical food to feed his physical body through which he relates to his environment.

Therefore, the word of God should be treated as a treasure, a goldmine full of nuggets waiting to be dug up. These were the very words spoken to create the universe and the same words that conceived Jesus in the womb of Virgin Mary. You see, I am praying that you will be able to grasp what I'm about to teach you;

and when you do, I pray by the Spirit of God through Jesus Christ to the Father that you will run with it and incorporate it into your life.

Apply the word of God to your life on a daily basis; it will empower you to activate the promises of God which are scattered all throughout the scriptures; you will believe without a shadow of doubt that the word of God is powerful. It is quick and it is sharper than any two-edged sword; also you will know that when you have the word of God on the inside of you, nothing will be able to stand against you. Nothing will be able to prevail against you; because the power of the universe, the power that controls and sustains the universe, is living on the inside of you. Oh, hallelujah. Oh, yes! The Son of the living God is living in you; and He has given you all these promises.

Beloved, all you need to do is to believe so as to activate them in your life.

The parable of the sower

By the time you finish reading this book, your life would be totally transformed. I'm going to teach you, by the grace of God, how to activate the word of God and apply them in your life. Jesus taught about a parable which was full of precious nuggets. It is called the parable of the sower. It says that there was a sower who went about sowing the seed. As he was sowing the seed, some fell on the wayside; some fell on stony ground, some among thorns; and others on good ground. So, there were four types of soil that the seed fell on.

Some of the seed fell on the wayside, and some fell on stony ground. The third was the thorny ground, or in the midst of thorns, and the last one was the good ground. When you analyze these grounds critically, you will realize some truths; divine truths that will change your life forever. This parable reinforces some universal truths about how seeds grow. The seed was the first thing that God created on the earth

(Genesis1:11); but it did not grow, because of the absence of rain (Genesis 2:5-6).

This establishes the truth that seeds can only grow in God-ordained conditions. Do you know that in the beginning when God created the heavens and the earth, the bible says that, at some point, God did not cause rain to fall upon the earth; because there was no man to till the ground? So the seed was in the ground until the rain came.

Even though the seed was the first thing that God created on the earth, (Genesis 1:11) it did not grow because there was no rain and also no man to till the ground until God caused rain to fall. The bible says in Genesis2:5 *"**This was before there were plants on the earth. Nothing was growing in the fields because the Lord God had not yet made it rain on the earth, and there was no one to care for the plants**."* **(ERV)** So nothing was growing even though the seed was in the earth. This tells you primarily that in order for every seed to grow, as I said earlier on, there needs to be moisture or water present in order for the seed to grow. Water is a life-giving force to all created things; and also everything that God created in the beginning was in the form of a seed as we just read. We know scientifically that there is a process known as photosynthesis whereby plants use the sunlight from the atmosphere and moisture in the soil to manufacture their food.

This is the principle that Jesus taught in the parable of the sower. This parable pointed out the spiritual photosynthesis which takes place when words are sown in the hearts of men through suggestions, either by oneself or other people. Words are spiritual seeds filled with power to create the very objects contained in them and they can only grow in the right and divinely ordained environment. Words, good or bad, can only flourish in the hearts of men when given the right ingredients to enhance growth. The promises of God are embedded in his word so when you take the word of God that pertains to your need and apply it to your situation it will manifest in your life. Take the word and hold onto it until something happens. Let it gain root in your heart and nurture it continually by meditating on it until it becomes flesh and manifest in your life. Just as the earth receives seed and holds onto it until the seed goes through the ordained processes, so likewise you can hold onto a promise in the word of God until it manifests in your life. The tenacity and the persistence with which you nurture the seed of the word of God in your heart, determines the outcome it will yield to you.

Recently archeologists found a 4,000-year-old Egyptian mummy. They were amazed to find several seeds of wheat held tightly in the palm of the mummy. The mummified body had withered, but the seeds were intact, held tightly in the ancient hand. If just one of those seeds had been planted in fertile soil and allowed to go through the normal cycles of growth and reproduction for fifty years, that one seed would have been able to produce the equivalent of the annual wheat harvest of the entire world. Instead, the seed rested inert for 4,000 years; secured in the mummified hand but not accomplishing what the seed was intended to do, which is to reproduce after its kind. Unrealized potential is a tragic indictment: the legacy of what might have been.

The seed was in the withered hand of the mummy for four thousand years but did not grow; because the seed was not in its proper environment, which is conducive for growth. So, in order for a seed to grow, there needs to be water. There needs also to be light; and then finally, there needs to be a fertile good soil. Jesus used the seed as an analogy, and as a symbol to explain how the kingdom of God works. This is how the kingdom of God works: that the seeds that are scattered are not going to benefit everybody; but only those who will position themselves to be good receivers of the seed.

Only those who will be able to apply the water to the word that they hear, and those that will be able to add the light to the word they hear, are the ones that are going to taste the goodness of God. It's not for everybody. If you look in the Old Testament, when God was bringing the children of Israel out of Egypt into the promise land, they all heard of the promise or the word of God; that He was taking them to the promise land: a land that flows with milk and honey. Many of them, however, did not believe. They did not add faith to what they heard. Therefore, it did not benefit them. As a result of that, out of the two million Jews that left the land of

Egypt, only two; I mean only two people from that generation were able to enter the Promise Land. What separated those two, or what set them apart from the rest?

These two were different because, they believed in the promise that was given to the patriarchs and also the promise giver. When God was speaking about these two that entered into the promise land, He said to Moses, *"Because all those men which have seen my glory, and my miracles, which I did in Egypt and in the wilderness, and have tempted me now these ten times, and have not hearkened to my voice; Surely they shall not see the land which I swore unto their fathers, neither shall any of them that provoked me see it. But my servant Caleb, because he had another spirit with him, and hath followed me fully, him will I bring into the land whereinto he went; and his seed shall possess it"* (Numbers 14:22-24).

The children of Israel did not believe the promise that God was taking them to the land that flows with milk and honey, but rather believed the negative report the ten spies brought about the land. God commanded Moses saying *"Send thou men that they may search the land of Canaan, which I give unto the children of Israel: of every tribe of their fathers shall ye send a man, everyone a ruler among them".*

(Numbers 13:1-2). When these men returned, ten of them had a bad report but Joshua and Caleb who had believed the promise of God, said unto the people *"The land, which we passed through to search it is an exceeding good land. If the Lord delight in us, then he will bring us into this land, and give it us; a land which floweth with milk and honey. Only rebel not ye against the Lord, neither fear ye the people of the land; for they are bread for us: their defence is departed from them, and the Lord is with us: fear them not"* These men had absolute faith in God and His promise unlike the others who believed what they saw instead of what God has said. Obviously, the ten spies walked by sight and not by faith in the word of God.

On the other hand, Joshua and Caleb had a different spirit in them that caused them to speak what they believe. It is called the spirit of faith. Apostle Paul said *"We having the same spirit of faith, according as it is written, I believed, and therefore have I spoken; we also believe, and therefore speak;"* **(2 Corinthians 4:13).** These two men (Joshua and Caleb) had the spirit of faith. They believed the promise and therefore they spoke according to what they believed. Believing with your heart and declaring with your mouth what you have believed, is called the spirit of faith. So, they had the spirit of faith. They believed the word of God and then they spoke based on what they had believed. The bible says this act pleased the Lord so much that He spared their lives and as a result, they were the only two, out of the two million Jews, that entered into the promise land.

They applied their faith to the promise they heard from God. They added water. They added the light. They added all these elements to the seed that they received; and when these things were added to the seed that they received, it germinated and bore fruit for them.

In the same way, every word of God that you will treat as a seed, that you receive into your heart, and then add the water and light of the word to, will bear fruit just as God has promised. As the rain comes from above and waters the earth and causes it to bud and grow, so shall the word that has proceeded out of the mouth of God not return unto Him void, but rather, it shall accomplish whatever it was sent to do. So, if you treat the word of God as a seed, which it is, then you can add certain elements to it to make the seed grow without being choked; without being trampled upon; without being on a shallow or stony ground; and it will surely yield fruit for you.

So now, with this in mind, let us examine the parable of the sower. What did Jesus mean by it? A parable is simply a story, an illustration using earthly things that we are all familiar with to explain spiritual truth. The word parable means double meaning. There is the obvious surface meaning of a parable and then there is a deeper spiritual meaning hidden from the casual listener. It is a style of teaching where truth is hidden from the casual listener who can only discover this truth when it is diligently sought. Parables work with the premise that; no knowledge is yours until you discover it with the inspiration of the Holy Spirit. So a parable was for those who were really serious about understanding what Jesus was saying.

Jesus said something so profound about this parable. He said if you do not understand this parable, how can you understand any other parable? We are going to examine what he meant also by that statement, so you will understand why this parable is the key to all parables. All the parables that Jesus taught was just a way of illustrating to us how the kingdom of God works. If this parable is the key to all parables, then it is the key to how the kingdom of God works. I believe that by the time you finish reading this book, your life would never be the same, and I pray that the Spirit of God would open the eyes of your understanding to comprehend these spiritual truths. The word of God has not lost its power, because our God changes not. He's the same yesterday, today, and forever. If He did it yesterday, He will do it again today; and He's going to do it again tomorrow. He is a promise and covenant-keeping God who is faithful through and through.

Let's look into the scripture. I'm taking this scripture from the Gospel of Mark chapter four. It is about the Parable of the Sower .This parable is filled with great nuggets, which we're going to dissect, taking each one of them at a time. Jesus said that, "*He who hears my words and does them is like a wise man who builds his house (life) upon a rock (the principles taught by Jesus).*" Meaning, the application of the word of God that we know, understand, and believe, is a spiritual key that unlocks all doors.

Also, the application of the word is more important than just hearing it. So, now, let's go to the scriptures and you'll see what Jesus' teaching is all about. Mark 4:1-9. "*And he began again to teach by the sea side: and there was gathered unto him a great multitude, so that he entered into a ship, and sat in the sea; and the whole multitude was by the sea on the land. And he taught them many things by parables, and said unto them in his doctrine, Hearken; Behold, there went out a sower to sow: And it came to pass, as he sowed, some fell by the way side, and the fowls of the air came and devoured it up. And some fell on stony ground, where it had not much earth; and immediately it sprang up, because it had no depth of earth: But when the sun was up, it was scorched; and because it had no root, it withered away. And some fell among thorns, and the thorns grew up, and choked it, and it yielded no fruit. And other fell on good ground, and did yield fruit that sprang up and increased; and brought forth, some thirty, and some sixty, and some an hundred. And he said unto them, He that hath ears to hear, let him hear"*

This parable is talking about how the sower, sows the word in the hearts of men. It says that some seed fell on the wayside, some fell on stony ground, some fell in thorns, and others fell on good ground. First of all, how many grounds did Jesus speak about? We will answer that question later; but for now, let us analyze this parable. So you ask yourself, 'Why would anybody go out to sow and then sow on the wayside? Or, why would somebody sow on the stony ground, or sow in thorns?' This is how it happened. The land of Israel is described as a land of various landscapes. It has hills and valleys, streams and rivers, coastal plains, and plateaus. With such a variety of soil types and climate zones, including parched desert in the south, and snowy mountains in the north, this land produced a remarkable variety of crops. When God heightened the expectation of the children of Israel about the promise land, He spoke of it as a very good land. *"For the LORD your God brings you into a good land, a land of brooks of water, of fountains and depths that spring out of valleys and hills; A land of wheat, and barley, and vines, and fig trees, and pomegranates; a land of oil olive, and honey;*

This scripture specifically mentions seven agricultural products namely: wheat, barley, vines, figs, pomegranates, olive and honey. These were some of the seeds that were capable of growing in the promise land. Since they didn't have mechanized farming in those days, the sower would have the seeds in a bag slung around his neck or in the fold of his garment. He then dipped his hand in the bag, takes some seeds and scatters them by throwing them carelessly. In so doing, some would fall on good ground and others did not. This is the idea or the mental picture that Jesus wants you to imagine. Some of these seeds needed different methods of planting. For example, barley grains were simply scattered abroad;

but wheat seeds, however, needed covering that was provided by being trodden down by yoked animals or by plowing of the field. The bible often refers to sowing, reaping, winnowing, threshing, and grinding of these grains. All these activities involved a lot of human effort that were added to the cultivation and harvest of these crops. In the same way, the word of God demands a lot of human effort to manifest physically.

When God gives promises to us, he speaks to all of us through the bible; but then, how we receive the promise, or how we hear the word, is what determines what we will do, and also get out of it. The things that we do with what we hear, will determine what will come out of it. As we continue, you will realize that Jesus will be teaching us in this context: our ability to receive the word in a proper and correct way, would determine how we apply the word of God in our life.

Jesus said something that was so profound. He said, "If you do not understand this parable, you will never understand any of the parables. Then also, "... *he said unto them, He that hath ears to hear, let them hear"*. What do you mean by that, Jesus? *"He that hath ears to hear, let 'em hear."* Do not all of us have ears? Yes, we all have ears but some are spiritually deaf. So what did He mean by saying, *"He that hath ears to hear, let them hear"*? Was Jesus implying that not everyone that hears the Word of God has the ability to comprehend what is heard?

Whatever He meant can only be ascertained when we consider the whole context, and so take note of this verse. *"And when he was alone, they that were about him with the twelve asked of him the parable. And he said unto them, Unto you it is given to*

know the mystery of the kingdom of God: but unto them that are without, all these things are done in parables: THAT SEEING THEY MAY SEE, AND NOT

PERCEIVE; AND HEARING THEY MAY HEAR, AND NOT UNDERSTAND;

lest at any time they should be converted, and their sins should be forgiven them. And he said unto them, Know ye not this parable?

And how then will ye know all parables? The sower soweth the word. And these are they by the way side, where the word is sown; but when they have heard, Satan cometh immediately, and taketh away the word that was sown in their hearts". Jesus explained to his disciples the reason behind the usage of parables as a teaching instrument. He said all these things are spoken in parables so that *"seeing they may see but they not perceive, and hearing they may hear and not understand"*. He said that the reason why He spoke in parables was to conceal the truth from the casual or lazy listener.

Perception is something that mostly comes from revelation. It is knowledge that resides beyond the senses. To perceive is to recognize, discern, envision or understand. Perception is a revelation and not an act of visualization. So this is the reason why Jesus spoke to them in parables; because there are people that hear but don't understand, and there are that that see but don't perceive. So what did He mean when He said, *"He who hath ears to hear, let them hear."*? What he meant was that he that have ears to hear and understand, let him hear and understand or he that have eyes to see and perceive, let him see and perceive; because, when you hear and do not understand, it does not benefit you.

A person truly hears when he understands what he has heard. Understanding, therefore, brings clarity which is the first law of learning and it comes from God. That's why he said, *"Unto you, it is given to know (understand) the mystery of the kingdom of God."*; but onto them that are without or outside of the kingdom, this is given to them in parables so that seeing they may see and not perceive and hearing they may hear and not understand. Unless it is given to you by revelation to know the mystery of the kingdom of God, you will hear, but will not understand, and you will see, but not perceive.]

CHAPTER 3

SPIRITUAL UNDERSTANDING GIVES LIGHT

So the first thing you should strive to attain when you hear the word of God is the ability to grasp the hidden and concealed message behind the word. The bible says in Colossians 1:9 *"For this cause we also, since the day we heard it, do not cease to*

pray for you, and to desire that ye might be filled with the knowledge of his will in all wisdom and SPIRITUAL UNDERSTANDING". Grasping the spiritual understanding of the word is like receiving the word of God in a whole new perspective that you haven't seen before. This is the moment when the Holy Spirit quickens the word of God in your human spirit and gives it special significance to you personally, thus making it very applicable in your life. Many people will hear the same message, but will come up with different interpretations. It takes illumination from God to understand His word. It has to be given to you. So when Jesus said that *"unto you it is given to know the mystery of the kingdom of God,"* he was making reference to the fact that it takes the illumination of the Spirit to understand spiritual things.

The Holy Spirit has given to Christians, the ability to comprehend spiritual truths but to the unbeliever it is not given. Apostle Paul prayed in Ephesians 1:17-18 *"That the God of our Lord Jesus Christ, the Father of glory, may give unto you the spirit of wisdom and revelation in the knowledge of him: that the eyes of your*

UNDERSTANDING BEING ENLIGHTENED; that ye may know..." Paul is telling us in this passage that revelation knowledge comes from God. Only God can give you knowledge through divine revelation. In life, there are three kinds of knowledge, namely: Formal knowledge, which comes from formal education whereby get formal educational knowledge such as in the social sciences, physics, chemistry and economics. Then there is experiential knowledge that comes from life experiences and the lessons they teach us; and finally, there is revelation knowledge, which comes from God. There are things that only God can reveal to you; therefore, revelation knowledge comes from the father of all creation. It is important to pray for revelation knowledge, which the Holy Spirit gives freely unto all who ask. Jesus said to the disciples in John 16:12-13, *"I have yet many things to say unto you, but ye cannot bear them now. Howbeit when he, the Spirit of truth, is come, he will guide you into all truth: for he shall not speak of himself; but whatsoever he shall hear, that shall he speak: and he will shew you things to come"*

This, He said in reference to the Holy Spirit who was not yet poured on all flesh; and when the outpouring happens, He brings revelation knowledge from Jesus to believers. So when you hear the word, strive to have an understanding of it; because the Holy Spirit has been commissioned to bring revelation knowledge to the saints. The understanding of the word of God would bring illumination, and give you the ability to appropriate it in your life. This can be attained by asking questions and searching the scriptures to connect the dots.

The bible says, *"The sower soweth the word."* I like what it says in the book of Luke 8:11which is Luke's account of the same parable. It says, *"Now…The seed is the word of God."* So, wait a minute. *"The seed is the word of God."* This parable talks about the process of sowing the seed of his word in the hearts of men, either by yourself or by others. This occurs when we hear the word of God through teaching, preaching, or reading. As we hear the word, the four categories of soils are the four types of heart conditions or hearts of people that received the word and how they heard it; and also, what they'll do with what they've heard. What you do with the seed, which has been encoded to reproduce after its' kind, when planted in the right circumstances, would determine the benefits you will derive from it.

Jesus proceeded to explain the parable by saying in Mark 4:15. *"And these are they by the way side, where the word is sown; but when they have heard, Satan cometh immediately, and taketh away the word that was sown in their hearts."* In this instance, when you hear the word of God; immediately, Satan comes and takes it out of your heart. He comes to steal the word that was heard. Wait a minute! If Satan can come and take away the word of God immediately, then why do we have to hear the word of God? If that's the case, then it's of no use hearing the word. Far from that; the Scriptures are always self-explanatory. When you read the account of Matthew, it sheds more light and brings clearer understanding about this scripture. The devil doesn't just come and steal what is heard; but rather he does so under certain prevailing condition. What is this condition?

It says in Mathew 13:19, *"When any one hears the word of the kingdom, and UNDERSTANDS it not, then cometh the wicked one, and catches away that which was sown in his heart. This is he which received seed by the way side."* So anyone hearing the word of the kingdom, and understanding it not, empowers the wicked one to come and steal it. This was the situation of the one that received seed by the way side. The one, who heard the word of God, but did not understand it, had it stolen from him by the devil. When you hear the word of God and don't understand it with your heart, the enemy will come and steal it from you. Until you understand and believe the truth in your heart, it is just a mere information in your mind. Satan cannot steal the word from your heart unless you do not understand it; but why is understanding so important that man should search diligently to attain? Understanding brings illumination to the mind, and it is the starting point of all our blessings in Christ. Without understanding of a concept, it cannot be applied. The salvation of man starts with an understanding of what Jesus has done for humanity. Understanding will fixate the word in your mind.

Apostle Paul said in Acts 26:17 that he had been sent by the Lord Jesus to the gentiles or the unsaved *"To open their eyes, and to turn them from darkness to light, and from the power of Satan unto God, that they may receive forgiveness of sins, and inheritance among them which are sanctified by faith…"* Paul said in this scripture that the *"opening of the eyes"* or illumination precedes deliverance from satanic oppression and forgiveness of sins; and it enabled the gentiles to see their inheritance in the Lord. When a person is not saved, the eye of his understanding is so darkened by demonic powers that he cannot receive the light of the gospel. Apostle Paul later reiterated the same truth in 2 Corinthians 4:3-4 *"But if our gospel be hid, it is hid to them that are lost: In whom the god of this world hath blinded the minds of them which believe not, lest the light of the glorious gospel of Christ, who is the image of God, should shine unto them."*

A veil is still covering the eyes of the unsaved and it takes the illumination from the word of God to remove it. Even when you are saved, the Holy Spirit, who is the author of the bible, has to open the eyes of your understanding to appropriate the mysteries of the kingdom of God. The Ethiopian eunuch in Acts 8 was saved, but did not understand the scriptures until the Holy Spirit sent Philip to open the eyes of his understanding. So Jesus, in the parable of the sower, referred to this truth by saying that, He speaks in parables so that hearing they (the unsaved) may hear, and not understand, and seeing they may see, and not perceive. On the other hand, He said, that it had been given to the saved the ability to perceive and understand the mysteries of the kingdom, or spiritual truths. Every Spirit-filled believer has been given the Holy Spirit who teaches us all things.

Mark 4:11-12 *"And he said unto them, Unto you it is given to know the mystery of the kingdom of God: but unto them that are without, all these things are done in parables: That seeing they may see, and not perceive; and hearing they may hear, and not understand; lest at any time they should be converted, and their sins should be forgiven them."* Therefore, only those that have spiritually opened ears will hear and understand, and those with enlightened eyes will see and perceive. This is why Jesus said *"He that have ears to hear, let him hear"*, which means he who has ears to hear and understand, let him hear and understand.

Jesus was, in this scripture, referring to an Old Testament scripture and also emphasizing the truth that it is only the word of God that has power to save and convert a person from darkness into light. The prophet Isaiah spoke about this state of the unsaved in Isaiah 6:9-10 *"And he said, Go, and tell this people, Hear ye indeed, but understand not; and see ye indeed, but perceive not. Make the heart of this people fat, and make their ears heavy, and shut their eyes; lest they see with their eyes, and hear with their ears, and understand with their heart, and convert, and be healed."* So, understanding brings illumination to the mind and causes man to perceive beyond what he sees with his physical eyes.

Why is it necessary to have understanding of the word before you can apply it to your life? Understanding would give you knowledge or information; and the skillful use of the knowledge or information you have acquired, is known as wisdom. The information or knowledge that you have acquired through understanding would be properly applied when God gives you wisdom as to how to use this knowledge appropriately. This is called godly wisdom. On the other hand, some information can be used wrongly through worldly advice and this is called earthly wisdom.

Understanding, just like all valuable and precious things in life, does not come easily. Precious stones are buried deep in the earth, yet man tunnels into the mountains and valleys just to lay hold on them. Likewise the most precious gem in life (the word of God) has to be desired in order for us to pursue it diligently. The bible says *"People know where to mine silver and how to refine gold. They know where to dig iron from the earth and how to smelt copper from rock. They know how to shine light in the darkness and explore the farthest regions of the earth as they search in the dark for ore. They sink a mine shaft into the earth far from where anyone lives. They descend on ropes, swinging back and forth. Food is grown on the earth above, but down below, the earth is melted as by fire. Here the rocks contain precious lapis lazuli, and the dust contains gold. These are treasures no bird of prey can see, no falcon's eye observe. No wild animal has walked upon these treasures; no lion has ever set his paw there.*

People know how to tear apart flinty rocks and overturn the roots of mountains.

They cut tunnels in the rocks and uncover precious stones.

They dam up the trickling streams and bring to light the hidden treasures. But do people know where to find wisdom? Where can they find UNDERSTANDING? No one knows where to find it, for it is not found among the living. 'It is not here,' says the ocean. 'Nor is it here,' says the sea. It cannot be bought with gold. It cannot be purchased with silver. It's worth more than all the gold of Ophir, greater than precious onyx or lapis lazuli. Wisdom is more valuable than gold and crystal. It cannot be purchased with jewels mounted in fine gold. Coral and jasper are worthless in trying to get it. The price of wisdom is far above rubies. Precious peridot from Ethiopia cannot be exchanged for it. It's worth more than the purest

gold "But do people know where to find wisdom? Where can they find

UNDERSTANDING?

It is hidden from the eyes of all humanity. Even the sharp-eyed birds in the sky cannot discover it. Destruction and Death say, 'We've heard only rumors of where wisdom can be found.' GOD ALONE UNDERSTANDS THE WAY TO WISDOM; he knows where it can be found, for he looks throughout the whole earth and sees everything under the heavens. He decided how hard the winds should blow and how much rain should fall. He made the laws for the rain and laid out a path for the lightning. Then he saw wisdom and evaluated it. He set it in place and examined it thoroughly. And this is what he says to all humanity: 'The fear of the Lord is true wisdom; to forsake evil is real UNDERSTANDING.' (Job 28 NLT)

As per this scripture, mankind has been able to mine for gold, silver and other precious stones that are buried deep in the earth. Man has been able to tap these resources and has achieved many great feats; but when it comes to seeking understanding, which is the foundational or solitary way that leads to wisdom, man does not have a clue as to where to find it. God, through his wisdom and grace, has given the pathway to wisdom, which is the ability to comprehend the word of God. The ability to eschew evil and revere the Lord can only be attained through fellowship with God in His word. Spiritual understanding will, undoubtedly, bring you illumination and clarity, which is the first law of learning.

The bible says "*Give me understanding, and I shall keep thy law; yea, I shall observe it with my whole heart.* The ability to observe the law or live by the word comes from understanding. We should always pray to God to give us spiritual understanding. Without understanding of the word, it will be impossible to apply the truth in your life. The bible also says in Job 32:8, "*there is a spirit in man: and the inspiration of the Almighty gives them understanding".* According to this verse of scripture, understanding comes as inspiration from God to our human spirit and it is the basis or the foundation of wisdom. A person can have understanding of the word of God and not necessarily walk in godly wisdom.

However, a person cannot walk in godly wisdom without having understanding of the word of God. Understanding of the word of God forms a belief system in your heart, but lack of understanding causes the word of God to become just an information in the mind. Proverbs 1:5 says "*A wise man will hear (understand), and will increase learning (knowledge); and a man of understanding shall attain unto wise counsels:*" When a wise man hears and understands the word of God, it increases his knowledge base and he applies it by giving wise counsels to others, making wise decisions and being very prudent in all his ways. What you don't understand, you can never apply, because understanding is a wellspring of life onto him that has it, and from this wellspring he draws knowledge that orders and directs his paths. Every problem in life becomes solvable in the presence of wisdom. What you don't understand, you don't know. But what you understand, the devil cannot steal from you.

Understanding, therefore, gives you knowledge (information), and the application or usage of the knowledge you possess through understanding is known as wisdom, which will set you free. The bible says in Proverbs 14:33 *"Wisdom rests in the heart of him that hath understanding"*. Therefore, understanding precedes wisdom or it gives birth to wisdom. It is also written in Proverbs 15:14 *"The heart of him that hath understanding seeks knowledge..."* So, according to these two scriptures, the person who has understanding seeks and pursues knowledge or information, which would be applied based upon the guidance from God. This is known as godly wisdom.

God will work with what you know and bring you direction as to how to use it.

Applying the knowledge you have based on biblical principles is known as wisdom.

The bible says *"and a man of understanding is of an excellent spirit"*. Daniel, according to the bible, always acted with integrity in all he did and we are to do the same. He was honorable in all his ways and had admirable qualities in character. Those who have developed in character like Daniel will excel in Godly values. They will live by God's principles and will not say one thing and then do another. They will seek the Lord about what He wants and will do and say what the Lord tells them as they are led; daily walking in the Spirit. Those who have an excellent spirit are very fruitful. They excel above the average Christian who seems to be more concerned about the things of this world than pleasing our Father. The fruit of the Spirit is easily seen by all, even outside the church. Those of an excellent spirit will hold to a higher standard than the world and even many in the church. It seems the church has lowered its standards drastically. We are to be an example of our Lord Jesus Christ in a way that attracts people to Him.

We read in the book of Daniel 6:3 that "... *Daniel was preferred above the presidents and princes, because an excellent spirit (spiritual understanding) was in him; and the king thought to set him over the whole realm"*. We can deduce from this scripture that Daniel had an excellent spirit because he had spiritual understanding which set him apart and above his peers in a foreign

42

land, even as a slave. The spirit of understanding that was in Daniel was referred to as an excellent spirit. Even unbelievers attested to this truth about him in Daniel 5:12 saying *"For as much as an excellent spirit, and knowledge, and understanding, interpreting of dreams, and shewing of hard sentences, and dissolving of doubts, were found in the same Daniel...".* He excelled above all his contemporaries and was made the leader of all the wise men in his days, because he had spiritual understanding or an excellent spirit. Understanding of spiritual principles set Daniel apart from his peers and elevated him above all of them; because the inspiration from the Spirit of God gave him spiritual understanding and wisdom. Understanding dissolves doubts, it interprets dreams and it promotes unfathomable and deep utterances that resonate in people's hearts as divine truth without any ambiguity.

This is the reason why the bible says that *"Wisdom is the principal thing; Therefore get wisdom. And in all your getting, get understanding."* From this scripture we can deduce, therefore, that wisdom is the end result or the fruit of understanding and as such we are admonished to get understanding if we want wisdom which is the principal thing. Also according to this scripture understanding is the seed and wisdom is the fruit. Understanding will lead you to wisdom. The bible says in Daniel 2:21 *"And He (God) changes the times and the seasons; He removes kings and raises up kings; He gives wisdom to the wise and KNOWLEDGE TO*

THOSE WHO HAVE UNDERSTANDING:" So knowledge is acquired from God through understanding. *"Who hath put wisdom in the inward parts or who hath given understanding to the heart?"* It is the Almighty God who gives wisdom through understanding onto man. Daniel is simply saying in this passage of scripture that God gives understanding which leads to knowledge; and the application of the acquired knowledge through godly guidance is called wisdom.

Wisdom, in a nutshell, is the skillful application of the word of God, which you understand, for successful living in this world of darkness. *"The fear of the LORD is the beginning of wisdom: a good understanding have all they that do his commandments: his praise endures forever*. Without good understanding, you cannot obey His commandments. God, in his bountiful mercies, has given unto us his word to enable us to partake in His divine nature. The most important thing worth having in life is a good working knowledge of the word of God, which comes through understanding; because a person can never rise above the level of his knowledge. Everything man would ever need is already embedded in the word of God. Therefore, study the word of God to attain understanding, and strive hard to apply it or live by the word.

Jesus said in Mathew 7:24-25 *"Therefore whosoever HEARS (understand) these sayings of mine, and DOES (applies) them, I will liken him unto a wise man (possessor of wisdom), which built his house upon a rock (teachings of Jesus): And the rain descended, and the floods came, and the winds blew, and beat upon that house; and it fell not: for it was founded upon a rock"* (**Emphasis mine**). Jesus likened the one who applies the word of God that he hears and understands, to a wise man or a possessor of wisdom. A person cannot apply or use what he doesn't understand. Therefore, seek to understand the word of God so that you can apply it to your life. All these scriptures are highlighting the importance of understanding of the word of God in our Christian walk.

Many people claim that knowledge is power, but it is a statement that is far from the truth; because it is only applied knowledge that gives you power. For example, let's say you are sitting in a room, which is equipped with an air-conditioner, and knows the cool refreshing air it can provide, and yet refuses to apply that knowledge by turning on the air conditioner; how could it benefit you? So your understanding of what you hear is very important; because it illuminates your mind and gives you the ability to apply it in your life. All the technological advancements that the world is enjoying now are simply due to the application of the physics, chemistry, biology, economics, and all the social sciences that we studied during our formal years of education. Some people took this knowledge and applied it, and therefore gained economic power. So use the knowledge that you have, and contribute to the welfare of society.

Understanding of the word gives illumination to the mind

The bible says in Psalm 119:130 "***The entrance of your words (God's word) gives light(illumination); it gives understanding unto the simple***" The Contemporary English Version (CEV) of the bible renders this same verse as "***Understanding your (God's)word brings light (illumination) to the minds of ordinary people***". This scripture is plainly equating understanding to light: meaning that understanding gives light and illumination to the mind of the one who possesses it. Understanding in any form brings illumination to the mind. In our everyday English, when somebody is giving you some information and you don't understand it you may say to them, "can you shed some light on what you are saying, or do you mind to shed more light on what you are saying"? This simply means: bring more understanding to it; but when we do not understand something, we say that we are living in the dark or we are living in ignorance.

So light is then equated to understanding and darkness is equated to ignorance. Just as physical light helps us to see and function in our environment, so also does spiritual understanding enable us to perceive and comprehend spiritual truths, which are not readily available to all. Without light, there would be no sight or vision. Human activities are always limited in total darkness. Man has to light up candles, lamps and light bulbs at night in order to be able to function. So without light, there would be total darkness, hindering man's ability to work. In like manner, without spiritual understanding, man cannot work the works of God. Jesus said in John 9:4 " ***I must work the works of Him that sent me, while it is day: the night cometh when no man can work*** " By this scripture, Jesus emphasized the truth that it is impossible to work in darkness. Light enables activities whilst darkness impairs. All truths are parallel; what is true naturally, is also true spiritually.

When you are living in ignorance, you are living in darkness. It is impossible for anyone to function properly in darkness. Without good information, it becomes very difficult to make good decisions. In darkness, we grope around just to feel our way; but when you are living in light, you are able to see and function based on the information that you are receiving; simply because you are living in understanding and enlightenment. Apostle Paul said in Ephesians 4:17-19 *"This I say, therefore, and testify in the Lord, that you should no longer walk as the rest of the Gentiles walk, in the futility of their mind, having their UNDERSTANDING DARKENED, being alienated from the life of God, because of the IGNORANCE that is in them, because of the blindness of their heart; who, being past feeling, have given themselves over to lewdness, to work all uncleanness with greediness."* In this scripture, Paul likened ignorance to darkness and it is the flip side of understanding. If ignorance is darkness, then understanding is light or illumination. He said the unsaved have their understanding darkened; because of the ignorance that is in them. Ignorance brings about darkness to the mind just as understanding brings light to the mind. Therefore, understanding is equated to, or symbolic of light and darkness is equated to, or symbolic of ignorance. Light enables us to see and function in our environment. Without light, there would be no sight, and without understanding, there would be no insight. It is light that causes us to see. This is the reason why God created light as the first law on the earth.

Spiritual photosynthesis

In life, there are some universal laws, which are applicable both in the spiritual realm as well as in the natural realm, and one of these laws is the law of sowing and reaping. This law governs almost every aspect of our lives. Some people call it cause and effect, action and reaction, and others call it boomerang; but in either case, it is pointing to one universal law of sowing and reaping. A law is a principle that works at all times. It is a rule of action. So this law of sowing and reaping demands certain conditions to be prevalent in order for the law to work. This is a universal principle that works in both the spiritual and physical realms. Just as in the physical realm a seed needs sunlight, moisture, a fertile soil, and a farmer to yield the desired fruit, so likewise, the word of God, which is a spiritual seed, also need these conditions in order to benefit the hearer. Just as light is very important to the growth of every seed ever sown, so also understanding (which is spiritual light) is very important in appropriating the word of God. Without light, a seed sown can never grow. Likewise, without understanding, the word of God sown in your heart cannot bear fruit.

Jesus was saying in this parable that the word of God is likened to a seed in the spiritual realm, or it is a spiritual seed, which is governed by universal sowing principles. In the natural realm, a seed needs a good soil, water and sunlight in order to germinate and bear fruit. Likewise, the spiritual seed also needs good soil, water, and light to bear fruit. This is a universal law; spiritual and natural laws, which govern the earth. There is a natural law called the law of gravity, which even though we don't see but we feel the effect of it. I'm sitting down right now; because of the law of gravity. I can stand up; because of the law of gravity. Even if I jump I will still come back down; because there is a gravitational pull that is being exerted on me to hold me in place. There is also the law of attraction, and the law of aerodynamics.

Also, we know that there's a law of sowing and reaping which is universal. This law states that whatsoever a man sows, so shall he reap, and also whenever you sow a seed in a good ground and in the right condition, it will yield fruit onto you. A seed sown in a good ground will not yield fruit on its own, but in conjunction with water and sunlight. The bible says in Job 14:7-9 *"Even a tree has more hope! If it is cut down, it will sprout again and grow new branches. Though its roots have grown old in the earth and its stump decays, (yet) AT THE SCENT OF WATER, IT WILL BUD and*

sprout again like a new seedling." (NLT) This scripture is indicating that, trees, plants and vegetation needs water to sprout, bud and grow. It is saying that, in the absence of water, trees wither; but by the scent of water, it will grow again. Jesus explained this principle subliminally in the parable of the sower. According to Jesus, in the parable of the sower, plants also need light from the sun to manufacture their food by a process known as photosynthesis.

If there is one process that sustains the backbone of living organisms in this world, it is photosynthesis. Whilst this process is critical to maintain the normal level of oxygen in the atmosphere, almost all aerobic life, either directly or indirectly, depends on it for energy. Although photosynthesis can happen in different ways in different species, some features remain the same. Photosynthesis is the process by which plants use the energy from sunlight to produce sugar, which in simpler words is the fuel used by all living things. Photosynthesis is a chemical process through which plants, and some bacteria, produce glucose and oxygen from carbon dioxide using light as the source. This glucose, an energy unit, helps trees and plants to survive and grow. Since most living creatures on earth, directly or indirectly, depend on these green trees, the process of photosynthesis is considered as a very important one. The process of photosynthesis that plants feed on, divides itself in two sets of reactions, namely lightdependent reactions, and light-independent reactions. As the names suggests, the light reactions need light to take place, while the latter ones can perform independent of the light. Nonetheless, the presence of light is of utmost importance for photosynthesis, since the light-independent reactions, also known as dark reactions, eventually uses the chemical energy produced in the light reactions. Photosynthesis, therefore, is arguably the most important biochemical pathway in the organic world; since nearly all life depends on it. The very fact that humans also get abundant oxygen to breathe; because of photosynthesis, deepens and amplifies the importance of this process.

Brethren, I am here to inform you that Jesus was the first scientist to explain the process of photosynthesis, and He did that in the parable of the sower. He made this obvious when He spoke about the parable of the sower. In the parable, Jesus made mention of the sun, which produces the light, and also the moisture or water in the soil. Who else would know this principle except the creator of the heavens and the earth? Jesus knew about photosynthesis and tried to explain it to His audience in the parable of the sower. He is the one who created the plants and, therefore, knows how it grows. He set this principle in motion, and he revealed it to the saints in the parable of the sower. He was indicating the need of sunlight by the seed to combine with the water in the soil to grow. The spiritual light that is needed by the spiritual seed is; understanding with your heart or spiritual illumination.

It is very, very important that before you can apply or even activate any word of God in your life, you have to have an understanding of the word. If you do not understand it, the word will not benefit you. You cannot use it. Who, in this world, can use or apply a principle or theory he doesn't understand? If you don't know how to drive, or don't understand how to drive you cannot drive. You are not a hair-dresser or a pilot; because you don't have the understanding of it, and there's nothing you can do about it until you formally acquire the skill to do so. You just don't know; but the beginning of you being able to do anything, is by understanding how it operates; for example, someone may desire to use the computer to do desktop publishing; but lack the technical ability and know-how.

One day, my younger daughter said to me, 'Hi daddy; can you teach me how to use the PowerPoint so that I can make a presentation?' I said, 'Okay, I will show you.' Then, I started explaining to her how PowerPoint works; but because she didn't have the understanding or the knowledge of how that software works, she couldn't use it. I was able to explain to her; because I understood how it works. So what you understand you know; and what you know is what you are able to apply. So the first thing we learn in our quest to appropriate all the promises of God in our lives is to have an applicable understanding of the promise. For example, let's say you are trusting God for healing; you search the scriptures and locate or identify the scriptures that pertain to healing, and make sure that you understand what the scripture is saying in the context.

For example, God said, in The book of Exodus that, *"If thou wilt diligently hearken to the voice of the Lord thy God, and wilt do that which is right in his sight, and wilt give ear to his commandments, and keep all his statutes, I will put none of these diseases upon thee, which I have brought upon the Egyptians: for I am the Lord that healeth thee"*. He said; I am Jehovah Rapha to those that diligently hearken to my voice or those that understand and apply what they hear from the voice of the Lord. He also said, in The Book of Isaiah, *"by his stripes we are healed."* He said also, in the second book of Peter, *"by his stripes we were healed."* All these scriptures are referring to healing, and also pointing to the truth that God wants his children to be healed; but if you don't understand that scripture in its entirety, and why God wants you to be healed, you cannot benefit from it.

So Jesus was saying in the parable of the sower that, it is very important not to be a wayside hearer. Being the wayside hearer means hearing the word without understanding. Without understanding there's no illumination to the mind. The entrance of the word of God or the unfolding, grasping and understanding of the word of God, will give you light and illumination. The entrance of God's word gives light to the simple. When the word of God is unfolded, it becomes personal or it becomes flesh. That is the Rhema word. The revealed word is the word that jumps at you when you're reading the bible or comes by the still small voice in your spirit. A Rhema is a word of God that has been quickened by the Holy Spirit to have a specific application in your life or your situation. It is a word of God tailor-made specifically for your personal application. This becomes possible when you have knowledge of the word of God so that the Holy Spirit will have something to work with.

The written word is the logos and the revealed word is the one that brings illumination, discernment, recognition, and understanding. Sometimes, when reading the bible, a word or a scripture jump out at you with understanding like never before. For example, I told you how I had a Rhema word of who Jesus is, and how the Holy Spirit led me through the scriptures from one scripture to the other; and there was an unveiling of truth to me about who Christ Jesus

50

is. Up until that point, I didn't know. I thought I knew; but I didn't. I only had head knowledge. No mortal man taught me who Jesus is; but the Holy Spirit. He taught me through scripture, precept upon precept; line upon line, here a little and there a little. So, when I had that understanding of who Jesus is and the principles that he taught, I was able to apply them in my life. It is very important. If you look into scripture, many people were given the spirit of understanding and wisdom by God. For example, look at Solomon. When, Solomon made a sacrifice unto God in The Book of 2 Kings, the bible said, *"At night God appeared unto Solomon and said; ask me anything that you want that I may give onto you"*. And Solomon said, *"Give me an understanding heart."*

He didn't ask for riches, fame or victory over his enemies as many people would have done. No, he did not ask for wisdom, he said, *"Give me an understanding heart..."* Understanding is the foundation of wisdom. Understanding would give you knowledge and the application of the knowledge you possess is known as wisdom. When you have an understanding of something, you know how to apply it; and did you know that understanding is a spirit or an anointing? The book of Isaiah 11:2 says

"And the spirit of the Lord shall rest upon him, the spirit of wisdom and understanding, the spirit of counsel and might, the spirit of knowledge and of the fear of the Lord." There are seven spirits that are mentioned in this verse and understanding is one of them. It is a revelation. When it comes to you and you take hold of it, nobody can take it from you; not even the devil can steal it from you; and, you'll be better placed to apply it. This is based on the fact that what you understand gives you knowledge, and what you know, you apply; which then becomes known as wisdom.

So understanding is the foundation of wisdom. Just as the natural seed needs light to grow, so also does the spiritual incorruptible seed of God need understanding to prosper in your life. Of course, there are other factors. The natural seed needs the light, good fertile soil, and water, in order to grow. This was exactly what Jesus was teaching in this parable. To wit, the spiritual seed likewise needs water, light, and a good soil in order for it to grow. So, the Parable of the Sower, is telling you about these things. He who has ears to hear, let him hear; meaning he who has spiritual ears to hear and understand, let him hear and understand. Jesus said, 'I'm speaking in parables so that hearing they may hear and not understand. The minds of unbelievers are not illuminated by the inspiration of the Holy Spirit to hear and understand spiritual truth. Their degenerated minds have not been enlightened. So they cannot understand spiritual truths. The word "hear" is translated from the Greek word " Akouo" which is pronounced "Akoo" . This word in the Greek means to understand or comprehend.

When you are not born again, your spirit remains inert and not connected to the Spirit of God to enable these spiritual truths to be downloaded into your spirit to illuminate, enlighten, and bring understanding to you. The spirit of God will have to download spiritual information into your spirit in order for you to have an understanding of it. Jesus said in Mark 4:11, it said, ***Unto you it is given to know the mysteries of the kingdom of God.*** It is given by the Spirit of God to believers to understand the mysteries of God. Those outside of the kingdom hear these truths in parables, so that seeing they may see and not perceive; and hearing, they may hear and not understand. You can see, but not perceive. Sometimes, for example, you'll be looking at somebody or talking to someone straight in the face, but your mind would not be involved. Even though, you are looking at them, it doesn't connect with your understanding or your mind. In order to perceive something, your vision has to correspond with your mind. These two faculties have to be in agreement in order for perception to take place.

When these are lacking, perception will not be available; but when you are looking and, at the same time, receiving what is coming to you in its entirety, you are receiving the truth with your heart. In the same way, you can hear something, but fail to understand it. Whatever you do not understand cannot benefit you. So that's what Jesus was saying. When you have understanding and you hear, it will be a blessing to you; but when you hear and do not understand, then the enemy comes and steals it from you; meaning the enemy cannot steal from everybody. He can only steal from those who do not understand what they hear. This is the person

Jesus described as a wayside hearer. At the wayside, nobody claims ownership.

The wayside is a no-man's land. When we say something is on a wayside, anybody can claim ownership; but nobody can claim ownership of what you understand; you are the only one who can claim ownership. You own what you understand. Yes, I own this, because I understand it. For example, when a person understands the concepts of nursing through formal education, no one can take it away from her, even if she chooses not to use it. So seek and pray to understand the word of God. The first and foremost principle Jesus was teaching in this parable, in order to equip you to activate the promises of God in your life, is to understand what the promise entails. Many people have accepted the person of Jesus; but are not applying the spiritual principles he taught. **The acceptance of Jesus Christ as our Savior guarantees our access into heaven; but the application of the principles He taught guarantees our successful living right here in this world.**

The children of Israel did not understand the promise that God gave to them; that He was taking them to a promised land. A land that was flowing with milk and honey, therefore, they did not enter into the promise land. They didn't understand and so couldn't believe. So they kept disbelieving him. He caused manna to fall from heaven; yet still, did not believe. He parted the Red Sea for them, but they still did not believe. Simply, they lacked understanding. The two that had understanding, Caleb and Joshua, had some godly characteristics that the rest didn't have. What was it that made them so successful? Their understanding of the promise of God spoken to the patriarchs set them apart from the rest. Their understanding of God, who owns all things, convinced them that He was able to do all that He has promised; because the gold is His, the silver is His, and so are the cattle upon a thousand hills. They understood that the earth is the Lord's and as such, He gives it to whosoever He chooses. This understanding made it easy for Joshua and Caleb to apply their faith to the promise; because faithful is He who has promised and He would do it.

So first and foremost, acknowledge that the entrance of God's word into your heart or the understanding of it will bring light and comprehension to the simple. This understanding is equated to the physical sunlight the natural seed needs to grow. Therefore, your spiritual seed, which is the word of God, also needs sunlight or spiritual understanding in your heart for it to benefit you or for it to have a nice, conducive atmosphere to grow. Spiritual understanding bypasses the mind and enters into the heart. **What you understand, you believe, and to believe is to accept something as true.**

The Bible is full of promises in both the Old and New Testament. The word testament means a covenant. In covenants, God gives promises, which are the blessings of the covenant, and expects the people He is in covenant with to activate them or apply them in their lives. However, many of us find it difficult to see the realization of these promises in our lives. Our inability to activate the promises of God is not because God does not keep his word or God is not faithful; but rather, it is our lack of understanding of the word and how to apply it. Know without a shadow of doubt that God is a faithful God.

He never changes, but we are the only variables. We are the ones that change. If only we can apply the word and do what is right in the sight of God, then we will have the benefits of everything that the word has promised us. Jesus used this parable of the sower to tell us much about ourselves, and how we receive the word of God. Parables are stories that use natural elements to explain spiritual truths. He employed natural elements or events to elaborate divine principles. On several occasions Jesus used a parable to carry out a point or bring his message across, and by so doing broke it down using common things around his audience; so that they could understand what he was teaching. Hence, in the sower parable, Jesus used the seed, which was very common at the time; because most of his audience were farmers.

So, they could relate to it when He used the seed as an analogy of the word of God. When a seed is sown in the right conditions it will germinate and grow; but if it's not in the right condition, it will not yield fruit. So, he used four different kinds of grounds, which were symbolic of the hearts of men to explain the conditions that need to be present for the seed, which is the word of God, to prosper or to benefit us in our lives. The bible says that, *"joyful is the person who finds wisdom, the one who gains UNDERSTANDING, for wisdom is more profitable than silver, and her wages are better than gold"*. Wisdom is found when we gain or acquire understanding of the word of God. That's the starting point. The bibles says what you don't understand, the enemy will steal from you, but the ones you do understand, he cannot; and understanding is likened to light.

In the natural realm, light transfers energy which plants use to make their food. If it were not for the sunlight, the earth would have been very cold, and as a result there would have been no life. This sunlight energy is used for photosynthesis, which creates all the starches and sugars that are used by both plants and animals to grow and sustain life. Light also transfers information by enabling us to interpret where things are in relation to other things; with our eyes and brain. Moreover, light enhances visibility and without light, every work, activity, and operation would not be possible. Nobody can operate, work, or be active in total darkness. A natural seed, therefore, needs sunlight to grow. Likewise in the spiritual realm, the word of God, which is a seed; the incorruptible seed of God needs the light of your understanding in order for it to manifest in your life. Without understanding, the word of God would not materialize in your life. There are other conditions that need to be present in order for the word of God to manifest or fulfill in our lives. Let us read on to find out.

CHAPTER 4

MEDITATING ON THE WORD THAT HAS BEEN UNDERSTOOD

The next ground that Jesus spoke about was the stony ground and I'm taking that scripture from Mark 4:5-6 *"and some fell on stony ground, where it had not much earth; and immediately it sprang up, because it had no depth of earth. But when the SUN WAS UP, it was scorched, and because it had no root, it withered away."* I like the way Apostle Luke explains it in the gospel of Luke 8:6 where it says, *"And some fell on a rock; and as soon as it was sprung up, it withered away, because it lacked moisture."*

"And some fell on a rock; and as soon as it was sprung up, it withered away, because it lacked moisture." When you put the two scriptures together, you notice that at the first reading (Mark 4:5-6), Mark said that some of the seed fell on the stony ground, which did not have much earth; because it was shallow and when the Sun came up (to produce sunlight that the seed needs to manufacture its food in a process called Photosynthesis), the seed withered away; because the stony ground lacked moisture. A critical analysis of this portion of scripture reveals that the main goal of the sun was to produce the sunlight, which the seed needs to be combined with the moisture or water in the soil to manufacture its food. Therefore, the absence of water and the presence of the sunlight presented a dilemma, which resulted in the destruction of the seed sown on the stony ground. Water is symbolic of meditation; because when a seed is planted, it needs to be watered continually in order to germinate and bear fruit. Likewise the word of God needs to be meditated upon continually in order for it to manifest in our lives. When we understand the word, but fail to meditate on it continually, it becomes difficult to

56

apply. Meditation, therefore, empowers you to apply the word, and the power of the word of God is in its application.

So the seed withered, not because of the rising of the sun and its accompanying heat; but rather, because of the dryness of the ground. A seed sown in a dry land or in the desert will not grow even though the sun is continually shining in the desert; because the land or desert lacks moisture. What is moisture? Moisture is the amount of water present in an object. Since light is equated to understanding and water is equated to meditation, the absence of either one of them will hinder the manifestation of the word in your life.

Likewise, the word of God will not benefit you if you understand but do not meditate upon it continually. When the seed was sown and the sun came up; because there was not much earth, and therefore, the seed was not deeply rooted, it withered away. Therefore, as soon as the sun came up, the seed withered away and fell apart; because it lacked moisture. So without water, the sun will cause the seed to dry up and wither, thus failing to germinate. Likewise without meditation, your understanding of the word of God would be limited or perish. The bible says that *"For lack of knowledge, my people perish"*. Lack of knowledge, which is a secondary effect or result of understanding, causes the children of God to perish. So understanding comes first, and then it gives you information or knowledge; and the ability to apply the knowledge that you possess only comes through continual meditation on what you know. You can never have knowledge without understanding. So, the seed that fell on stony ground lacked moisture, which is literally water; and that's the reason why this seed failed. A seed can never grow without the presence of water.

Likewise, many of us would have basic understanding of the word of God, but if we fail to meditate upon it continuously to absorb the good nutrients from it, our understanding will wither away at some point. Just as your physical body digests food and absorbs all the nutrients that your body needs, so also meditation on the word of God, which you understand helps you to spiritually digest the word in order to absorb the good nutrients from it. Scriptures can be interpreted literally, figuratively, and symbolically. So what does the sun represent in this scripture? Although it represents the sunlight which the seed needs to photosynthesize its food literally, it also symbolizes the temptations, persecutions, and trials that will come as a result of the word.

The heat and pressure that would be exerted by life circumstances, when the word becomes prominent in our lives would be the acid test to prove us. The bible says in the book of Proverbs 24:10 that *"If thou faint in the day of adversity, thy strength is small"* If you fail in a time of adversity, your strength is small". This means the seed failed, because it lacked moisture in the soil, or it was weakened; because of the absence of water. Also, it means that, adversity comes to test our strength; because the trial and proving of your faith works out endurance, steadfastness, and patience. Finally, the sunlight figuratively refers to illumination or understanding to the one who comprehends a concept.

This scripture is telling us that, when we hear the word of God and understand it; but it does not become deeply rooted in our hearts by meditating on it continually day and night, it will not bear fruit in our life. You see, the more you think or meditate on the word, you begin to experience or act upon what you are thinking. What you do or think about continually will become part of you, or it will become flesh like your second nature or your habit. A habit is something that you do without thinking consciously about, and it is built progressively when it is done continually like driving, walking, and playing a musical instrument. So when you understand something, it does not become a habit automatically until you think about it diligently and continually for a long period of time. For example, when nailing a pin on a wall, the first tap only fastens the nail on the wall, but not deep enough. However, to drive the nail deeper into the wall, you need to keep tapping the nail until it becomes completely driven into the wall. Likewise, understanding of the word only plants the word in your mind; but it takes continuous thinking or meditation on the word you have understood to drive it into your heart.

You see, the word of God can be in your mind without being in your heart, but it cannot be in your heart without first being in your mind. What you understand in your mind will only be transferred into your heart when you dwell on it continually day and night through meditation. A man would become what he continually thinks about, and it will influence his actions. The bible says in the book of Proverbs that *"as a man thinks (continually) in his heart, so is he"*.

In life, what you think about continually is what you eventually say. What you speak to yourself continually, you will believe. What you believe steadfastly, you will receive. Until you believe the truth in your heart, it is just information in your mind. Information or knowledge can be in your mind and not in your heart, but it can never be in your heart without first being in your mind. Therefore, you have to convince your heart to believe the truth by speaking it continually through meditation.

If you want to change your thought process, start talking. Talking occupies your mind more than thinking. Talking aloud will change the way you think. It is difficult to talk about one thing and think about something else. This is the reason why the bible is telling us to think more about the word of God, meditate upon it through self-talk; and reflect upon it so we will have a deeper understanding of it. Even though there may be rocks or stones in the stony ground, which are symbolic of the mental blocks or hindrances in our minds, through the meditation on the word, these blocks and hindrances will be crushed. Meditation involves self-talking, imagination, diligent study, and pondering the truths in the word of God. All these activities impregnate the heart, which is very creative.

Every opposition melts or crumbles in the presence of the word of God. The bible says *"Is not my word like as a fire? saith the Lord; and like a hammer that breaks the rock in pieces?"* The word of God is like a hammer breaking through the rocks. Even though, there are stones (mental blocks) in the ground (heart), when you meditate on the word, it will break through the rocks; and then the meditation will cause you to be well-rooted and deeply grounded in the word, and the word, in you.

Jesus went on further to explain and clarify the characteristics of this type of ground by talking about meditation in Mark 4:24 *"And he said unto them, take heed what you hear: with what measure ye mete, it shall be measured to you: and unto you that hear shall more be given.*" Take heed what you hear, with what measure ye mete, it shall be measured to you, and unto you that hear shall more be given. What was Jesus talking about? Take heed what you hear for with what measure ye mete, it shall be measured back onto you, and he that hears shall be given more. What does it mean? Ask yourself questions like this when reading the bible, and then start probing and looking at scriptures in other translations to bring clarity to it. Then you will get a better understanding of what the word is saying.

When you read the same scripture in the amplified bible, it says *"And He said to them, be careful what you are hearing. The measure [of thought and study] you give [to the truth you hear] will be the measure [of virtue and knowledge] that comes back to you--and more [besides] will be given to you who hear."*

Hallelujah. In this scripture, Jesus is saying that the more you meditate (thought and study) upon the word, more understanding, virtue, and knowledge will come back to you. Why? Because the more you meditate on the word, more understanding will be given to you as you are giving the Holy Spirit more raw materials to bring revelation to you. Unto you that hear and understand, more understanding will be given through meditation; meaning, the one who understands and meditates upon the word that he understands will get more understanding and deeper revelation knowledge. You see, when you are meditating upon the word of God you are giving the Holy Spirit the raw materials to work with, and download more revelation knowledge to your spirit.

So as you are meditating on the word, you are digging deeper roots, for deeper understanding. The bible says in the book of Psalms chapter of 1 that, *"blessed is the man that walks not in the counsel of the ungodly nor sits in the seat of the scornful nor stands in the way of sinners, but his delight is in the law of the Lord: and in his law he meditates day and night"*, and as a result of his meditation in the word day and night, *"he shall be like a tree planted (by God) by the rivers of water that brings forth his fruit in his season; his leaf also shall not wither* (because he is planted

60

by the rivers of water, there is constant supply of water); *and whatsoever he does prospers.*" It is apparent in this scripture that, meditation on the word of God, has many blessings attached to it, and it is a gem. Meditation is this scripture is likened to water that causes the tree (man) to grow. It's something that many of us have not come to the realization of. The more you meditate upon the word of God, the more you build yourself up, as you put the power of God on the inside of you.

It's like putting God, literally, inside of you; because the word of God is God. Jesus said *"these words that I speak unto you, they are spirit and they are life."* So when you have this word in you and you meditate on it day and night, you're incubating the word in your spirit. You are incubating the word. You incubate the word until it becomes flesh within you, and when you apply it, or when you speak it, it comes with power. This is Meditation. I'm talking about meditation; biblical meditation. I'm not talking about meditation during, which you cross your leg and sit down and chant some mantras and try to empty your mind of all things. No, that's not what I'm talking about.

I'm talking about biblical meditation, where you put the word of God in your heart through your mind by thinking about it day in and day out; and in so doing, you build up your spirit man by incubating the word inside of you; and brethren, great things will come to you. When Moses died and Joshua took over as the leader of the children of Israel to bring them into the promise land, God gave onto Joshua the key to be successful in his assignment. Moses' assignment was to take the children of Israel out of Egypt, and then Joshua's assignment was to bring them into the promise land; but then when Joshua was taking over, God gave him this profound instruction.

He said *"This Book of the Law (bible) shall not depart out of your mouth, but you shall meditate on it day and night, that you may OBSERVE TO DO according to all that is written in it. For then YOU shall make YOUR way prosperous, and then YOU shall deal wisely and have good success"* (Joshua 1:8) Let not this book of the law depart out of your mouth." By that, Joshua was to keep the word in his mouth and meditate on it day and night.

According to the Hebrew translation, the word "**HAGAH**" which is translated as "**meditate**" means to murmur, imagine, mutter, speak, ponder or study. It is an act of transferring the word from your mind into your heart through self-talk. Since your heart is the spiritual matrix or womb where all issues of life are conceived. The ability to experience good in your life depends on what you feed your heart through continual thinking on whatever you desire. You see, the word of God can be in your mind and not be in your heart; but it cannot be in your heart without first being in your mind.

So, Joshua was to transfer the word of God from being head knowledge into a spiritual force issuing out of the abundance of his heart. Out of the heart proceeds the issues of life and in order to observe and apply the word, it has to be in his heart. Then *he* (Joshua) will make his way prosperous (not God, but Joshua; because it was his personal responsibility), and whatever he does, he will have good success since his life would be ordered by the word of the Lord.

Meditation would give him deeper understanding of the word, which will empower him to obey and apply the word. As long as you are meditating upon the word and applying it to your life, success would be inevitable. Can you believe that? God himself said it. The only way that you are going to succeed in activating the word of God in your life is to keep on meditating upon it. This is what Moses did, and this is what you should do to ensure success in your life. If you look through the bible, there are different types of meditation. For instance, there is the meditation whereby you consider the work of the hands of God in creation (Psalm 8); and there is the type that ponders about the majesty and holiness of God. Then, there is the type that ponders, meditates, and studies the word of God and its power in the affairs of men. This latter type was referenced when Moses said to the children of Israel "*For this commandment which I command you this day is not too difficult for you, nor is it far off. It is not [a secret laid up] in heaven, that you should say, who shall go up for us to heaven and bring it to us, that we may HEAR and DO it? Neither is it beyond the sea, that you should say, who shall go over the sea for us and bring it to us, that we may HEAR and DO it? But the word is very near you, in your MOUTH and in your MIND and in your HEART, so that you can do it" (Deuteronomy 30:1114) AMP.*

The word of God, first of all, has to be in your mouth, then in your mind by thinking about it and speaking it to yourself, before it can be in your heart. Moses told the children of Israel to meditate on the word by keeping it in their mouths, minds, and hearts. This was exactly what God said to Joshua after the death of Moses. There is nothing in this world more powerful than the knowledge of this universal principle. This is the spiritual key known as biblical meditation, and it is a spiritual exercise that should be a part of every believer who wants to activate the promises of God in his/her life. Hearing the scriptures is important. Reading the scriptures is also important. Studying the word is important as well, and memorizing the word is also important; but all these disciplines, do not empower us to grasp and apply the word of God in our lives until it culminates in meditation. Hearing the word of God, reading it, studying, and memorizing it without meditation is like trying to grasp an object with four fingers without your thumb. It is a very difficult thing to do.

Do not chase after other things, but rather seek God through His revealed word. Everything we need for life and godliness has been given to us through precious promises scattered throughout the bible; but it is our responsibility to search it out. The bible says in Proverbs 25:2 *"It is the glory of God to conceal a thing: but the honor of kings is to search out a matter"* It is the honor of believers who are also kings to search out what the King of kings has concealed in His glory.

The bible says in Revelation 1:6 that Christ Jesus has made us kings and priests onto God. Therefore, God, the King of glory, has concealed precious things in His promises all throughout scriptures so that we can diligently search and study, meditate, and then apply them. We are supposed to search through the scriptures by studying to show ourselves approved onto God, and then meditate and apply the word in our lives. We should take the promise, whatever it is talking about, and then acquire a good working knowledge through understanding and meditation, which will make it easier to apply it. **Many Christians are going to heaven without impacting the earth for Jesus simply because they fail to apply the principles of the kingdom of God on earth**.

Knowing and having a relationship with Jesus only gives you a ticket to heaven, but to live the abundant life, which He came to give you entails the application of the principles, which He taught in the word of God. This is the reason why many believers are living a life of mediocrity.

Everything you will ever need is already provided in the word for you. If it is about your health, your prosperity, your protection, whatever it is, make sure you search the bible to understand what is expected of you, and then meditate on it; as you make sure first and foremost that you understand what the promise is about, and under what circumstances was the promise given. For example, Psalm 1 talks about the blessings of the man that meditates on the word of God. It also mentions his lifestyle as someone who avoids evil in all forms and shapes. So, you cannot expect the blessing of God without living a life, which is pleasing to God. So study the word and observe how it applies to you; and once you know that; meditate upon it, think about it all day, and night, day in and day out. Think about it over and over and over. Jesus said. *"Be careful what you are hearing. For, the measure of thought and study you give to the truth you hear (understand) would determine the measure of knowledge and virtue that comes back to you"*. So, when you meditate on the word, it builds up your faith because faith comes by hearing.

As you hear yourself speaking to yourself through meditation, it builds up your faith tremendously. After going through this process for a while, the word becomes written upon the tablets of your heart, thereby making it possible to observe and obey. David said that *"Thy word have I hid in mine heart, that I might not sin against thee."* When we hide the word of God in our hearts, it becomes a point of reference and a tool of conviction to us. Therefore, the measure of meditation that you will give to what you are hearing will be the measure of virtue and knowledge, that will come back to you and more...more... more understanding, more knowledge will be attained by the one who hears and understands through meditation.

Let's look at some other scriptures to shed more light on meditation. Psalm 119:98100 reads *"You (God), through your commandments, make me wiser than my enemies, for [Your words] are ever before me. I have better understanding and deeper insight than all my teachers, because your testimonies (words) are my meditation. I understand more than the aged, because I keep your precepts [hearing, receiving, loving, and obeying them]"*

I'm going to paraphrase that. He says, you through your commandments have made me wiser than my enemies, for your words are ever with me. I have more understanding than my teachers, because your words are my meditation. I understand more than the old, because I keep your words. Hallelujah. I understand more, because the more I meditate, the more wisdom, knowledge, and understanding I gain.

So you see, the seed that fell on the stony ground lacked moisture, and therefore didn't grow. Meditation is symbolic of the watering of a planted seed, and when you are meditating on the word you are watering the seed of the word of God. In the natural, when you plant a flower, you have to continually water it in order for it to grow. So also does the word of God, which is a spiritual seed need watering in order to grow, and meditation is the act of watering the word of God that you have sown in your heart.

When you are meditating upon the word, you are watering the seed that is sown in your heart. So when you meditate upon the word, what you are doing is that you are pouring more water on the fertile soil of your heart, where the word of God is sown. When the water is present and the sun comes up, the seed will grow and come to maturity; the seed will grow and it will bear its fruit. The bible tells us that our God is not a man that he should lie, has he said it and will he not perform it? Isaiah 55:10-11 says " *For as the rain cometh down, and the snow from heaven, and returneth not thither, but WATERETH (moistens) the earth, and maketh it bring forth and bud, that it may give seed to the sower, and bread to the eater: so shall my word be that goeth forth out of my mouth: it shall not return unto me void, but it shall accomplish(by watering) that which I please, and it shall prosper in the thing whereto I sent it."*

We know that every word that has proceeded out of the mouth of God is sure to come to pass; but the only hindrance or obstacle is how we apply it. You will see subsequently, when we start looking at the other grounds that they were all different by the absence or lack of something that caused the crop to fail, except the one that fell on a good ground. What made it a good ground? We are going to look into all of that, and you will see that if you want the word of God to work in your life, the word of God works when you work it the right way. Make sure that when you hear the word that you won't be like the wayside hearer who doesn't claim ownership of what he's hearing by understanding it. Therefore, the enemy comes and steals it away. In the parable, the birds of the air came and devoured the seed that was sown on the wayside. This means that the seed was visible to the birds; it was not buried or received into the ground and was on the surface of the ground and not in the ground. This is the only reason why the birds of the air were able to see the seed

The stony ground hearer also does not have much earth or depth in himself. He is very shallow and superficial when it comes to the things of God, because he doesn't meditate deep on the word. So, any time temptation comes his way, he stumbles and falls and the word does not benefit him. He had understanding but failed to meditate on it. Jesus said that "when the sun came up", it caused the seed to wither because of lack of moisture. There was sunlight, which is equated to understanding but lack of moisture, which is symbolic of meditation caused the failure of the seed. He had understanding (which is symbolic of the sunlight) but lack of meditation (moisture) caused the seed (word) to fail. You cannot apply something that you don't understand. Not just simply understanding, but having a spiritual understanding or insight of it. I don't know much about Archimedes' principle in physics of course. I don't understand it. During my school years, I realized that, science was not for me, so I stayed away from science, because I couldn't understand it.

The scientific formulas in the physics and the chemistry were too much for me; but when it came to other subjects like administration, economics and management, I excelled; because I had an understanding in those subjects. So, the things that you understand, you are able to apply them easily. It is very important in life to have the grace to accept the things you cannot change, the boldness to change the things that you can, and the wisdom to differentiate between the two conditions. What you do not understand you cannot apply. If you understand the scriptures pertaining to the situation you are going through, then you can meditate upon it. Then, let the word infuse and dominate your thinking by building a tabernacle on that particular word. This simply means that you should dwell on the word continually and permanently. The word will illuminate you by bringing you out of the darkness of ignorance into his marvelous light of spiritual understanding. Let the word bless you.

Meditate upon it, and then keep going back to God with questions. Why did you say this here, instead of that; because, if you don't ask the Holy Spirit questions, He will not bring to you revealed knowledge even though He is your teacher. So first of all, you need spiritual understanding and insight of the word, and then you have to do biblical meditation, which will give you deeper understanding and knowledge. These are symbolic of the water and the light. Biblical meditation is the water that is needed by the word of God so as to prosper in our lives.

Now, let us look at one more scripture that will shed more light on the truth that the word of God is also used to water the word.

Meditation is equated to watering of the word

Isaiah 55:10-11says "*For as the rain comes down, and the snow from heaven, and do not return there, but water the earth, and make it bring forth and bud, that it may give seed to the sower and bread to the eater, so shall My word be that goes forth from My mouth; It shall not return to Me void, but it shall accomplish what I please, and it shall prosper in the thing for which I sent it.*" Hallelujah!!! Just as the rain and snow come from heaven, and do not return back up to heaven, but waters the ground that it may cause it to bud and grow, so shall the word of God not return unto God empty but it shall prosper in its assignment. As a matter of fact, let us look at the same scripture but in a different translation. It will give us a better understanding. The bible says that the word of God is like a two-edged sword. Every day that you read the word of God, you get a different revelation, but when you read different translations they give you different perspectives of understanding, and when you put it all together you get a perfect picture. You get a complete picture of what the bible is talking about.

So here, let's read the same scripture in the New Living Translation. It doesn't change the context. The meaning is still the same, but worded differently. Now let's read to what it says. "*The rain and snow come down from the heavens and stay on the ground to water the earth. They cause the grain (seed) to grow, producing seed for the farmer and bread for the hungry. It is the same with my word. I send it out, and it always produces fruit. It will accomplish all I want it to, and it will prosper everywhere I send it.*"(**Emphasis mine**)

This is God saying that I sent my word to water the seed of my word. So the word of God, which is a two edged sword, is the seed. This same word is also the light, and the water; and this same word is sown in your heart, which is the ground or spiritual womb. Just as the seed in the natural realm need a good fertile ground, light, water, and good keeping of the ground, in order to grow; so likewise does the spiritual seed, which is the word of God need these things. All these things are the different facets of the same word of God. The bible also says in Job 14:7-9: "*Even a tree has more hope! If it is cut down, it will sprout again and grow new branches. Though its roots have grown old in the earth and its stump decays, at the scent of water it will bud and sprout again like a new seedling.* Even a stump of a tree has more hope of growing again, as long as, its water supply is not cut off. The word of God has many facets. The word is the light, the seed, and the water; all three in one. Just as there is a natural law that governs sowing and reaping, there is also a spiritual law that governs how the word of God works; and that is what I am teaching you right now. The parable of the sower was a demonstration of the spiritual photosynthesis that governs the word of God.

CHAPTER 5

CARES OF THE WORLD CHOKES THE WORD

Now, let us look at the remaining grounds and how they received the word. Let us examine the next ground, which is the thorny ground. What is the concept of the thorny ground, and how do you appropriate it? What do you have to do that you do not become like a thorny ground hearer? You see, this whole parable is revealing how we hear and apply the word of God in our life.

Jesus said in Mark 4:7 that "*And some fell among thorns, and the thorns grew up, and choked it, and it yielded no fruit*" Some of the seed fell among thorns and the thorns grew up and choked the seed. The thorns competed for the limited nutrients in the ground and therefore deprived the seed from growing. Jesus afterward explained to the disciples the meaning of this parable by saying "*And these are they which are sown among thorns; such as hear the word, and the cares of this world, and the deceitfulness of riches, and the lusts of other things entering in, choke the word, and it becomes unfruitful*".

The scripture says this seed fell among thorns; meaning the thorns were present before the seed fell amongst them. Apparently, this hearer had other issues in his heart before he heard the word. The cares of this world like monthly obligations such as rent and other utility bills, coupled with the deceitfulness of riches like get-rich-quick-schemes, got the most of his attention and focus, leading him to neglect the word of God which he had heard. It is very obvious that this hearer had no faith in the word of God because, his focus and attention was not on the word. Therefore, he did not mix faith with what he heard but rather concentrated on his physical and

explain to him the statement, "who is this scripture referring to in this context? Is it talking about himself, or talking about somebody else?" Make sure you understand because, what you understand the enemy cannot steal from you, and what you understand, becomes easy to apply.

No law or ordinance is mightier than understanding. Understanding, therefore, comes through diligent study of the word of God. The word of God does two major things in a believer's life: It provides food for the spirit, creates light for understanding and awareness in the mind. Christians need and deserve a mindset, which is widely awake and offers them the spiritual understanding of how the kingdom of God works. Understanding can overcome any situation, however mysterious or insurmountable it may appear to be. A man may imagine things that are false, but he can only understand truth; and the word of God is truth. When something is false, the apprehension of the falsehood is not the understanding of it.

Many people say that knowledge is power, but it's not true. Applied knowledge is power. What you know and don't apply doesn't empower or benefit you. When you do not understand what the buttons in your car will do for you, it will not benefit you. You can be driving around with foggy windshields without knowing that the defrost button can get rid of the fog. On the other hand, if you know about the defrost button but fails to deploy it, you will not benefit from it either. Knowing and not applying the knowledge makes it worthless.

Knowledge alone would not be good enough for me, but I have to apply the knowledge that I have. In the same way, you can have the knowledge of something, but when you don't apply that knowledge, it becomes useless. So, knowledge isn't power per se, but applied knowledge is power. Knowing the scriptures is simply making sure that you understand. Why? Because you need to understand it better so that you will be able to apply it. The knowledge that you get through spiritual understanding, you will be able to apply. Jesus wants you to understand this parable because it is the key to all parables; and as such we are having an in-depth study of the whole of Mark chapter 4; because when Jesus was speaking he spoke in a complete context.

After the parable, he went on to say other things, to elaborate or bring more light to what he was saying, and believe me you are going to be tremendously blessed. The bible is full of words loaded with power to create your own world. The very words that were spoken to create this whole universe, the very words that God used to create the worlds, these very words are available to you in the bible; and if only you can assimilate them into your spirit, meditate upon them to build your faith in them, then you'll be tremendously blessed.

Therefore renew your mind to see things from God's perspective. Begin to see things the way God sees them, and then as you do and you study the word continually and fellowship with other Christians, your life will undergo total transformation.

Lack of knowledge

The bible says in Hosea 4:6 that *"My people are destroyed for lack of knowledge*: If lack of knowledge of the word destroys God's people, then on the other hand, having knowledge of the word would tremendously empower you for success. Without knowledge, you cannot wage a good warfare. Without good or spiritual understanding of the word, you can't do much. Consider this scriptural verse as a coin with two sides. On one side is the effect of ignorance of the word of God which is destruction and on the other side is the benefit that comes with knowledge of his word which is blessing. You need to understand the word because, out of the mouth of God, comes knowledge, wisdom and understanding. So know your entitlements? What are the benefits of the promises of God to you? What are the things God has promised you?

When you don't know, you cannot lay hold of them. To activate the promises that God has given to us, we must be able to practically put the word of God into action. The Bible said that we have a better covenant built on better promises. So in the old and new covenants, there are thousands of promises that God expects each and every one of His believers or blood- bought saints to appropriate in their life. The only prerequisite is our knowledge of the faithfulness of God and His promises. The knowledge that God is faithful and can never lie should be our motivational force that drives us to activate the promises or put the word of God into practice. God is also a covenant-keeping God. Knowing the character of God, gives us an assurance that His word is ever sure, and will manifest in our life, if we apply it.

Making sure that we are able to activate these promises in our life is the theme of this work. Remember that we've been studying from the parable of the sower. This is a parable that Jesus used to explain to us or to teach us how the word of God works in our life. Also, there are three parables that Jesus spoke in Mark chapter 4 and all three of them dealt with the word of God as a seed from different perspectives, but in continuity. Mark 4:1- 32 reads "*And he began again to teach by the sea side: and there was gathered unto him a great multitude, so that he entered into a ship, and sat in the sea; and the whole multitude was by the sea on the land. And he taught them many things by parables, and said unto them in his doctrine, Hearken; Behold, there went out a sower to sow: And it came to pass, as he sowed, some fell by the way side, and the fowls of the air came and devoured it up. And some fell on stony ground, where it had not much earth; and immediately it sprang up, because it had no depth of earth: But when the sun was up, it was scorched; and because it had no root, it withered away. And some fell among thorns, and the thorns grew up, and choked it, and it yielded no fruit. And other fell on good ground, and did yield fruit that sprang up and increased; and brought forth, some thirty, and some sixty, and some an hundred.*

And he said unto them, He that hath ears to hear, let him hear. And when he was alone, they that were about him with the twelve asked of him the parable. And he said unto them, Unto you it is given to know the mystery of the kingdom of God: but unto them that are without, all these things are done in parables: That seeing they may see, and not perceive; and hearing they may hear, and not understand; lest at any time they should be converted, and their sins should be forgiven them. And he said unto them, Know ye not this parable? and how then will ye know all parables?

The sower soweth the word. And these are they by the way side, where the word is sown; but when they have HEARD, Satan cometh immediately, and taketh away the word that was sown in their hearts. And these are they likewise which are sown on stony ground; who, when they have HEARD the word, immediately receive it with gladness; And have no root in themselves, and so endure but for a time: afterward, when affliction or persecution ariseth for the word's sake, immediately they are offended. And these are they which are sown among thorns; such as HEAR the word, and the cares of this world, and the deceitfulness of riches, and the lusts of other things entering in, choke the word, and it becometh unfruitful. And these are they which are sown on good ground; such as HEAR the word, and receive it, and bring forth fruit, some thirtyfold, some sixty, and some an hundred.

And he said unto them, is a candle brought to be put under a bushel, or under a bed? and not to be set on a candlestick? For there is nothing hid, which shall not be manifested; neither was anything kept secret, but that it should come abroad. If any man have ears to HEAR, let him HEAR. And he said unto them, Take heed what ye HEAR: with what measure ye mete, it shall be measured to you: and unto you that HEAR (AND UNDERSTAND) shall more be given. For he that hath, to him shall be given: and he that hath not, from him shall be taken even that which he hath.

And he said, So is the kingdom of God, as if a man should cast seed into the ground; And should sleep, and rise night and day, and the seed should spring and grow up, he knoweth not how. For the earth bringeth forth fruit of herself; first the blade, then the ear, after that the full corn in the ear. But when the fruit is brought forth, immediately he putteth in the sickle, because the harvest is come.

And he said, Whereunto shall we liken the kingdom of God? or with what comparison shall we compare it? It is like a grain of mustard seed, which, when it is sown in the earth, is less than all the seeds that be in the earth: But when it is sown, it groweth up, and becometh greater than all herbs, and shooteth out great branches; so that the fowls of the air may lodge under the shadow of it."

In these parables, Jesus used the word of God as an analogous seed that when given the proper conditions, would germinate and grow in our lives. In life, we are governed by laws. There are different kinds of laws that govern our lives; our everyday lives are ordered by different laws. There are physical laws, civil laws, marital laws, traffic laws, and all other kinds of laws.

There are also laws that pertain to the word of God, but the law of seedtime and harvest, which the Bible talks about in the book of Genesis 8:22, is the principal law, as far as the seed is concerned. The Bible says *"While the earth remains, seedtime and harvest, and cold and heat, and summer and winter, and day and night shall not cease"* This law was decreed after the flood in the days of Noah, and it established the truth that there are seasons in life. According to the scripture that we just read, we have days and we have nights, we have summer and we have winter, we have cold and we have heat. All these seasons are interchanging one another according to the ordinations of God, who works according to principles. The seed also has a law that, there's a season for a seed to be sown and there's a season for a seed to be harvested. Sandwiched between these two seasons of sowing and reaping is the natural process that the seed goes through. So there is a law that governs and regulates seeds.

When a seed is planted, the Bible also tells us that there's a set of conditions that need to be present in order for the seed to grow. When Jesus was using this as an analogy in the parable of the sower, he gave six different types of grounds in which the seed was planted. But then only three out of the six or 50 percent of the seed grew in the ground. Fifty percent (50%) of the seeds sown did not yield fruit because of unfavorable conditions in which it was sown. So it is obvious that a seed needs certain favorable conditions in order to grow. Likewise the word of God which is an incorruptible seed needs certain favorable conditions in order for it to yield and produce the desired results. Jesus spoke so many parables in which he used natural elements to explain spiritual truths. He had to come to our level of comprehension so that his message could be understood by the targeted audience. Many of His parables taught us how the kingdom of God works in the hearts of men. However, he emphatically said this parable is the key to understanding all parables; because it indicated the supremacy of the word of God in his kingdom.

Everything God created came out of the word as it was spoken. All his creation were done through the word. The conception of Jesus by Virgin Mary was spoken by His messenger angel Gabriel. Everything God ever did or is going to do, will be done through the spoken word. That is the reason why this parable is paramount in our Christian walk. Jesus knew the needs of men and as such gave unto them the ways, means and ability to attain it. In the beginning, God gave to Adam the seed (His word) as man's means of sustenance. *"And God said, Behold, I have given you every HERB- BEARING SEED, which is upon the face of all the earth, and every tree, in the which is the fruit of a tree- yielding seed; to you it shall be for meat."* Genesis 1:29.

I want you to take note of something mentioned in this scripture. It said, God gave unto man, the herb-yielding seed for his provision or meat and to the wild animals, birds and the cattle he gave the herbs as their food. Therefore, man needs the seed (the word of God) to survive both physically and spiritually. The physical seed is meant to nourish and sustain his physical body and the spiritual seed to sustain his spirit. This concept was reiterated when Jesus said in Mathew 4:4 *"Man shall not live by bread alone, but by every word that proceeds out of the mouth of God "*.

So man's dependency upon the word of God cannot be understated. This is why Jesus taught this parable to emphasize the importance of the word of God in our lives and how to hear, understand , meditate and apply it correctly so as to benefit and have good success. This parable pointed to the truth that; seeds need right environmental conditions to grow, and therefore, the word of God, which is a spiritual seed, also needs a good spiritual environment to grow. When you understand, meditate, and mix faith with the word of God when you hear it, virtue and revelation knowledge would be added onto you, thus empowering you to apply and activate the word in your life. But the absence of these virtues was the idea Jesus was sending across to his audience when he told this parable.

Lack of understanding

Earlier, we talked about the seed that fell on the wayside and as soon as it fell the enemy came or the birds of the air came and then devoured it. It means that, this seed fell on hard ground and was very visible to the birds of the air, so they came and devoured it. If this seed was received in the heart or buried in the ground, it wouldn't have been seen by the birds of the air. Seeds are meant to be buried in the soil and not on the ground where it would be visible. No bird can dig out a seed out of the ground unless it is visible on the surface of the ground. So this seed failed because it was not received into the soil. This is symbolic of the devil coming to steal the word away from us when we don't understand it, and therefore fail to hide the word in our heart.

The enemy can only steal the word when there's no understanding. One of the reasons why the word of God fails in people's life is because of lack of understanding. And we've established that understanding is equated to light, illumination or insight. Understanding of the word comes through inspiration from God, and also through diligent studies. It gives knowledge or information to the possessor. It Illuminates our spirit man to divine principles and makes these truths easy to apply. Just like in the natural realm the seed needs light to photosynthesize its food, so likewise when you hear the word of God, the light of spiritual understanding has to be present to help the seed to materialize in your life. It is one of the conditions needed by the spiritual seed of the word of God to grow.

Lack of meditation

Secondly, we talked about the seed that fell among the rocky ground or the stony ground. A stony or rocky ground lacks moisture and therefore very shallow. There was dryness, because there were rocks that have taken much of the soil to make it shallow, so as soon as the seed fell, it was received immediately in the shallow ground and started growing but because it had no depth of soil, it withered away when the sun arose. Normally, a seed needs sunlight in addition to water in the soil to manufacture its food in a good fertile ground but not to wither away. Although, the sun came up, but due to lack of moisture in the soil, the seed did not grow. Moreover, the absence of moisture in the soil, did not make it a fertile ground thus rendering it unfavorable for seed growth.

This means that the dryness of the stony ground caused the seed to wither away when the sun arose. If there was moisture or water in the soil, then the seed would have grown when the sun came up; because the seed needs the sunlight to manufacture its food. So when you hear the word of God and don't gain a deep rooted understanding of it by meditating continually on it, the moment affliction comes or persecution comes as a result of the word, you falter. There was understanding, because the sun came up but the crop failure was due to lack of moisture. Meditation on the word that you have understood would bring about deeper understanding and revelation knowledge.

Understanding would give you knowledge but meditation would give you revelation knowledge. There are three types of knowledge namely; formal knowledge which we acquire through formal education, experiential knowledge, which we acquire through life experiences, and finally, revelation knowledge which is given by God through the Holy Spirit. Formal knowledge comes through understanding that we acquire from studying but revelation knowledge comes by inspiration from the Holy Spirit through meditation. When you meditate on the word of God, you give the Holy Spirit some raw materials to work with in order to bring about revelation knowledge. Lack of meditation also causes the word of God to be unfruitful in your life. In the subsequent chapters I, through the grace of God, would show you the dynamics of these principles.

Lack of faith

Then there's the one that fell among thorns. The Bible said that the thorns chocked it and it did not bear fruit. And Jesus explained by saying that these are the ones that when they receive the word, allow the cares of the world and the deceitfulness of riches, which were present before the word was received, to compete with the word for attention. The thorns were present before the seed was sown because the bible says *"and some fell among thorns"* These already present concerns (thorns) shifted his attention and focus from the word of God to these distractions, and therefore, choked the word. Since the thorns were present before the seed was planted on the ground, they competed for the limited nutrients in the ground thereby choking the life out of the seed.

Many of us have our own cares, issues and things that we're stressing about, things that we're worrying about, strongholds that are governing the way we think and behave. Due to the presence of these preconceived cares and wants, when we hear the word of God, our focus turns away from the Word and focuses on the cares that are present already in our lives. The cares of this world and the deceitfulness of riches like get-rich-quick schemes, entices us away from focusing on the word of God. This indicates that there was lack of faith, because when you have faith you'll cast all your cares onto God by believing and trusting that He will supply all your needs according to his glorious riches in Christ Jesus.

When you have faith, you will not be anxious or worry about anything because God is your source. The bible says in 1 Peter 5:7*"Casting all your cares upon him; for he cares for you'*. When the children of Israel were in the wilderness after leaving Egypt, their focus was not on the manifold blessings which God miraculously bestowed on them but their focus was on mundane things, which they were accustomed to in the past. They did not have faith in the word of God but kept their focus on the cares of this world such as good food, and good homes, and were not ready to believe in the word of God. They did not cast their cares onto God, but rather, they served to sway their focus away from God. Likewise, the seed that fell among thorns did not bear fruit because the thorns choked it due to lack of faith. When you worry about the cares of the world, it is a sign of faithlessness.

The cares of this life can cause the word of God to be unfruitful. When you have faith, you will cast your cares onto God, because He cares for you. Faith in God gives us the assurance that, although we do not know what tomorrow has in store for us, but because we are strongly anchored to the One who knows and controls tomorrow, we believe that our future is safe and secure in His hands. Jesus said *"Therefore I say to you, do not worry about your life, what you will eat or what you will drink; nor about your body, what you will put on. Is not life more than food and the body more than clothing? Look at the birds of the air, for they neither sow nor reap nor gather into barns; yet your heavenly Father feeds them. Are you not of more value than they? Which of you by worrying can add one cubit to his stature? So why do you worry about clothing? Consider the lilies of the field, how they grow: they neither toil nor spin; and yet I say to you that even Solomon in all his glory was not arrayed like one of these. Now if God so clothes the grass of the field, which today is, and tomorrow is thrown into the oven, will He not much more clothe you, O you of LITTLE FAITH? Therefore do not worry, saying, 'What shall we eat?' or 'What shall we drink?' or 'What shall we wear?' For after all these things the Gentiles seek. For your heavenly Father knows that you need all these things. But seek first the kingdom of God and His righteousness, and all these things shall be added to you"*.

When we seek God first in all our ways, He will never leave nor forsake us, but rather, supply all our needs according to His glorious riches in Christ Jesus. It is, therefore, apparent that the seed did not grow in the thorny ground because the presence of the weeds choked the seed from growing. When there are all kinds of mental blocks serving as hindrances to the manifestation of the word of God in our life, it drains faith in the word. Most of the seeds failed, because the hearers lacked faith, understanding and meditation on the incorruptible word of God.

So where there's lack of faith, where there's lack of meditation, and where there's lack of understanding, the word of God will

not prosper. Faith is very important because without it, we can never receive anything from God. Faith is the spiritual currency by which things are bought and obtained in the spirit. It is a medium of exchange in the spiritual realm. Everything that man seeks can be obtained through faith. Everyone has been given the measure of faith which needs to be exercised in order to grow. Faith is like the muscles in your body. Everyone has muscles but it is only those who go to the gym or in some way exercise their muscles can develop big, strong muscles. Likewise, until you engage your faith, it will never grow. We have to mix faith with the word of God, we have to meditate on the word, and we have to strive to understand it in order for the seed of the word of God to germinate in our life and bear good fruit.

CHAPTER 6

GOOD FERTILE GROUND

Now, let us take a look at the good ground. The bible says in Mark 4:8 *"And other fell on good ground, and did yield fruit that sprang up and increased; and brought forth, some thirty, and some sixty, and some an hundred"*. This seed fell on the good ground where it sprung up, increased and then brought forth fruit. Some of them yielded thirty fold, some sixty and some a hundredfold. First of all, the seed sprang up and then afterward increased before it brought forth fruit. This means that it was a process. It did not bear fruit overnight but rather it went through a gradual process of growth.

The seed that was sown on the good ground bore fruit because of the presence of favorable conditions. When you consider the three gospel accounts of this parable, you can safely conclude that favorable conditions were present. In Mark 4:20, Jesus explained this hearer by saying " *And these are they which are sown on good ground; such as hear the word, and RECEIVE it, and bring forth fruit, some thirtyfold, some sixty, and some an hundred."* (Emphasis mine) And then in Mathew 13:23, He says " *But he that received seed into the good ground is he that heareth the word, and UNDERSTANDETH it; which also beareth fruit, and bringeth forth, some an hundredfold, some sixty, some thirty.* (Emphasis mine)

Also in Luke 8: 15 He says *"But that on the good ground are they, which in an honest and good heart, having heard (understood) the word, keep (meditated on) it and bring forth fruit with patience."* (Emphasis mine)

84

When you analyze these scriptures carefully, you notice that the seed was received, understood, kept, and meditated upon with patience for the growing seed to manifest. The seed did not grow overnight and moreover it engaged the effort of the hearer by receiving, meditating and keeping the seed. All these words were "action" words on the part of the hearer. These actions were added to the word bore fruit or moved from a mere seed into a fruit. For example, the verb "keep" in Luke's account denotes maintenance and retention of the seed with diligence and continuity. So there was understanding, and what was understood was meditated upon whilst being mixed with faith.

The most important thing that I want you to take note of is that the seed did not yield equal harvest. In all three accounts, some yielded thirty-fold, some yielded sixty-fold and some yielded hundredfold. Why was it that the good ground that had moisture, sunlight and absence of thorns or weeds, didn't yield equal harvest? It did not yield fruit equally for all of them. Some yielded thirty-fold of what was sown whilst some yielded sixty-fold of what was sown, and others yielded hundredfold of what was sown. Why is it that it did not yield equally to all of them? We will find out later.

Jesus proceeded to explain the reason why He spoke in parables by saying "*Because it is given unto you to know the mysteries of the kingdom of heaven, but to them it is not given. For whosoever hath (understanding), to him shall (revelation knowledge) be given, and he shall have more abundance (through meditation): but whosoever hath not (understanding) , from him shall be taken away even that he hath. Therefore speak I to them in parables: because they seeing see not; and hearing they hear not, neither do they understand. And in them is fulfilled the prophecy of Esaias, which saith, By hearing ye shall hear, and shall not understand; and seeing ye shall see, and shall not perceive: For this people's heart is waxed gross, and their ears are dull of hearing, and their eyes they have closed; lest at any time they should see with their eyes and hear with their ears, and should understand with their heart, and should be converted, and I should heal them. But blessed are your eyes, for they see: and your ears, for they hear. For verily I say unto you, that many prophets and righteous men have desired to see those things which ye see, and have not seen them; and to hear those things which ye hear, and have not heard them"* (Emphasis mine, Mathew 13:11-17). Jesus made it emphatically clear that it is through the Holy Spirit that understanding in the word of God is given to believers. Unless a person is born-again, he cannot understand spiritual things.

A person only hears what he understands. Jesus said; He speaks in parables so *"That seeing they may see, and not perceive; and hearing they may hear, and not understand;* that seeing, they may see, but not perceive; and hearing they may hear, but not understand. The reason why I'm speaking in parables is because those who really want to hear and understand will have to put in an effort to hear and understand. A parable is a style of teaching where truth is hidden from casual listeners until when they are ready to discover it. The purpose of a parable is not to lay bare the truth but to hide the truth because the speaker is working with a principle based upon the premise *"nothing is truly yours until you discover it."* This points to the truth that it takes inspiration and illumination from the Holy Spirit plus an effort from you to understand spiritual truth. The word of God is something that you cannot just hear and easily understand. It takes the Spirit of God to explain the word. So, you have to give it time and study, and then understanding of the word will come. A light of illumination would be turned on in your mind when understanding comes.

Then, meditating on the word that had been understood would build up your faith in that particular word, and bring to you deep revelation knowledge which will make it possible to apply the truth. Whatever you think about continually will manifest in your life. This is a spiritual principle. The bible says that *"as a man thinks in his heart, so is he"*

As you think more on these things in the word of God, you will become the very thing that you're thinking about. I want to point something out to you about what Jesus said to the disciples which was very, very powerful. From the verse eleven in the same scripture, Jesus said *"Unto you it is given to know the mystery of the kingdom of God: but unto them that are without, all these things are done in parables: That seeing they may see, and not perceive; and hearing they may hear, and not understand; LEST AT ANYTIME THEY SHOULD BE CONVERTED, AND THEIR SINS SHOULD BE FORGIVEN THEM'* **(Emphasis mine)**. Jesus is saying that if His listeners understand His message, the word can transform them and cause them to repent so that their sins will be forgiven.

The word of God is powerful and able to convert one from destruction into salvation. The word of God is capable of turning your situation around for the better. The word of God is capable of turning your darkness into light and your mourning into dancing. Moreover, it takes inspiration from the Spirit of God to understand the word of God. The Holy Spirit must open the eyes of your understanding before you can truly know and rightly interpret His truth. His truth is available only to those with a regenerate spirit and in whom He dwells, for only the Spirit can illumine Scripture.

The spirit of man is the candle of the Lord

Furthermore, this scripture can be understood better when you compare it to what Jesus said in the twenty-first verse. And he said unto them, *"Is a candle brought to be put under a bushel, or under a bed? and not to be set on a candlestick? For there is nothing hid, which shall not be manifested; neither was anything kept secret, but that it should come abroad.* Wait a minute! Let me read these two scriptures again.

First it said, I'm saying this unto you in parables, because unto you it is given to know the mysteries or secrets of the kingdom of God; but unto them that are without or outside all these things are done in parables. Jesus said to them "I'm telling you these things in parables because you have the power and the ability to understand; since you have been enlightened by the spirit of God to understand these things. But those that are outside they don't understand". Then he went on and asked *"is a candle brought to be put under a bushel or under a bed and not to be set upon a candlestick?"* Why is He talking about a candle and what does it have to do with anything? This is what he meant; it is written in Proverbs 20:27 *"**The spirit of man is the candle of the Lord, searching all the inward parts of the belly**"*. The candle, according to the bible, is the spirit of man by which the Lord searches the inward parts of a man's belly or heart. The bible also says *"**...there is a spirit in man: and the inspiration of the Almighty gives them understanding**"* This verse is saying that understanding, illumination, and insight comes from above into our spirit through the Spirit of God who illuminates our human spirit and gives to us the ability to understand the mysteries of the kingdom of God.

So Jesus was talking about the spirit of man, that we have not been born again or spiritually regenerated to be deprived of the hidden things and mysteries of God but rather we have been born-again to be set on a candlestick which is symbolic of the Holy Spirit, who then reveals the mysteries of God to us. Once you have your spirit man born again then, you are connected to the Holy Spirit who will unveil a lot of these things unto you. So when Jesus was saying "Is a candle brought to be put under a bushel or under a bed and not to be set on a candlestick, He was talking about the rejuvenated spirit of man. When a candle is lit we don't hide it under a bed but rather we put it on a candlestick; and a candlestick in the Bible is symbolic of the Holy Spirit of God. So when your spirit becomes born again and rejuvenated and then connected to the Spirit of God, He will bring unto your understanding, a lot of these things that you hear and you'll be able to apply it to your life.

The bible says in Zechariah 4:1-6 *"**And the angel that talked with me came again, and waked me, as a man that is wakened out of his sleep, And said unto me, What seest thou? And I said, I have looked, and behold a CANDLESTICK all of gold, with a bowl upon the top of it, and his seven lamps thereon, and seven pipes to the seven lamps, which are upon the top thereof: And two olive trees by it, one upon the right side of the bowl, and the other upon the left side thereof. So I answered and spake to the angel that talked with me, saying, what are these, my lord? Then the angel that talked with me answered and said unto me, Knowest thou not what these be? And I said, No, my lord. Then he answered and spake unto me, saying, this is the word of the Lord**"* *unto Zerubbabel, saying, not by might, nor by power, but by my spirit, saith the Lord of hosts".*

We can conclude from the preceding scripture that the candlestick is the Spirit of God who empowered and anointed Zerubbabel to do the work that God assigned him to do. So what was Jesus talking about then, or how does this relate to what Jesus was saying? It takes the revelation and empowerment of God to be able to appropriate or put these things into practice and also be able to plant the promises in our hearts, knowing that God, who has promised, is faithful to bring it to pass. So He has already done his part, all He expect of you is to make sure that you position yourself so that these things will come to pass in your life. The promises of God will definitely manifest in your life if you diligently apply these principles. So in the whole of Mark chapter four, Jesus talked about three different parables all referring to the seed.

These three different types of parables were all referring to the word of God as a seed. He showed in different ways how the seed should grow in our life and I'm going to delve into that so that you'll get a better understanding of how to activate the word or promise of God in your life. Now let's see why the seed which was sown on the good ground, did not yield equal harvest; but some yielded thirty fold, some sixty and others, hundredfold.

Mark 4:24-25 said *"And he said unto them, Take heed what ye hear: with what measure ye mete, it shall be measured to you: and unto you that hear shall more be given. For he that hath, to him shall be given: and he that hath not, from him shall be taken even that which he hath."* And he said unto them, take heed what you hear; with what measure ye mete, it shall be measured unto you and unto you that receive or unto you that hear shall more be given. For he that hath (understanding), to him shall more (understanding) be given and he that hath not (understanding), from him shall be taken even that which he hath (like the wayside hearer). It says take heed what you hear. Why? According to this parable, we know that the sense of hearing is one of the entry points into our hearts. Okay, it says take heed what ye hear, for with what measure ye mete it shall be measured to you and unto you that hear shall more be given. For he that have, to him shall more be given, and he that have not from him shall be taken away even that which he have. What is Jesus talking about?

What kind of measure is He talking about here? The measure of meditation, the measure of attention, the measure of thought and study you give to what you hear will determine the measure of grace, virtue and knowledge that will be measured back to you. He that hears and understands shall more understanding be given; for he that has understanding, shall more understanding be given through meditation; But he that have not understanding, even what he has shall be taken away from him. So that is what we saw in the first instance, the seed that fell on the wayside because he had no understanding even what he heard was taken away from him. That's what Jesus was talking about here. I like the way the amplified version of the bible renders this verse.

So let's read what Amplified bible says. *"And he said to them, be careful what you are hearing. For the measure of thought and study you'll give to the truth you hear (understand) will be the measure of virtue and knowledge that comes back to you and more besides will be given to you who hear. For to him who has (understanding) more will be given. And from him who has nothing (no understanding) even what he has, will be taken away by force"* (Emphasis mine). So we realize that the devil was able to take away from them because they did not have understanding of what they heard. It also says *"unto him that have (understanding) shall more be given"*. Why? It 's because the one that have understanding and meditate on what he knows, more understanding will be given to him by the Holy Spirit.

The Bible says in Psalm 119: 97-100 *"Oh, how I love your law! it is my meditation all the day. You, through your commandments, make me wiser than my enemies; for they are ever with me. I have MORE UNDERSTANDING than all my teachers, for your testimonies (words) are my MEDITATION. I understand more than the ancients, because I KEEP (or meditate on) your precept".* David said in this psalm, you through your commandments, has made me wiser than my enemies for your (God's) words are ever with me. I have more understanding than all my teachers because your testimonies (words) are my meditation. Since your testimonies or your words are my meditation, I have more understand than the ancient because I keep, meditate, think and ponder your precepts or words. What does this mean? He said I have more understanding, because your word is my meditation.

When you keep the word of God or meditate upon the word of God, it will cause you to increase in your understanding and have deep revelation knowledge. In Luke 8:15 it says " *But that on the good ground are they, which in an honest and good heart, having heard the word, KEEP it, and bring forth fruit with patience*" When you compare Psalm119:97-100 with Luke 8:15, you realize that both scriptures talked about meditation by using the word to KEEP in reference to meditation. The good ground hearer was the one who understood the word, meditated on it, and as a result bore fruit based on the measure of meditation. In Mathew's gospel, he rendered the good ground as "*But he who received seed on the good ground is he who hears the word and understands it, who indeed bears fruit and produces: some a hundredfold, some sixty, some thirty*." Therefore, putting the three gospel accounts together, you realized that the good ground hearer understood the word, kept and meditated upon it before it bore fruit based on the measure of attention devoted to the word. The word "*KEEP*" is translated from the Greek word "KATECHO", which means to "keep in memory or retain". So the good ground hearer is the one that understood the truth, meditated on the truth and mixed faith with the truth. This eventually led to a bumper harvest.

This is what Jesus was talking about in the parable of the sower. In order to obtain your desires from the word of God, you have to understand the truth and dwell on the truth continually until it becomes one with you or your second nature. This is to say, the truth has become a habit in you. This can be achieved when we meditate on the truth day and night. Moreover, we have to mix faith with the truth. This explains the parable of the sower. Whatever you understand and think about all the time would influence your lifestyle and you will eventually become what you are continually thinking about. Paul said in Philippians 4:8 " *Finally, brethren, whatsoever things are true, whatsoever things are honest, whatsoever things are just, whatsoever things are pure, whatsoever things are lovely, whatsoever things are of good report; if there be any virtue, and if there be any praise, think (meditate) on these things.*" (Emphasis mine) Meditate on these good virtues and they will manifest in your life because as a man thinks in his heart, so is he. Meditation, therefore, is likened to the watering of the seed of the word of God that is sown in your heart. Now, let us look at the other parables that Jesus spoke about in the same context to shed more light on the power of the incorruptible seed of the word of God.

CHAPTER 7

PARABLE OF THE GROWING SEED

Jesus went on further to talk about another parable that also concerns the seed. This time around, He talked about how the seed grows. This parable should not be taken independently but as a continuation of the parable of the sower. It is inevitable that the seed of God's word will grow when it is received, by faith into the heart of the hearer. The seed grows independently in the ground. The supernatural power inside the word of God is released when it is received, then mixed with faith, understood and meditated upon until it manifests. When you plant the seed of the word of God in your heart, you should not expect the seed to bear fruit instantly, but wait for God to do His part. Just like in the natural realm, when you sow a seed, you don't expect it to bear fruit or reap it instantly. Likewise when you sow today you're not going to reap your harvest today, but you have to give it time to grow. Man does not control how and when the seed should grow; but it is rather in the powerful hands of God.

Mark 4:26 says *"And he said, So is the kingdom of God, as if a man should cast seed into the ground; And should sleep, and rise night and day, and the seed should spring and grow up, he knoweth not how. For the EARTH brings forth fruit of herself; first the blade, then the ear, after that the full corn in the ear. But when the fruit is brought forth, immediately he puts in the sickle, because the harvest is come."*

What is Jesus talking about here? In this parable, Jesus presumed that the conditions that are needed for the seed to grow were present in this soil. There was a fertile ground, adequate sunlight, moisture and the absence of unwanted weeds, so growth was inevitable. In other words, there was spiritual understanding of the word, which was meditated upon and then mixed with faith, until it manifested in the life of the hearer. Jesus did not explain this parable like the parable of the sower; because the meaning of it had already been given. The seed was still representative of the word of God and the ground was still the hearts of men. However, this time around, it is a man that casts seed in his own heart.

So He proceeded from seed sown on fertile ground in the parable of the sower into this parable, whereby the planted seed goes through the laws of natural growth. He then talked about the principle of seed time and harvest as it was mentioned in Genesis 8:22. In that principle it states that, there is a time of growth between sowing and reaping. A season when the planted seed goes through the natural process of growth in the ground. This is the time that meditation and watering of the word becomes very important. The seed would grow only when the right conditions are present. When man tills the land and strip it of all unwanted weeds thus making conditions favorable for seed growth. Moreover, He is saying that, there are two dimensions to a seed. There is the natural aspect as well as the supernatural aspect. There is the role that man plays in planting and watering the seed, and the role that God plays by causing the planted seed to grow.

The bible says in 1 Corinthians 3:6 "*I planted, Apollos watered, but God gave the increase.* So when you sow the word of God in your heart, even on fertile ground, do not expect to have your harvest instantly. When you plant it today know that the rest is in the hands of God. Whilst waiting for the seed to grow, keep meditating on the word or watering the seed until it germinates and bears fruit. Just like when you sow a seed in the natural realm, you don't sow today and reap today. You sow today and you sleep, wake up, sleep, and wake up again until you see the blade start to grow gradually. Science has taught us that when you plant a seed before it grows, it dies first. And then the first activity that happens is the root start growing. The root will come out of the seed and then dig deep into the ground and as it goes deep into the ground in search of nutrients to promote growth, the blade will shoot out of

94

the earth. So before you see the blade coming out of the earth, the root had already been developing for a while.

This parable dealt with the growth period between sowing and reaping when we apply our understanding, faith and meditation to the word of God. This is the season when the effects of the sun, water and the absence of weeds come into manifestation. Our input at this point, would determine our output. What we do at this point, would determine the result or harvest we will get from the seed. Man cannot completely control the growth of the seed. The bible says *"As you do not know what is the way of the wind, or how the bones grow in the womb of her who is with child, so you do not know the works of God who makes everything. In the morning sow your seed, and in the evening do not withhold your hand; for you do not know which will prosper, either this or that, or whether both alike will be good"*.

This scripture is comparing the growth of the seed of man (sperm) in the womb of a woman to how seed grows in the ground. In both instances, patience becomes an important virtue; because man cannot determine how the seed grows and is, therefore, compelled to wait on God to do his part. Whilst you are waiting, keep watering it by meditating on it, using other scriptures to under-gird or support it. The Bible says that just as the rain and the snow comes down from above and waters the ground and causes it to bud or grow, likewise the word of God will water your ground and cause your ground to bud and grow. The word of God has the power to water your ground or soften your heart and cause your seed to grow. Just as the rain comes from above and waters the ground, so shall the word of God that have proceeded out of His mouth, not return unto Him void; but it shall accomplish its purpose.

Meaning every word that proceeded out of the mouth of God has the ability to water your ground, and your heart, softening the heart, to give it the right condition for the seed to grow. The word of God has the power to transform your life when you apply it correctly. It is a spiritual seed that has been encoded with the ability to reproduce after its kind. Every situation or issue that we encounter in life has a corresponding bible verse that pertains to it.

They are all embedded in the bible which is our manual for successful living. Whatever you need, is in the word of God. They have been given to us through precious promises. The bible says in 2 Peter 1:2-4 that *"**Grace and peace be multiplied unto you through the KNOWLEDGE of God, and of Jesus our Lord, According as his divine power hath given unto us ALL THINGS that pertain unto life and godliness, through the KNOWLEDGE of him that hath called us to glory and virtue: Whereby are given unto us exceeding great and precious PROMISES: that by these (promises) ye might be partakers of the divine nature, having escaped the corruption that is in the world through lust"***

This scripture is confirming that, God has given to us all things that pertain to life and godliness through our knowledge of Him who has called us. In His calling, He has given to us exceedingly great and precious promises that through them (promises), we will partake, share and participate in His divine nature. This means, our knowledge of God empowers us to know the promises, which have been given to us in His word. Our knowledge of God through His word unveils thousands of precious promises scattered throughout the bible. These promises cover every area of our lives and when we sow the promise in our hearts in the right condition, we can rest assured believing that God would cause it to grow in our heart and manifest in our life. You will not know how the seed will grow in your heart and manifest in your life but simply believe it.

I remember years ago when my wife left Africa and went to America, I stood on the word of God continually until we were re-united. I stood on the scripture, which says *"**what God has put together, let no man put asunder**"*. This was my prayer and meditation. I believed it was the will of God for married couples to stay together and so for my wife to be in America and I in Africa was not the will of God. I believed that God will not put us together, and then later on put us asunder, therefore, it was against His word or will for us to be separated. So for about three years I meditated, prayed and thanked God dwelling mainly on this scripture. Eventually, God mysteriously, opened the door for me to join my wife in America. So the word of God works when you work it continually, believing that He is a faithful God who watches over His word to perform it.

When God called Abraham, he gave him promises that had been extended to all of us through his seed Jesus Christ. Therefore, it is very important to have a good knowledge of God's word so that grace and peace will be multiplied in your life. The more you know about God, the more grace and peace you get. The more promises that you know and actively apply would determine the virtue and glory that comes back to you. The level of your knowledge about God, determines the level of faith and understanding you possess.

Everyman is limited by his own knowledge. Since everything had been given to us through promises, our knowledge of the promises becomes paramount to our success in life. If you do not know about a pain killer that can cure your headache, it cannot cure you. This is the reason why God said "*My people are destroyed for lack of knowledge (of my promises)*" (Emphasis mine). On the other hand, the people that know their God and His promises shall do exploits. What you don't know, can kill you, and what you know and don't apply will not benefit you. Therefore activating the promises of God in one's life should be the primary desire of every blood-bought child of God. It is for this very reason that Jesus was crucified on the cross so that the blessing of God would be made available to all men. I pray, in the name of Jesus, that you will assimilate these truths. I pray that you'll be able to assimilate these truths and apply them to your life; and that you will realize that every time you apply this truth it will bring great success to you; because this is the word of God which never fails.

Everything that God has said in his word is true and if we will apply them to ourselves, it will be done unto us according to the promise. Therefore, find a scripture of promise that pertains to your situation and firstly, ensure that you have total understanding of it. Begin to put it on the inside of you by memorizing the scripture and taking note of the context in which it was used. Build a spiritual edifice or tabernacle on the scripture by dwelling constantly and totally on it. Repeat and review the scripture until it becomes personalized by putting your name in the context instead of people in the bible. Then picture the concepts by using your imagination and seeing yourself already in full possession of this promise of God. Turn each part of the scripture into prayer to God the father through the name of the Son, Jesus Christ.

Finally apply the truth to your life. The power of the word of God is manifested in its' application. Keep on holding on by meditating on it continually and eventually it will manifest in your life. This is a universal principle which ensures that whatever thought you hold in your mind for a long time, will sink through spiritual osmosis into your heart which is your spiritual "womb", and whatever is conceived in your heart

(spiritual womb) will be given birth to or manifest in the natural. You may not know how; but it will definitely manifest if you do precisely as has been stated in the bible.

When God promised Abraham a son, he waited for twenty five years before the manifestation of the promise. The seed had to grow into maturity. When God told Abraham that the land of Canaan would be given to his descendants, Abraham did not wait for his descendants to possess the land in the future; but he activated his faith by buying a piece of the land to be used as a burial ground for him and his immediate family. As a result of his action, Abraham, Sarah, Isaac, Rebecca, Jacob and his wife were all buried in the cave of Machpelah. Genesis 23: 8-10 says *"**And he spoke with them, saying, if it is your wish that I bury my dead out of my sight, hear me, and meet with Ephron the son of Zohar for me, that he may give me the cave of Machpelah which he has, which is at the end of his field. Let him give it to me at the full price, as property for a burial place among you.**"*

The bible tells us Abraham bought this piece of land as a burial ground for his family when Sarah died. Though, the land of Canaan was not yet possessed by his descendants until four hundred years later, but yet Abraham, the father of faith, by faith bought a piece of the land as a burial ground. He demonstrated his absolute trust in God and His word. He understood that once God has spoken, He is faithful to accomplish His word and as such he (Abraham) planted himself as a seed on that land. He willed in his heart to possess the land for his descendants by his faith in what God had promised. As a result of this action, Abraham, Isaac, Sarah, Rebecca, Jacob and Joseph were all buried on this very piece of land, which was bought by Abraham. Abraham received the seed of the promise and he mixed it up with faith, and then continually meditated on the promise until it manifested.

In Genesis 49:29-33 the bible says *"And he (Jacob) charged them, and said unto them, I am to be gathered unto my people: bury me with my fathers in the cave that is in the field of Ephron the Hittite, In the cave that is in the field of Machpelah, which is before Mamre, in the land of Canaan, which Abraham bought with the field of Ephron the Hittite for a possession of a buryingplace. There they buried Abraham and Sarah his wife; there they buried Isaac and Rebekah his wife; and there I buried Leah. The purchase of the field and of the cave that is therein was from the children of Heth. And when Jacob had made an end of commanding his sons, he gathered up his feet into the bed, and yielded up the ghost, and was gathered unto his people."* The patriarchs planted themselves as seed in their death on the promise land, because they believed in the promise of God even though the manifestation was in the future. Whenever God saw their remains in the land of Canaan, it reminded Him of His covenant with Abraham, Isaac, and Jacob. Moreover, it reminded God of their faithfulness; because they believed and acted upon the promise until death.

Indeed, Abraham had faith in God and believed in His words. Even though, the manifestation did not come until four hundred years afterward, he knew something about the immutability of the word of God, and chose to depend totally on it. You too can depend on the word of God by sowing it in your heart and letting it go through the normal growth process. The word of God is so sure that it will never fail if only we can apply it to our lives and do what we're supposed to do with all diligence, it will never fail because our God is faithful and He changes not. He's the same yesterday, today, and forever. Waiting patiently for the manifestation of the promises of God in your life is very important. Jesus said that when the word of God is sown in the ground, it takes time to grow according to the laws of nature. The benefits will come gradually, but surely.

Just as a natural seed is encoded with natural DNA to reproduce after its kind in a miraculous way, so likewise, the incorruptible seed of the word of God is encoded with spiritual DNA to produce what it was sent to do. Everything in the universe was created by the word of God out of nothing. So the word of God was the primary raw material that was used to create the whole universe. This same raw material is at your disposal to be used to create your own universe just as it was used in the beginning by God. No man knows this raw material more than Jesus Christ who was with God during the creation of the universe. He is enlightening us to the supremacy of the word. It is sure to reproduce after what it is meant to do so patiently wait and it will not be too long.

The bible says that all shall pass away except the word of God. Everything you see around you would expire one day; but the incorruptible seed, would never corrupt or expire. The earth, where the seed is sown would pass away but the seed would not. The farmer who sows the seed would pass away, but the seed would not. All shall pass except the word of God, which is eternal. So yearn for this incorruptible seed and let it be part of you that you too would have eternal life. Not everyone has what it takes to carry this seed in his heart. In the parable of the sower, we noticed that, not all the grounds yielded fruit when the seed was sown. Fifty percent of the grounds failed to produce; because they lacked certain conditions, which prevented them from yielding fruit. So when you look at those scriptures and look at those truths you realize that Jesus was teaching about spiritual photosynthesis.

The word of God will be preached to all people; but then some will receive it in good faith and some will not receive it. Whenever you hear the word of God, anything that will cause doubt, unbelief, and things that will not benefit the word, should be removed. Get rid of them out of your life and your mind and patiently wait for the manifestation of your desire by meditating and thinking about it continually. Then the blessings will flow and then the manifestation of the word will come. You rid your mind of all these negative things by renewing your mind with the word of God through meditation.

The one who has understood the word and has studied, meditated upon it, and mixed it up with faith, would wait patiently because faith is the substance of things hoped for; the evidence of things not seen. He may not see the fruit immediately when the seed is sown, but by faith he has the substance or proof of it. Coupled with prayer, he would assuredly see the manifestation of the word or promise in his/her life. The person who has faith will pray, speak the word, and confess the word. The person who has faith will meditate upon the word and build up his faith. The person who has faith would wait patiently for the manifestation of the promise. This is the meaning of the parable of the growing seed; after a seed has been sown on a good fertile ground, it takes time to grow and manifest and therefore patience becomes an important virtue at that point. What you do at this point of growth, will determine the kind of harvest you will reap.

CHAPTER 8

PARABLE OF THE MUSTARD SEED

Lastly, Jesus spoke of the kingdom of God as a grain of mustard seed. *"Then He said, "To what shall we liken the kingdom of God? Or with what parable shall we picture it? It is like a mustard seed which, when it is sown on the ground, is smaller than all the seeds on earth; but when it is sown, it grows up and becomes greater than all herbs, and shoots out large branches, so that the birds of the air may nest under its shade."*

This parable is better understood when we compare it with what Jesus said on other occasions to His disciples. On two occasions, He compared their faith to a grain of mustard seed, which has the potential to grow when planted in the right condition. The mustard seed, although tiny, is real, specific, and tangible. The point of the comparison of the mustard seed and faith is that faith must be more than just a concept in your mind. It must be real, it must be specific and it must be tangible with substance. This is why Jesus mentioned a specific tangible seed, the mustard seed. It is real, tiny, and yet carries the power to reproduce. Likewise, faith must be real, sizable, and carry the ability to manifest in the natural from the unseen.

Unlike the other two parables about the seed, this parable named a specific seed which was known to His listeners. By this, Jesus was telling His listeners that faith is real and not an illusion. It must be tangible and not abstract. It must produce results in your life; something real that you can attribute to God's compassion for you. Jesus said that if they had faith as a grain of mustard seed, they could do the impossible. This means that if we have faith in the word of God and sow it in our heart, it will grow to accomplish greater things that would benefit the world with all its evil inhabitants.

Every seed has a specific condition or ground in which to sow it. For example, the seed of man (sperm) can only be sown in the womb of a woman so as to grow. You cannot sow the seed of man in the womb of any other mammal. Likewise the word of God can only be sown in the hearts of men which is the spiritual "womb". The heart is the vital part of every man that reproduces whatever is planted in it through thought, and out of the spiritual "womb" flow the issues of life. The word of God has been programmed to yield results in your life so long as you sow it in your heart under all the needed conditions. Jesus used the mustard seed to illustrate the principles of the Kingdom of God for several reasons.

A seed carries within itself the DNA or the blueprint of the parent plant. An acorn produces an oak tree not a mulberry tree. A mustard seed is going to produce a mustard plant. Likewise, the Word of God will produce the Kingdom of God within you. The kingdom of God is not with observation, but it is within you. It is in your heart. So when we sow the word in our hearts, it will give birth to the kingdom of God within us. When we mix faith with the word or the promise of God that we hear, understand and meditate on, it will grow into something greater that will benefit all.

Therefore, the mustard seed faith is the kind of faith that has the ability to grow when exercised appropriately. It is a living faith with physical and tangible results. Faith is like a muscle in your body and it grows when it is exercised or utilized. Everybody has muscles in their body, but it is only those that exercise their muscles continually that can develop big and strong muscle. Likewise, faith grows when we continually exercise or use it. When you exercise your faith in all life situations, it will grow and be beneficial to many who are under the bondage of the evil one. God would bless you so that you will be a blessing onto others. Start, therefore, by exercising your faith with little things, and then gradually move on to bigger things.

The bible says *"Now faith is the substance of things hoped for, the evidence of things not seen"*. This means that whatever you are hoping for has substance through the word of God and it is a reality, because of your faith. The word of God is the evidence of what you hoped for. Your expectation is real and has substance in the word. By the word of God, you can actualize what you are hoping for through faith. It is also said that "*So then faith comes by hearing, and hearing by the word of God.*

When you put these two scriptures together, it can be paraphrased like this "**faith, which comes by hearing the word of God, is (presently) the substance (tangibility, physicality, reality and embodiment) of the things we are hoping for in the future. It is also the evidence and proof of the things we do not yet see with our physical eye because it is in the future but we only see it with an eye of faith.**" Or, it can be paraphrased "**Now the word of God is the substance of things hoped for, the word of God is the evidence of things not yet seen with the naked eyes**".

Whatever you are hoping for in life can be actualized through faith in the promises of God. The word of God would give you the substance and evidence of what you're hoping for, and it will be your assurance that you already have it. When you have an orange seed, it gives you the assurance that one day the seed would become an orange tree if it is sown in the right environment and condition. Likewise, the word of God gives us the assurance that we have what it promises if we apply the right principles to it. God can never lie. Every promise that He has given you in the bible is "yea and amen". Therefore, trust in Him and His promises so as not to be disappointed.

Abraham had a promise from God that He (God) was going to give the land of Canaan to his descendants in the future.

Abraham believed the word of God and it became his evidence or proof. He therefore bought a piece of that land and used it as a burial ground four hundred years before the fulfillment of the promise of God (Genesis 23:8-10). Even though, the promise was given to Abraham, but the benefit has overflowed to all mankind. All the patriarchs were buried on the land of Canaan more than four hundred years before their descendants possessed the land; simply because Abraham believed in the word of God without any limitations, and, most importantly, acted upon his belief. Faith is also acting upon the word of God that you have believed; so start acting upon the word that you have believed and do not waiver. The truth that God can never lie, should be your fortress, strength and foundation to build your faith on.

Jesus, in this parable, compared the kingdom of God to our faith in the word of God which guides, leads, and point us to His kingdom. In the absence of the word of God, we will not know the kingdom of God and its righteousness. The kingdom of God started with a handful of men in a small obscure part of the world some two thousand years ago; but it has grown to become a giant tree and people who were oppressed by the devil are finding shelter under this tree of the kingdom. Faith in the word of God caused the kingdom to grow beyond measure. It all started with faith, which had substance as a mustard seed, even though it was tiny; but it was also tangible with physical results, which had caused the blind to see, the deaf to hear, the dumb to speak and the lame to walk; and it had also grown to become a powerful force that causes the enemy to tremble. It has brought deliverance to millions of people; but it all started from a small place in Israel as a spiritual force within the hearts of men. The kingdom of God is within you; it is resident in your heart through the word of God.

The bible says that everything shall perish except the word of God. So trust in God and believe in His promises which are scattered throughout the bible because without faith it is impossible to please God; everyone who comes to Him must believe that He is the great I AM. You used the same faith to believe that Jesus is the Son of God and you made a confession that He is your Lord and Savior. You used the same faith to believe that you have received the Holy Spirit when you asked. You used the same faith to believe you have received wisdom when you asked. You used the same faith to believe God hears you when you pray. You used the same faith to believe you are made righteous and justified after you were born again. This same faith flows through you with power and conviction when you lay hands on people and pray for others to receive healing or deliverance. But it all started with a simple belief in the word of God.

*"And Jesus said unto them, Because of your unbelief: for verily I say unto you, If ye have faith as a grain of MUSTARD SEED, ye shall SAY unto this mountain, Remove hence to yonder place; and it shall remove; and nothing shall be impossible unto you (Mathew 17:20) " .*Again he said *"...If ye had faith as a grain of MUSTARD SEED, ye might SAY unto this sycamine tree, Be thou plucked up by the root, and be thou planted in the sea; and it should obey you (Luke 17:6).*

In these scriptures, Jesus shed more light on the mustard seed faith. In both instances, the presence of the mustard-seed faith led them to speak to their problems out of faith. They spoke to the impediments and they were removed. This means that the mustard-seed faith is the faith that would result in mountain and tree moving power when we understand, believe, meditate, and incubate the word in our hearts; which is our spiritual "womb", and speak it out of our mouth with boldness, conviction and confidence. Jesus said *"if you have faith as a grain of MUSTARD SEED, ye shall SAY ..."* This means mustard seed faith causes us to speak, declare and decree. If you have not understood, believed, and meditated on the word of God until it sinks into your heart through spiritual osmosis, you cannot speak it out with confidence, boldness and faith.

The only time that you can speak to mountains and trees is when you have understood, believed, and meditated on the word of God to the point that it has become fused into your spirit, and therefore, proceeds out of your mouth with the spiritual force which is encoded in that particular word. Mustard seed faith utters and declares power-filled words, which had been incubated and nurtured in the heart. Just as the mustard seed has to be planted, watered and nurtured to maturity, so also the word of God has to be planted in our hearts by understanding, believing, meditating, and mixing it with faith till it grows to become a giant tree of the kingdom.

Jesus explained how we can speak to mountains to be removed with success in the gospel of Mark 11:22-23 when he said

"...Have faith in God. For verily I say unto you, That whosoever shall say unto this mountain, Be thou removed, and be thou cast into the sea; and SHALL NOT DOUBT IN HIS HEART, but shall BELIEVE that those things which he saith shall come to pass; he shall have whatsoever he saith. This is how the mustard seed faith works. It starts in the heart as a tiny substance, where it is incubated and meditated upon until it grows to become one with our being. When such a word is released, it comes with power and filled with a spiritual force; because at this point, you have believed totally in the power of the word and have spent days and months meditating and musing on the word. You will speak therefore based on your conviction and belief in that particular word. These power-filled words would minister grace to your listeners and bring deliverance to those that are bound. The mustard seed faith would speak the word of God to bless others, cast out demons, and bring deliverance to the captives. These words are not spoken out of doubt in the heart but in total conviction of the power of the spoken word. Words that are believed in the heart, and meditated upon long enough are normally spoken with faith and conviction, thereby bringing to pass the intended purpose.

The mustard-seed faith is what apostle Paul referred to as the spirit of faith in 2

Corinthians 4:13 *"We having the same spirit of faith, according as it is written (in Psalm 116:10), I believed, and therefore have I spoken; we also believe, and therefore speak;* The mustard-seed faith believes in the heart and speaks it out of the mouth based upon conviction, and so the words come out with power. Jesus compared the word of God to a mustard seed to illustrate that they are both meant to be planted, understood (which is illumination), meditated upon (watered), and nurtured (mixed with faith) until it manifests openly. Just as a natural seed needs certain conditions to be present before it can grow, so also the word of God needs certain conditions in order to manifest in our lives.

It is only through the preaching of the word of God that those oppressed by the devil can be saved and find refuge in the kingdom of God. The bible says in Romans 10:10 *"For with the heart man believeth unto righteousness; and with the mouth confession is made unto salvation"*. The mustard seed faith begins in the heart and comes forth from the mouth, when we confess what we have believed in the heart. This is how salvation, which is the entry point into the kingdom, takes place. When one believes in the heart and confesses with the mouth that Jesus died and resurrected for his sins, he enters into the kingdom of God. The word salvation was translated from the Greek word "soteria" which means, deliverance, protection, salvation, healing, and prosperity. Therefore, you can believe in your heart unto righteousness and with the mouth make confession unto deliverance, protection, salvation, healing, prosperity, or whatever your need is.

Putting it all together, you will realize that Jesus spoke in one context about the incorruptible seed, using three parables to illustrate how the kingdom of God works. First of all, He spoke about how the seed needs certain conditions to be present before it could grow (spiritual photosynthesis). Secondly, He spoke about how the seed eventually grows on a fertile ground during the period between planting the seed and reaping the harvest, how we are supposed to water and clear out all the weeds on the ground to promote growth. How the seed grows on its' own accord without any influence from man and thirdly, He spoke also about how the seed can grow to become something greater and be a blessing to those who are under the bondage of the enemy. So the seed progresses from growing in the right environment, then grows according to God's own ordinance of seed, growth time, and harvest. Finally the seed or word of God grows to become a powerful force to bless all humanity through understanding, meditation, mixture of faith and confession.

It is very important to note that, throughout these parables, meditation or watering of the seed was a common thread that ran through all of them. In the parable of the sower, the one who heard the word with understanding, and then kept and nurtured it, had harvest coming back to him based upon the degree of attention devoted to the word. Some received thirty fold, some sixty, and others received a hundred fold harvest based on the measure of meditation, attention, and diligence given to what was heard. In the parable of the growing seed, the one who continued to water or meditate on the word that had been planted in his heart, eventually saw the harvest.

Finally, in the parable of the mustard- seed, the one who had a tangible evidence of the word by dwelling on it continually spoke to minister grace to others to bring them to repentance. The common thread running through all these three parables is the attention given to the word. The act of dwelling on the word continually in their hearts, yielded great recompense to all of them. All the three gospels accounts of the parable of the sower shared some unique details, which fits perfectly together. In these accounts, the one who bore fruit was described as someone who received, understood and kept the word in his heart patiently, until the manifestation of the word in his life.

CHAPTER 9

THE SEVEN PRINCIPLES

There are seven powerful principles that you should learn from these three parables that Jesus taught. These are divine principles that should be grasped and incorporated in your life. I believe it will yield tremendous results for you.

PRINCIPLE # 1

THE HEART IS YOUR SPIRITUAL GROUND

The first principle we learned from these parables is that your heart or inner man is the spiritual "womb" where the word of God is planted. Every seed has a specific environment in which God has ordained for it to prosper. The seed of the word of God can only grow in the hearts of men. Likewise, the seed of men (sperm), can only be planted and grow in the womb of a woman. The human heart is extremely creative and non-judgmental. Whatever is planted in the human heart and nurtured continually would be reproduced supernaturally. Jesus, in these parables likened it to the earth, ground or soil where seeds of ideas, innovations and concepts are planted and birthed out. The heart, as mentioned in the bible, is not the physical organ that pumps blood to the rest of your body; but rather your subconscious mind. Scientifically, it is proven that, the human mind functions in two dimensions namely; the conscious and subconscious.

The conscious mind is the "awake-mind" - which is only used when we are awake and it controls and regulates the activities of the body over which a person has voluntary control like, lifting up of holy hands, singing praises to the Lord and prayer. The subconscious mind, on the other hand, goes on working 24 hours of every day. It is not a tangible entity, and therefore not visibly located anywhere in the physical body. It cannot be seen with the naked eye, or with microscope. It cannot be measured, weighed, or taken apart for scientific research, analysis, and study. It is rather a spiritual phenomenon. The human body is like a powerful mechanical and complex entity that is governed by an engine in the inside of it called the mind, which has two functional parts namely; conscious and subconscious.

The subconscious mind is likened to a garden and the conscious mind is the gardener.

These two work harmoniously together. Whenever these two agree, great things occur. The conscious is likened to the male specie that impregnates the subconscious or the female specie. Nothing gets into the subconscious mind except through the conscious mind. In other words, nothing gets into your heart except through your mind.

Whatever you dwell on or think about continually in your conscious mind, will eventually sink through a process similar to osmosis, into your heart or subconscious mind. By thinking continually about something in your mind, you are watering that seed of thought. Thoughts are seeds that we consciously or by neglect plant in our hearts or subconscious mind.

Until a person accepts that the subconscious mind was created and given to man by God, and it is not a new age phenomena; he cannot learn to use it to his advantage. It is, sometimes, called the spirit man or inner man. It regulates and controls certain body functions that a person cannot voluntarily control such as, respiration, circulation of blood through the vessels and digestion of foods. Let us do some illustration at this point to differentiate between these two functions of the mind. I want you to STOP BREATHING for a minute; yes! Stop breathing for a few seconds. By your conscious mind, you will be able to stop your breathing instantly but only for a short time and then your subconscious mind will take over again when you stop focusing on your breathing. With your conscious mind, you were able to control your breathing voluntarily; but it lasted only for a short time before your subconscious mind took over again. You have been breathing unconsciously since you started reading this book.

At the moment, your subconscious mind is controlling your respiration without any effort from you. Last night, whilst you were sleeping, the Lord kept your heart beating by the function of the subconscious mind .It is the part of your being that controls the involuntary functions of your body. The subconscious mind kept your physical heart beating, exchanging oxygen for carbon dioxide and digesting ingested food. Moreover, the subconscious mind or your heart is the seat of your emotions, imaginations, the storehouse of information or memory bank, and countless others. The subconscious mind, to some extent, can be influenced by your conscious mind.

Unfortunately, the subconscious mind does not know the difference between what is real and what is not. It doesn't know the difference between right and wrong; positive or negative; it doesn't know the difference between success and failure; but it will accept any statement that you keep repeating to it through thought processes, meditation or through words. It will only accept information as true when the conscious mind believes that information as true, and also when it is mixed with emotion like faith, desire or fear. It operates like a modern day computer, but has a storage capacity and memory system that supersedes ordinary computers in general. The subconscious mind is like a personal computer and you are the computeroperator. It records everything that happens in the personal, sensory, and intellectual world – from the day of conception until the day of death. It takes directions and instructions from the conscious mind and follows these directions implicitly. It is called "man's most obedient servant". It can only say "yes" and it has no limitations. It is a massive power source without direction. This is the reason why the bible places so much importance and emphasis on the conditions of your heart which is known as your subconscious mind in the secular world.

As the subconscious mind is the womb in which the seed of suggestion is sown, the conscious mind is the gardener who plants the seed. These seeds can be sown by yourself or by others through suggestion. We saw this truth in the parable of the sower where the word was suggested or planted in the conscious mind. But until the conscious mind accepts and dwells on the suggestion or thought long enough, it cannot be transferred into the heart or subconscious mind. Every thought becomes part of the never-failing memory system of the subconscious mind. EACH INIVIDUAL IS WHAT HE THINKS CONTINUALLY.

We ought to be careful and selective with our choice of thoughts; because God has given us full and absolute control over our minds. The only thing that man has absolute and total power of control over is his conscious mind which in turn controls the subconscious mind. We alone choose our thoughts and our thoughts create and shape our world. The bible entreats you to guard your heart with all diligence; because, out of your heart comes the issues of life. This is how you know that the word "heart" in the bible is what is known in our modern day as the subconscious mind.

I made this observation by studying the functions and attributes of the heart in the bible. There are so many references made in the bible in regards to the heart. And upon close examination one can ascertain and determine what the word "heart" means in the bible. After all the scriptures that mention the "heart" were gathered and studied, one may deduce that the heart consists of the emotions; the memory; and the imagination. Jesus mentioned "understanding with their heart" in John. 12: 40 and Mathew 13:15. This means that, the intellect or reasoning ability resides in the heart and mind. The bible also speaks of the heart possessing emotion in John 14: 1.

Emotions such as joy, love, and desire are emotions said to emanate from the heart as stated in John. 16: 22; Mathew 22: 37; 5: 28. The language "pricked in their heart" or "convicted in their heart" is an allusion to the conscience or that part of the heart that pains us when we do wrong (Acts 2: 37). These, then, are the attributes of the heart to which the bible makes reference. Sometimes a particular scripture that mentions "heart" may be referring to the emotions; sometimes the intellect or conscience may be the main thought. However, all these are the functions of the subconscious mind as scientists have proven with numerous experiments, and it corresponds and conforms to the biblical definition. In Hebrew, the word "LEB", which is translated as heart in English, has a variety of usage like: the inner man, mind, will, understanding, inner part, knowing, thinking, reflecting, recalling, feelings, passions and appetites. In the Greek, the word "KARDIA" also has a variety of usage just like in Hebrew. Now, having established what the heart consists, let us now analyze some relevant truths about the heart.

(A) IT IS YOUR RESPONSIBILITY TO KEEP YOUR HEART

Many people seem to forget that God places certain responsibilities upon man and HE (God) will not perform these matters for man whereby he (man) will be free from any responsibility. You are responsible to keep your heart or subconscious mind by guarding it consciously. Listen to the wisdom of King Solomon: "*Keep (consciously) your heart (subconscious mind) with all diligence; for out of it are the issues of life*" (Emphasis mine Prov. 4: 23). From this inspired command, we learn several truths. First of all, man must keep and safeguard his own heart by being conscious of what he thinks about at all times and secondly, he must do so diligently or consistently. He must be very disciplined and self-controlled in his thoughts. Moreover, out of the heart proceeds or flows all the issues of life. So the responsibility is totally given to man to determine the input and output of his heart. God has given to man the sole and absolute control of his own mind, which controls what enters into the heart or subconscious mind.

Whatever you put in your subconscious mind through the conscious, would determine what it will reproduce back to you. Negative thoughts come into our minds automatically, because of our fallen nature; but positive thoughts have to be consciously planted in our minds. Therefore, keep out the negative thoughts consciously and plant positive thoughts in your subconscious mind by thinking on positive things continually. The Bible also speaks of a people "*that set not their heart aright*" (Ps. 78: 8) to do the right thing before God. They made a decision consciously not to do right by God. God, however, will assist a man who seeks to prepare and keep his heart by the word of God (Ps. 10: 17; 51: 10, Ezra 7:10, Daniel 1:8).

The ability to keep your heart or subconscious mind is in your power because you choose voluntarily or by neglect what information to feed it. Jesus said in the parable of the sower *"take heed what you hear"*; because information is sent to your conscious mind through your five senses; but the information that you dwell on continually or your dominant thought will be imprinted in your subconscious mind, and will eventually manifest in your life. Repetition is one of the methods that impresses or communicates to the heart. This is the reason why, God told Joshua to meditate on the word DAY AND NIGHT repeatedly and continuously. Therefore, biblical meditation engages, impresses and feeds your subconscious mind with positive things from the word of God; and it is in your absolute power to determine what you think about or meditate on. Worrying is a negative form of meditation, which also has the power to bring to pass the object of your dominant thought. Job said in Job 3:25 that *"For the thing which I greatly feared is come upon me, and that which I was afraid of is come unto me."* This is a very powerful spiritual principle that works all the time irrespective of the kind of thought, whether good or bad.

The subconscious mind is the seat of our emotions so be careful not to harbor any negative emotions; because it will manifest in your life. Knowledge of this truth would empower you to heed the advice of Jesus Christ to take heed of what you are hearing from your own conscious suggestions or from others. The bible also instructs us to pull down strongholds, cast down imaginations and every high thing that seeks to exalt itself against the knowledge of God; and bring into captivity every thought to the obedience of Christ through our conscious mind. We are the door-keepers of our hearts or subconscious mind, which is the spiritual womb in which all kinds of seeds are planted and nurtured into maturity through continuous and persistent thoughts or suggestions either by ourselves or by others. This truth was evident in the parable of the sower; because the word of God was suggested by the sower and the responsibility was upon the hearers to do whatever they choose with what they have heard.

(B) GOD LOOKS AT THE HEART AND NOT THE OUTWARD APPEARANCE.

Regarding the heart of man we read, "*For He God, knows the secrets of the heart*" (Ps. 44: 21). The word of God is said to be "*a discerner of the thoughts and intents of the heart*" (Heb. 4: 12). Our Lord Jesus Christ is presented as "*he which searches the reins and hearts*" (Rev. 2: 20-23). Hence, God knows our will, our emotions, intellect, and conscience. All things are laid open to our Lord; nothing is hidden from Him who shall be the righteous judge of all men (2 Cor. 5: 10). The bible also said of Jesus, "*And needed not that any should testify of man: for he knew what was in man*" (John. 2: 25). As evidenced by the many recurrences in the bible, the term "heart" is a very important word; because God is so deeply concerned about the inner man or the condition of the heart. Out of the heart proceeds the issues of life and it is the seat of the spirit man. Whereas man looks at the outward appearance to judge, God looks at the heart, which is hidden to the natural eye. You cannot continually think about evil, and expect your heart to be pure. What you entertain consciously in your mind would eventually be stored in the heart. Therefore, think and meditate on positive things, which will give birth to positive manifestations.

1 Samuel 16:7 said "*But the LORD said to Samuel, "Do not look at his appearance or at the height of his stature, because I have rejected him; for God sees not as man sees, for man looks at the outward appearance, but the LORD looks at the heart."* The heart cannot be trusted unless it has been fed continually with positive ideas, thoughts and principles through the word of God. It is very creative and, therefore, we have to be diligent in keeping it; because it would manifest whatever we plant in it.

Jeremiah 17:9-10 also says "*The heart is more deceitful than all else and is desperately sick; Who can understand it? I, the LORD, search the heart, I test the mind, Even to give to each man according to his ways, According to the results of his deeds".*

The heart is desperately wicked because it does not have the ability to make moral judgments as to what is right or wrong but rather whatever is fed into the heart would be reproduced either good or bad. Moreover, these passages teach us that the Lord looks at and searches the heart, the inner person. They also emphasize the truth that we are totally responsible to keep our hearts. Why is the heart so important? It is so, because the issues of life: our actions, works, pursuits, motives, attitudes etc., and all proceed from the heart (Pr. 4:23; Matt. 6:21; 12:34; 15:18). What we do in word and deed is first of all a product of what we are on the inside.

Jesus said in Mathew 5 that *"Ye have heard that it was said of them of old time,*

Thou shalt not kill; and whosoever shall kill shall be in danger of the judgment: But I say unto you, That whosoever is angry with his brother without a cause shall be in danger of the judgment: and whosoever shall say to his brother, Raca, shall be in danger of the council: but whosoever shall say, Thou fool, shall be in danger of hell fire". He also said *"Ye have heard that it was said by them of old time, Thou shalt not commit adultery: But I say unto you, that whosoever looks on a woman to lust after her hath committed adultery with her already in his heart".*

What was the Lord teaching the people when He made these statements? He was calling their attention to the moral precepts they had been taught by their religious leaders for years, precepts that had their source in the Old Testament Scriptures. But then, with the words, "but I say to you..." He readdressed those same issues as, first and foremost, matters of the heart. When you look at a woman lustfully, you are fantasizing or imagining in your heart (subconscious mind); but the subconscious mind or heart receives this as true, because it does not know the difference between reality, fantasy and assumption. Therefore it is considered done in your subconscious mind because it doesn't know the difference between reality, imagination and fantasy. This is the reason why a person can play with himself to stimulate the genital organs and achieve sexual pleasure by simply fantasizing about someone else. Using your imagination is a very powerful tool.

The subconscious mind will give back to you the recorded results or reactions associated with every action with which you have had prior experience. So, Jesus was saying, when you lust after a woman in your heart (subconscious mind), you have already committed adultery; because your subconscious mind does not know the difference, and therefore you are guilty as charged. Biblical Christianity centers in an inward, intimate walk with God by faith. Anything else is nothing more than religious hypocrisy.

For instance, Jesus teaches us that adultery and murder begin in the heart; because the issues of life proceed out from the heart. You may not have literally committed adultery, but if you look at a woman or a man with that in view, you have already committed adultery. Where? In your heart! (Matt. 5:28). Our walk with God is always a matter of the heart. Jesus also said in Mathew 15:17-20 *"Do not ye yet understand, that whatsoever entereth in at the mouth goeth into the belly, and is cast out into the draught? But those things which proceed out of the mouth come forth from the heart; and they defile the man. For out of the heart proceed evil thoughts, murders, adulteries, fornications, thefts, false witness, blasphemies: These are the things which defile a man..."* Another bible version (ERV) renders this very portion of scripture as *"Surely you know that all the food that enters the mouth goes into the stomach. Then it goes out of the body. But the bad things people say with their mouth come from the way they think. And that's what can make people wrong. All these bad things begin in the mind(subconscious): evil thoughts, murder, adultery, sexual sins, stealing, lying, and insulting people. These are the things that make people wrong. Eating without washing their hands will never make people unacceptable to God (Emphasis mine)"*

(C) GOD'S WORD IS DESIGNED TO BE IN YOUR HEART

David said, *"The law of his God is in his heart; none of his steps shall slide"* (Ps. 37: 31). The prayer of the Psalmist was, *"Incline my heart unto thy testimonies, and not to covetousness"* (Ps. 119:

36).The bible also says that "*And these words, which I command thee this day, shall be in thine heart*". The residence of God's law in our hearts suggests our minds, emotions, will, and conscience are all involved and saturated in the matter of God's laws. It also says in Job 22:22 "*Receive, I pray thee, the law from his mouth, and lay up his words in thine heart.* All these scriptures are entreating us to hide the word of God in our hearts.

We need to feed on the word to be healthy Christians; we need to study the word to be intelligent Christians; we need to memorize the word to be skillful Christians; we need to apply the word to be obedient Christians; and we need to meditate on the word of God to be prosperous Christians. For this reason, endeavor to fill your heart or subconscious mind with the positive and pure unadulterated word of God that will eventually bring positive manifestations and results into your life. When you fill your heart or subconscious mind with the word of God, you fill it with the Holy Spirit of God. The bible says in Colossians 3:16 "*Let the word of Christ dwell in you richly in all wisdom; teaching and admonishing one another in psalms and hymns and spiritual songs, singing with grace in your HEARTS TO THE LORD*". When you compare this scripture to Ephesians 5:18-19 "*And be not drunk with wine, wherein is excess; but be filled with the Spirit; Speaking to yourselves in psalms and hymns and spiritual songs, singing and making melody in your HEARTS TO THE LORD*;"

It is very noticeable from these scriptures that, the end result of being filled with the word of God and the Spirit of God is the same. In both instances, utterances were made in psalms, hymns and spiritual songs in the heart unto the Lord. This means that when you fill your subconscious mind with the word of God, positive utterances filled with the word of God would be made to God. The mouth speaks out of the overflow of the heart and when the heart is filled with the word of God to an overflow, the mouth would speak based on the contents of the heart. This also reiterates the truth that when you fill your heart with the word of God, you fill it with the Holy Spirit of God. God and His word are one. Jesus said "*the words that I speak unto you, they are spirit, and they are life"*. So when God looks at your heart, what will HE see? Would He see a reflection of Himself or something other than His word? For this very reason therefore, feed your spirit man with the incorruptible seed that would bear unto you tremendous fruits.

(D) YOUR WORDS ARE REFLECTIONS OF YOUR HEART

Jesus asked some of the Pharisees, "O generation of vipers, how can ye, being evil, speak good things? For out of the abundance of the heart the mouth speaks". Many times we hear it said that "this person has corrupt speech but his heart is good" (Eph. 4: 29). Jesus says one cannot have bad speech and a good heart. Corrupt speech is indicative of a corrupt heart. A good man, out of the good treasures that he had consciously stored up in his heart (subconscious mind) through repetition and persistence, brings forth good things; and an evil man, out of the evil treasures that he had stored in his heart, brings forth evil things.

A man's words are indicative of what is in his heart. The bible says that sweet and bitter water cannot come out of the same fountain; nor can an apple tree bear orange fruit. It also says that death and life are in the power of the tongue and they that love it, will enjoy the fruit or benefits thereof. So, be careful what you put in the inner man or in your heart, because it will find its way out of your mouth. This is the reason why meditation on the word of God is very important to renew or program the subconscious mind. What you store in your heart continually, would find its way out of your mouth and it will shape your destiny.

(E) YOUR HEART CAN BE WRONGLY INFLUENCED

Finally, many do not realize that what they "feel in their heart" is not authority in religious matters, except the word of God that has been consciously stored in the heart. The bible says in Deuteronomy 11:16*"Take heed to yourselves, that your heart be not deceived, and ye turn aside, and serve other gods, and worship them;"* The heart or subconscious mind can be deceived by the wrong information that you feed it because it is non-judgmental and non-analytical. It does not scrutinize, verify and analyze information to see if it is true or not, as long as you believe it, the heart would accept as true. Working in the medical field as a Surgical Technologist, I have seen how the human body can be deceived to accept bone grafts like auto-graft and allo-graft bones as the body's own broken bones, and then the body will work tirelessly to bring healing to the supposedly broken bones. The subconscious mind is totally responsible for self- preservation of the physical body.

The placebo effect happens when the treatment of a patient is based on a known inactive substance like a sugar pill, distilled water, or saline solution rather than a substance with real medical value. The recipient or patient may still experience an improvement merely because his/her expectation to do so was very strong. Placebo effect is a medical phrase that suggests that a person can be deceived to think and believe that a sugar pill can cure his sickness and as long as they believe it, the sugar pill will cure him of his sickness. So the cure was not achieved by the sugar pill but by the patient's own belief.

Whatever is believed as true by the conscious mind, would be accepted as true by the heart, and therefore trigger the desired results because the heart or subconscious mind is the creative medium in every man. Through the subconscious mind, the body brings healing to itself. For example, when you cut yourself accidentally with a kitchen knife when preparing a meal, the wound would heal through the sublime workings of the subconscious mind. It does not matter what religion you belong to; as long as you are alive, healing will surely take place. The subconscious mind has been ordained by God to renew the physical body as the agent of healing and regeneration. In the same vein, it has been ordained by God to create and manifest any thought that has been held continually and diligently in the conscious mind irrespective of the kind of thought; whether good or evil.

The heart is not so smart and can be easily deceived by others through suggestions. Listen to what King Solomon said, "*He that trusts in his own heart is a fool; but whoso walks wisely, he shall be delivered*" (Prov. 28: 26). The one that trusts in his own heart, the bible says, is a fool; but who so walks wisely shall be delivered because he walks according to the word of God. You see, God is not a respecter of persons but a respecter of His word, and therefore deals with men according to His word. Jesus said that *"Therefore whosoever heareth these sayings of mine, and doeth them, I will liken him unto a WISE man, which built his house upon a rock:"* According to this scripture, the one that walks by the words of Jesus is considered wise. The person that trusts in his own heart as opposed to the words of Jesus is a fool, as per the bible.

Therefore do not trust in your own heart except when it is filled with the word of God. One's heart can erroneously approve of him when he is wrong; and one's heart can condemn him when he is right (Prov. 28: 26; I Jn. 3: 18-21). The heart or subconscious mind must be properly educated in the truths of God's word before it can be of great use to us in our service to the Lord. If you do not put the word of God in your heart continually, it becomes easy to be misled by what you feel in your heart. David said *"Thy word have I hid in my heart that I might not sin against thee"*. Hide the word of God in your heart through meditation and it will help you to eschew evil. The word of God when hidden in your heart would serve as a point of conviction and steer you away from sin.

It is evident that the heart or subconscious mind is a very important part of your being that affects every area of your life. Knowledge of this immortal part of your being is very important. It is not metaphysical; neither demonic nor new age phenomena. There are many things that the bible reveals about the heart. It is a place of storage or the memory bank of information as Jesus mentioned in Mathew 12:35.The bible also says that *"The heart is deceitful above all things, and desperately wicked: who can know it?"* The truth of this scripture becomes very obvious when you consider that the subconscious mind or the heart does not know the difference between reality and fantasy.

This is the reason why, it is very important to keep your heart with all diligence; because whatever you feed it, would be accepted as truth. This is a universal truth that is applicable to both Christians and non-Christians alike. Moreover, this explains why visualization and imagination are as effective and successful as they are in programming the heart or subconscious mind. The importance of the heart was very much emphasized in the three parables that Jesus spoke in Mark chapter four. In the parable of the sower, the heart or the ground was the determining factor which dictated the end result of the seed. I will extensively deal with this aspect of the heart subsequently in the chapters to come.

When we do visualizations and confessions, we do it only in the present tense and we only see the end result, as though it has already happened. The bible says that, "*God calls those things that be not as if they ARE*". It also says that "*NOW faith IS the substance of things hoped for…*" The highlighted words in the preceding scriptures, indicates that the heart deals always in the present. If it is dealing with something in the future, it will consider as being done. Whatever you present to it, when filled with strong emotions like faith, desire, hope or fear, would be manifested unto you. This is the message that Jesus was teaching us in the three parables in Mark chapter four. Whatever we feed our hearts, as long as they are mixed with faith (which is one of the powerful emotions), it will eventually bring it to pass. It is very important to acknowledge your heart as the spiritual womb, ground, earth or soil where seeds of ideas, innovations, creativity and all issues of life are planted. Whatever is planted in it would be reproduced by the heart; because it's very creative.

When you put evil in your heart, it will reproduce evil and when you put good in your heart, it will reproduce good. The heart is very creative based on whatever you feed it intentionally or by neglect, either by yourself or others. Jesus said "*A good man out of the good treasure of the heart brings forth good things: and an evil man out of the evil treasure brings forth evil things*". This means whatever you store consciously through your conscious mind (gardener) into your subconscious mind (spiritual garden) or your heart would be accepted as either good or bad, and it would influence your life. Likewise when you put evil in your subconscious mind, it will reproduce evil, and good will reproduce goodness. It does not discriminate and therefore it is very wicked and cannot be trusted. It does not know right from wrong but whatever is presented with emotions like faith would be reproduced. Jesus spoke a parable about the subconscious mind in which He called it the "unjust judge". In that parable, Jesus called the subconscious mind as the unjust judge and said that if your subconscious mind or heart can give things to you without restraint, how much more would not God, the heavenly Father, give you good things when you ask for them.

When you analyze that parable, it highlights the characteristics of the subconscious mind as being non-analytical, but only responds to continuous systematic pressure by which information is delivered, and when the information is emotionalized. That is the reason why a person can watch a movie, knowing very well that it is fiction and yet become sad or even cry based upon the events in the movie. This becomes possible; because the subconscious mind does not know the difference between what is real and what is fiction. As long as you believe what you are watching, the subconscious mind would accept it as true and therefore bring to pass a reaction based upon the emotions associated with events in the movie.

This person believed the events in the movie or film and therefore the subconscious mind brought about the natural reaction to the specific event. This explains why Jesus said "*all things are possible to those who believe*". He did not say all things are possible to those who believe in God. An unbeliever can have a strong belief in certain objects like voodoo rings, beads and amulets around the waist and it will produce results for him. It is actually his belief that brought to pass the expected result. These objects might have been given by a fetish priest but their belief in it brings results to them. That is why there are so many belief systems or religions claiming to be the right way with many followers; because the subconscious mind or heart is also the seat of the belief system. Whatever you believe as truth, would be accepted as truth by your heart; but there is only one truth and it can be found in Jesus Christ. In order to understand how wonderfully God created you, it is imperative to recognize the functions of the subconscious mind.

When we meditate on the word of God, we are renewing our subconscious mind with the word of God. It is one of the most important gifts that God gave to man. In Mark chapter 4, Jesus spoke about the word of God as a seed in three parables. The first one, (Parable of the sower), deals with how we receive the word of God in our heart and what we do with the word when we hear it. The second parable, (parable of the growing seed) deals with how the seed grows in our heart or subconscious mind when it is sown; and the last one,(parable of the mustard seed) deals with the potency of the word of God when it is sown or incubated in our hearts to produce the spirit of faith. He taught these parables to emphasize the importance of meditation on the word of God. The bible says "As a man thinks (*meditates*) in his heart (*subconscious mind*), so is he".

You will become whatever you think about continuously,. Therefore Jesus said "*take heed what you are hearing for the measure of thought and study (meditation) you give to what you hear, would determine what you will get out of it*". Meditation makes it easier to apply the word of God because the more you think about the word continuously and repetitively, you are planting the seed of the word in your heart or subconscious mind. Once the word is planted in your heart, you will not know how the seed will grow in your subconscious mind and bear fruit. Turn it over into the hands of God who created your heart or subconscious mind to do the rest. He will cause it to yield results. So when you meditate on the word, you are transferring information from your conscious mind into the subconscious mind, which is the spiritual womb in which the seed of the word of God is sown.

In conclusion, the word heart in the bible is not the physical, blood-pumping organ found in our chest but rather the subconscious mind. The bible "heart" involves the mind, beliefs, emotions, and memory vault of man. God's acceptance of man is based on man's heart (Prov. 3: 4 ff.). Moreover, God demands our whole heart (Ps. 119: 34, 69). Finally, "*whatsoever ye do, do it heartily, as to the Lord, and not unto men*" (Col. 3: 23). Your heart is the spiritual womb in which the word is sown and words are spiritually encoded to reproduce after their kind. The word of God is a creative power in your mind, heart and mouth. Every seed has a specific ground where it can grow. The word of God, which is a creative power, can only be sown in the human heart or subconscious mind where it would be incubated to create whatever it has been encoded and ordained by God to accomplish. This was the message of Jesus in Mark chapter four when He taught about spiritual photosynthesis.

PRINCIPLE # 2

FIVE SENSES ARE THE GATES TO YOUR HEART

The second principle is that, the gates or entry points into the heart or subconscious mind are your five senses; what you're hearing, seeing, tasting, touching and smelling. These are the entry points of information into your conscious mind. When information is in your conscious mind and you dwell on it continually, it becomes transferred through a spiritual osmosis into your spirit man or into your heart which is also your subconscious mind. The word of God becomes flesh or fuses in your heart through persistence and then you begin to do it naturally or habitually. When you meditate on the word long enough, it becomes second nature or a habit, which you do without thinking about it consciously. The power of your words cannot be understated especially if it is scripture-based. The spiritual world operates in the realm of sound. Sound is Vibrations that travel through the air or another medium and can be heard when they reach a person's or animal's ear.

Sound is the activating force in the spiritual realm. It takes spoken words to activate spiritual beings. The universe was created through sound which came through the spoken word. Before Jesus our savior was conceived, the spoken word was released through sound. The born-again phenomenon starts in the heart and ends in our confession which is also sound. So what you're hearing is very important because it has the potential to influence what you would confess to shape your world.

126

Moreover, the bible entreats believers to keep the word of God before their eyes at all times. It says "*My son, attend to my words; incline thine EAR unto my sayings. Let them not depart from thine EYES (or keep it before your eyes at all times); keep them in the midst of thine heart. For they are life unto those that find them, and health to all their flesh*.(Proverbs 4:20-22) The preceding scripture mentioned the ears and eyes as two of the entry points into the heart. It is saying that it takes your hearing and seeing continually to keep the word in the midst of your heart. What you are seeing and hearing continually can affect your life. The first principle we learned from this parable is that your heart is the spiritual womb or ground where the word of God is sown; secondly, your sense of hearing is one of the entry points into your heart. As we know, faith comes by hearing the word of God and so also fear comes from hearing negative or evil report. The bible says in 2 Peter 2:8 "*for that righteous man Lot, dwelling among them, tormented his righteous soul from day to day by SEEING and HEARING their lawless deeds*

Lot dwelt among sinners in Sodom and Gomorrah. As a result, his spirit was continually vexed within him by seeing and hearing their sinful deeds. What a man hears has the power to influence his life. God moves within the realm of sound. Everything God does, it's done through sound. He created the whole universe by His words and expects believers also to know the power of their words. Every word that you speak, you also hear with your inner ear and therefore has the power to influence you either positively or negatively. When you meditate on the word of God, you speak the word of God to yourself by muttering and the more you hear the word of God, it builds up your faith. That's why Jesus said be careful what you hear, take heed what you hear for the measure of thought and study you give to what you hear will determine what will come back to you.

SPIRITUAL UNDERSTANDING BRINGS ILLUMINATION

The third principle we learned from these parables is that understanding the word of God you hear, is the spiritual illumination or light that helps the seed of the word to grow and manifest in your life. Sunlight causes the natural seed to grow and likewise understanding with your heart causes the word to benefit you. Understanding with your heart simply means accepting some information as true beyond your reasoning process or having an "aha" moment when you grasp a truth. Your understanding of the word of God that you hear is symbolic of the light, which causes the word of God to yield fruit.

God must open the eyes of your understanding before you can truly know and rightly interpret His truth. His truth is available only to those with a regenerate spirit and in whom His Spirit dwells, for only the Spirit can illumine Scripture. Just as the physically blind cannot see the sun, likewise the spiritually blind cannot see the Son of God who is hidden in the scriptures. Both lack proper illumination, which comes through understanding. There are few humans who receive the truth completely and wholly by an instant illumination. The majority of us receive illumination progressively. Precept upon precept; line upon line; here a little, and there a little; so shall men acquire progressive illumination. What you do not understand, you cannot apply to your life profitably and what you do not understand, you will not believe. Just as a natural seed without sunlight cannot grow, so likewise the spiritual seed without understanding in the heart would not prosper. When you understand with your heart, it is devoid of human reasoning or logical analysis; but full of divine illumination and insight, which causes a light to be turned on in your mind. The bible says one shall chase a thousand enemies and two shall chase ten thousand.

This simply means, there is strength in unity but mathematically, it does not make sense. That is why you have to understand spiritual things with your heart. Jesus said to Nicodemus that except a man is born again, he cannot enter into the kingdom of God; but he could not grasp the truth, because he heard it but did not understand. In life, a person only hears what he understands; because all truths are easy to understand once they are discovered. The most important point is to discover them. When God told the children of Israel to walk around the wall of Jericho in order to defeat that city, they understood with their heart. In the natural, it did not make any sense; but it was the instruction and their obedience that gave them victory. Whatever you cannot understand, you cannot possess, and with understanding you can overcome any situation, however mysterious or insurmountable it may appear to be.

In the parable of the sower, Jesus made it clear that the seed needed sunlight in order to grow when He said in Mark 4:6 that *"But when the SUN WAS UP, it was scorched; and because it had no root, it withered away"*. The seed withered when the sun arose; because the ground lacked moisture. The absence of water in the soil caused the seed to wither when the sun arose. Sunlight was meant to be used by the seed in addition to the moisture in the soil to manufacture its' food but instead, it dried up the seed. When a seed is sown in a desert, it will not grow because of the absence of moisture. Understanding with your heart, would give you knowledge and the application of the knowledge you possess is known as wisdom. In other words, wisdom is the ability to use knowledge which you have understood and apply it profitably. Understanding, therefore, is the founding pillar of wisdom. When God appeared to king Solomon in a dream and told him to ask for whatever he wants, king Solomon did not asked for wisdom as many people think; but rather he asked for an understanding heart.

The bible says king Solomon said" *Give therefore thy servant an understanding heart to judge thy people…"*, Then God responded *"Because thou hast asked this thing, and hast not asked for thyself long life; neither hast asked riches for thyself, nor hast asked the life of thine enemies; but hast asked for thyself*

UNDERSTANDING to discern judgment; behold, I have done according to thy words: lo, I have given thee a wise and an understanding heart; so that there was none like thee before thee, neither after thee shall any arise like unto thee. And I have also given thee that which thou hast not asked, both riches, and honour: so that there shall not be any among the kings like unto thee all thy days.

King Solomon asked for an understanding heart from God because in the lips of him who has understanding, wisdom is found. The bible says that a man of understanding has wisdom. Consequently, King Solomon became the wisest man that ever lived even though, he did not ask for wisdom. So understanding of the principles of the kingdom of God is very vital in our life. The bible also says that *"The wise also will HEAR (understand) and increase in learning, and the person of understanding will acquire SKILL (knowledge) and attain to sound COUNSEL [so that he may be able to steer his course rightly].*

A wise man hears and his understanding leads him to increase in knowledge or information that can be applied to ensure successful living. Also a man of understanding shall attain unto wise counsel to order his life righteously and most importantly, a man of understanding is of an excellent spirit. Even though, wisdom is the principal thing that we've been entreated to seek; but the scripture says emphatically that, understanding would lead us to wisdom. The bible says in Proverbs 4:7 *"Wisdom is the principal thing; therefore get wisdom: and with all thy getting get understanding."* With all thy getting, get understanding because it will lead you to the principal thing which is wisdom. We understand with our conscious mind but when we dwell or meditate on the understanding continually, the information is then transferred into our hearts which is the subconscious mind.

PRINCIPLE # 4

MEDITATION BREEDS REVELATION KNOWLEDGE

The fourth principle is that your meditation of the word, will give you more revelation knowledge or RHEMA which would empower you to activate the word in your life. A RHEMA is a word of God that has been quickened by the Holy Spirit to specifically apply to your need or situation. A RHEMA makes the word of God very applicable to you personally. So when you meditate upon the word of God, it gives the Holy Spirit the needed materials to bring specific revelation knowledge to you. God always gives unto us according to our ability to comprehend or according to the depth of our knowledge. The bible says in Ephesians 3:20 *"Now **unto him that is able to do exceeding abundantly above all that we ask or think, according to the power that works in us**,"* This scripture is telling us that God is able to do exceedingly abundantly above all that we ask or think based on the power (knowledge) that is at work in us. Knowledge is power, so God works effectively in our life based on our depth of knowledge. For example, Apostle Paul was very knowledgeable in the law or the Torah before his divine encounter with Jesus on the road to Damascus. He sat under, and learned from, the great minds of his time. Because of the depth of his knowledge, the Holy Spirit was able to give more revelation knowledge to him than all the other apostles. As a result, he singlehandedly, wrote more than two thirds of the New Testament even though, he did not walk with Jesus during His ministerial years on earth. Paul was a man who meditated on the word of God continually as he also admonished us to think on the word continually.

Paul besought us to renew our minds by thinking soberly in Romans 12:2-3. He also said we should be gatekeepers of our minds by being conscious of our thoughts at all times in 2 Corinthians 10:4-5. Meditation on the word of God, therefore, would bring more revelation knowledge to you, and it is symbolic of the spiritual water needed by the spiritual seed, which is the word of God, to prosper in your life. The bible says that through meditation, more understanding is given to us. We become wiser than even our teachers when we meditate on the word day and night.

"For My thoughts are not your thoughts, nor are your ways my ways," says the Lord. For as the heavens are higher than the earth, so are my ways higher than your ways, and My thoughts than your thoughts. For as the rain comes down, and the snow from heaven, and do not return there, but water the earth, and make it bring forth and bud, that it may give seed to the sower

and bread to the eater, so shall My word be that goes forth from My mouth; It shall not return to Me void, but it shall accomplish what I please, and it shall prosper in the thing for which I sent it."

The ways and operations of God are higher than your ways, thoughts and operations. Therefore, exchange your ways and thoughts for a higher way of operation through the meditation and application of the word of God.

PRINCIPLE # 5

MEASURE OF MEDITATION DETERMINES THE MEASURE OF REWARDS

The fifth principle is that, the measure of thought and meditation you give to what you hear (understand) will determine what will come out of it to you. The Amplified bible says in Mark 4: 24-25 *"And He said to them, Be careful what you are hearing. The measure of thought and study you give to the truth you hear will be the measure of virtue and knowledge that comes back to you-- and more besides will be given to you who hear. For to him who has will more be given; and from him who has nothing, even what he has will be taken away by force* .What is Jesus saying here? Take heed what you hear; because what you are hearing will enter your heart; and the measure of thought and study (meditation) you will give to the truth you hear with your heart, will determine the measure of virtue and knowledge that comes back to you. Likewise the measure of thought and study you give to the evil report you hear through worry, would determine the level of damage that would come back to you.

When Jesus said that the measure that you give to what you hear, would determine the measure of what you will get back, he was referring to meditation as the preceding scripture clearly indicates. So now if you read these verses in the Amplified bible, it says that the measure of meditation you give equals the knowledge you get back in return. The Amplified version clarifies it by what Jesus said unto them; be careful what you are hearing for the measure of thoughts and study (which is meditation) you give to the truth you hear will be the measure of virtue and knowledge that comes back to you; and more besides will be given to him who hears, for to him who hear and understand, shall more understanding be given through meditation, and from the man who has nothing or who doesn't have understanding, even what he has shall be taken away from him.

This is why Jesus said that the seed that was sown on the wayside because the hearer did not understand, the devil came and stole the word from him. What you do not understand, the enemy would steal from you. But the one who understands, more knowledge will be given to him through meditation. Also, the level of meditation, determines the level of fruitfulness. The parable said that, on the good ground, some yielded thirty-fold, some sixty and some hundredfold. They yielded fruit based on the measure of meditation devoted to what was heard and understood. This is the reason why the good ground did not yield equal harvest to all but rather , some yielded thirty, some sixty and others hundred. The measure of meditation, determined the measure it yielded to each one of them.

PRINCIPLE # 6

PATIENCE IS NEEDED AS AN ELEMENT OF FAITH

Now the sixth principle says the word of God that you hear, understand and meditate on, must be mixed with faith in order for it to manifest in your life. When you successfully sow or cast the word in your heart (subconscious mind) through repetition of thought and words, you should not expect it to manifest in your life instantly; but rather wait patiently for it to grow roots in your life before manifestation; since there can never be faith without patience, and belief that the desired results would be attained eventually. The heart (subconscious mind) is highly impressed upon by thoughts that are emotionalized or mixed with emotion because it is the seat of our emotions. Prayers that are very effective are those that are emotionalized or mixed with emotion and faith is one of the most powerful emotions. The power of belief is so tremendous that it can move mountains.

Therefore, have faith and consider the end as already accomplished by calling the things that do not appear as if they are. Jesus said in Mark 11:23 " *For assuredly, I say to you, whoever says to this mountain, 'Be removed and be cast into the sea,' and does not doubt in his heart, but believes that those things he says WILL BE done, he WILL HAVE whatever he says* ". Belief in the heart (subconscious mind) is paramount to obtaining our desires in life and it also empowers the subconscious mind to bring it to pass by creating our strong cravings and desires. This is the way God ordained it. This is how God created man; when we believe with our heart, it brings empowerment either good or bad. The power of belief can never be understated.

Jesus said something, which was very profound in Mark Chapter four. He spoke about the seed in three different ways. The first parable dealt with, how to consciously sow the word of God as a seed in the fertile garden of your subconscious mind or heart. In the second parable, he said that when a seed is sown it doesn't grow the same day. When you sow a seed, you have to give it time to germinate through patience. First of all, it has to die before it germinates and begin to develop root; then after it has been well rooted, the blade will shoot upward towards the sun. This means that after you have understood the word and have meditated upon it and mixed it up with faith through prayer, you have to wait patiently for the manifestation of the promise. Once the word has been planted in your heart or subconscious mind through repetition of thought and words, it will automatically be manifested in your life. You may not know how this will happen but the expectation, the belief, the assurance and the conviction of your faith will cause the subconscious mind or heart to bring it to pass.

Just as in the natural, a seed does not grow overnight but goes through the natural growth process; so also the spiritual seed has to go through the spiritual growth process. Therefore, give the word of God time to grow and manifest in your life. Do not plant today and expect it to grow or see results tomorrow but rather wait patiently for its manifestation in time.

The bible says *"Just as you cannot understand the path of the wind or the mystery of a tiny baby growing in its mother's womb, so you cannot understand the activity of God, who does all things. Plant your seed in the morning and keep busy all afternoon, for you don't know if profit will come from one activity or another—or maybe both.*

"Jesus also said, "The Kingdom of God is like a farmer who scatters seed on the ground. Night and day, while he's asleep or awake, the seed sprouts and grows, but he does not understand how it happens. The earth produces the crops on its own. First a leaf blade pushes through, then the heads of wheat are formed, and finally the grain ripens. And as soon as the grain is ready, the farmer comes and harvests it with a sickle, for the harvest time has come." The farmer waited patiently and expectantly for the harvest and he obtained the desired results. Whilst waiting, he kept watering the seed until he sees the harvest.

These two scriptures are simply telling us not to be concerned about how God miraculously causes seeds to grow in the earth, heart (subconscious mind) and in the womb of a pregnant woman because they are out of our control. Once a man sows the seed, the rest is in the hands of God. All he has to do is to believe that the seed would bear fruit. How the seed would grow in the soil is beyond his control. We have done our portion by planting the seed or the word of God in our heart, and it is now in the hands of God to cause it to grow. All that is needed at this point is to wait patiently, knowing and believing that it will come to pass. Most importantly, you must believe. The atmosphere of faith and expectancy is very vital to the growth of the seed, and it is in this environment that the subconscious mind thrives. The subconscious mind only receives information that is mixed with emotion. Love, faith and desire are the most powerful emotions that greatly influence the subconscious mind. It also shows us that, there is a natural responsibility as well as supernatural responsibility, which involve man and God respectively in the growth of a planted seed.

God is a covenant keeping God who will always keep his promise; because He watches over His word to perform it. The bible says in 1 Corinthians 3:6-9 *"I planted the seed in your hearts, and*

Apollos watered it, but it was God who made it grow. It's not important who does the planting, or who does the watering. What's important is that God makes the seed grow. The one who plants and the one who water, work together with the same purpose. And both will be rewarded for their own hard work. For we are both God's workers. And you are God's field. You are God's building. (NLT)

It is the responsibility of a man to plant a seed and cultivate the land but it is God who causes the seed to grow. Therefore, it is important to trust in the word of God and its ability as the incorruptible seed to transform lives for the better since God would never fail. He watches over his word to perform it in our lives. The word of God is the conveyor, conduit and container of His power that is why it is exalted above all His names. It is through the word that we know His names. The whole universe was created by the breath of His mouth. The word of God is so powerful, because it has been encoded to reproduce whatever it was sent to do. So, everything that you need has already been deposited in you in Christ Jesus; because the kingdom of God is within you. So, why is it that, the word of God is not manifesting in your life.

The very words that created the heavens and the earth has been given to you as the raw material to create and frame your own world. You have been made a god on the earth; because you have been given the word of God to create, invent and bring to pass whatsoever you desire, according to the word of God. So long as your desire does not violate the word, God would make sure that His word manifests in your life. The bible says in John 10:34-35 *"Jesus answered them, Is it not written in your law,*

I said, Ye are gods? IF HE CALLED THEM GODS, UNTO WHOM THE WORD

OF GOD CAME..." The faithfulness and power of the word of God is what makes God who He is and this very word has been given to us therefore making us gods as well. Jesus was once addressing his audience and said something very profound to the effect that if the scripture called the people unto whom the word of God came to as gods, then they are the children of God indeed.

136

Therefore, He (Jesus) was not blaspheming when He said that he is the Son of God. Many Christians do not know their privileges as sons of God in Christ Jesus. Many have accepted Jesus as their Lord and savior; but are not applying the principles that he taught. Many are going to heaven without impacting the earth for Jesus. We were born again to manifest and conform to the image of Jesus Christ, who is the firstborn of many brethren. Your acceptance of Jesus as your Lord and savior only entitles you to enter into heaven and spend eternity with Him; but if you do not apply the principles that He taught while on this physical earth, you will not live the abundant life, which Jesus came to offer you. It takes faith to know and patiently wait for the manifestation of the word in your life. Abraham waited twenty five years for his promise son; because he believed and had faith in the word of God.

There are two faces of the gospel. There is the Son of God and the System of God. There is the person of Jesus Christ, and the principles of Jesus Christ, which He taught. Many had accepted the person of Jesus Christ; but are not living according to the principles that he taught. One of the principles that Jesus taught was the ability as a child of God to see the word of God become real and applicable in your life. He said in John 15:7 *"If ye abide in me, and my words abide in you, ye shall ask what ye will, and it shall be done unto you."* Asking what you need should be done according to the word that is already in you. So once you abide in Christ and his word abides in you richly, then you can make demands based on the word which abides within you and it will be granted to you.

Whatever you are demanding should align with what God has already provided for you in His word through Christ Jesus. It is very important to have a very good working knowledge of the word of God; because whatever you need is already provided in the word. Grace and peace would be multiplied unto you through your knowledge of the word of God. Lack of knowledge causes many to perish. On the other hand, the presence of knowledge causes many to prosper. It is all about knowledge which comes to us through understanding with the heart; and the application of the knowledge and information that we possess, will bring us prosperity and success. It is, therefore, very, very important to have knowledge of the bible more than anything else in the world. Every solution to life's problems has been placed in the bible for our use. It is our manual for life. Believing in the bible is the wisest decision anybody can make. You can believe in any other thing you desire, but none is as powerful as the word of God. Therefore, wait patiently for the manifestation of the word; because it will surely come to pass.

PRINCIPLE # 7

THE POTENTIAL ENERGY OF THE INCORRUPTIBLE SEED

Finally, the seventh principle: The word of God as an incorruptible seed is encoded with potential energy waiting to be unleashed when sown in the right and desired environment. This was the message of Jesus when he spoke the parable of the sower where he likened the kingdom of God to a seed that was sown by a farmer. Many of the seeds fell on grounds that were not conducive for the growth of the seed. The seeds failed because the conditions on these grounds were not favorable. Jesus spoke in parables so that His message could not be easily understood. It takes the illumination of the Spirit of God to comprehend some of His deep sayings. In his teachings, he likened the word of God to an incorruptible seed; but what similarities does a seed have with the word of God? They are both impregnated with potential energy that can only be released in the right environment. The word of God can transform a life if it is applied correctly.

Likewise, a natural seed can also transform a life if it is sown correctly. One orange seed can become a whole forest of orange trees that would bring financial gain to the farmer and reward his efforts, when it is sown properly in the right condition. The orange seed has the potential to become an orange tree with hundreds of orange fruits on it. In each of these fruits, there are more seeds that would be replanted to reproduce after its kind more orange trees, which have hundreds of fruits with seeds. If this process continues for a few years, the single seed can be multiplied a million times over. So also is the word of God. It has been encoded to reproduce after its kind. Everything that you will ever need in life has already been deposited on the inside of you in a form of a seed in Christ Jesus. These seeds of ideas, concepts, thoughts and innovations need to be planted in our hearts or subconscious minds and nurtured continually till it bears fruit in our life. The process of sowing the seed of ideas, concepts, thoughts and innovations embedded in the word of God into our hearts or subconscious mind is the theme of the parable of the sower.

Different kinds of seeds require different environmental conditions to grow. For example, the seed of a man can only be planted in the womb of a woman. This is the only designated and ordained environment conducive for the growth of this seed. Likewise the seed of ideas, thoughts, concepts and innovations embedded in the word of God can only be planted in the hearts of men, which is the subconscious mind. This spiritual seed can be sown personally in your own heart based on your needs. The assurance that God watches over His word to perform it should also motivate and encourage you; that the seed would never fail if planted in the right environment.

Therefore, plant the seed in your heart and nurture it to grow into the desired fruit. When you apply the principles that Jesus taught in this parable correctly, then you shall surely and definitely prosper in everything that you do. The only variable in this equation is the human factor. Just as in the natural realm, a farmer has to plant a seed in a fertile ground and then keep tending the land to get rid of all weeds that would impede the growth of the seed, likewise, when we sow the word of God in our hearts we have to keep our heart chaste and pure so as to ensure the growth of the word in our life.

Negative heart conditions like unforgiveness, bitterness, malice, envy and other unrighteousness, would hinder the growth of the seed. We learned that, it takes understanding of the word of God, and then meditation on the word we have understood for deeper revelation to be attained. Meditation on the word is done repetitiously to empower you to obey and apply the word. When we mix unwavering faith to these two disciplines, we would definitely see the manifestation of the word in our lives. God created the human heart in such a way that it responds to emotional impulses speedily. When our words, prayers and thoughts are filled with emotions, they impregnate the heart and it eventually gives birth to whatever it has conceived.

This is the reason why we are admonished to have faith, trust and believe in the Lord in all things because whatever we believe we can achieve. The bible tells us that, *"with our heart we believe..."* This means that the heart or subconscious mind is the seat of our emotions and it is the only language the heart or subconscious mind understands and speaks. Therefore, the heart only accepts information that is mixed with emotion and faith is an emotion. Desire is the strongest of all emotions that influences the heart. The subconscious mind is also impressed upon through repetition.

Moreover, the subconscious mind only accepts information that has been accepted by the conscious mind, which is the gate-keeper of the subconscious mind. This was exactly the main theme of Jesus when he compared the kingdom of God to a seed in the parable of the sower. This is the reason why meditation has to be done day and night on a continuous basis thus ensuring repetition which is one of the means used to impregnate the subconscious mind. This is also how we appropriate the word of God or transfer it from the spiritual realm in Christ Jesus into our physical life. We have also learned that these disciplines represent the light and water that the seed needs in order to grow plus our ability to have faith in God and his word.

It is very important that we understand these principles so as to apply them in our lives. It is also very important that we know how to meditate on the word of God. So, I'm going to spend some time to talk about biblical meditation, its importance and how to do it.

CHAPTER 10

BIBLICAL MEDITATION

Meditation is the most important Christian discipline that elevates believers to the level that God expects them to attain. Due to the truth that salvation of man is threefold, namely: the salvation of the spirit, the salvation of the soul and the salvation of the body; every Christian is expected to work out his/her own salvation. The salvation of the human spirit is a one-time event; but the salvation of the soul is a lifetime process which is the sole responsibility of every Christian, and until a born-again believer embarks upon the journey of renewal of his soul, which comprises the mind, will and emotion, he can never experience the abundant life that Jesus came to give onto him.

The salvation of the physical body is also a one-time event, which will take place in the future as stated in Romans 8:23, when we will put on the incorruptible body. Both the salvation of the spirit and the body are one-time events that God Almighty works in every believer beyond our control and influence. So the only part that true Christians are required to play is the renewal of the soul, which comprises the mind, the will and the emotions. Until these faculties of our being are completely, entirely and wholly surrendered to the Lord, we cannot experience the abundant life.

Jesus made reference to this truth when He said in one of His parables in the gospel of Mathew 13:33 *"Another parable spake he unto them; the kingdom of heaven is like unto leaven, which a woman took, and hid in three measures of meal, till the WHOLE was leavened"*. Jesus said that the kingdom of God is likened onto leaven or yeast which is a substance that causes fermentation and expansion of dough, when baking bread. This leaven was hidden in *"three measures of MEAL until the WHOLE was leavened"* (Emphasis mine). According to this parable, the three measures of meal is equal to one whole; that is, it takes the three measures to make one whole meal. Just as it takes, the spirit, soul and body of a believer to make him whole as Paul mentioned in 1 Thessalonians 5:23 " *And the very God of peace sanctify you WHOLLY; and I pray God your WHOLE SPIRIT and SOUL and BODY be preserved blameless unto the coming of our Lord Jesus Christ .* So, according to this scripture, the totality of man comprises the spirit, soul, and body; and the good news of the gospel is supposed to affect all these areas of our Christian life. The word "whole" means complete, entire, intact, total, undivided, unbroken or non-fragmented. So according to Jesus, it took the three measures of meal to make one complete, entire, non-fragmented, and whole meal.

But, we cannot completely understand this parable unless we uncover what Jesus meant by the word *"LEAVEN"*. According to Mathew 16: 6 &12, *"Then Jesus said unto them, Take heed and beware of the leaven of the Pharisees and of the Sadducees... Then understood they how that he bade them not beware of the leaven of bread, but of the DOCTRINE of the Pharisees and of the Sadducees"* So, according to this scripture, Leaven was symbolic of a religious doctrine because it can influence the attitudes and behavior of those who embrace it just as leaven can affect the composition of the dough it comes in contact. Therefore, Jesus was making reference to the doctrine of the kingdom of God, which is supposed to ferment, intoxicate, infuse and inflame our whole spirit, soul and body to make us whole and fit for kingdom purposes.

Jesus also said that *"no man putteth new wine into old bottles: else the new wine doth burst the bottles, and the wine is spilled, and the bottles will be marred: but new wine must be put into new bottles.* This statement was also pointing to the same truth that the kingdom of God cannot be contained in our old sinful nature but rather with a renewed mindset. All through the New Testament, references were made by the apostles about the renewal of the mind. Apostle Paul spoke about it in almost all of his epistles; but it is only through meditation that the mind can be effectively renewed. True and effective renewal of the mind only takes place in the heart or subconscious mind, which can only be reached and imprinted upon through biblical meditation. It is in the heart where all information are stored or the heart is the seat of the faculty of the memory.

Biblical meditation, therefore, is a spiritual discipline or activity that can cause you to prosper in whatsoever you do. It is an assured and guaranteed way of channeling the power and blessings of God into your life. The bible says in Psalm 1:1-3 that *"**Blessed is the man that walketh not in the counsel of the ungodly, nor standeth in the way of sinners, nor sitteth in the seat of the scornful. But his delight is in the law of the Lord; and in his law doth he meditate day and night. (As a result of his continual meditation on the word)... he shall be like a tree planted (stability) by the rivers of water (satisfaction), that bringeth forth his fruit in his season (significance); his leaf also shall not wither (superiority); and whatsoever he doeth shall prosper (success)"**.*

According to this scripture, meditation brings about stability, satisfaction, significance, superiority and success (I call them the five S's). These are some of the manifold blessings of meditation. Moreover, it says in the book of Joshua 1:8 that meditation would bring into your life prosperity and success. These two scriptures are among the numerous scriptures that talks about success and prosperity. Most importantly, they were mentioned in connection with meditation. The spiritual discipline of biblical meditation will also give you deep understanding and wisdom far above your peers. The bible says in Psalm 63:5-6 *"**My soul shall be SATISFIED as with marrow and fatness; and my mouth shall praise thee with joyful lips: When I remember thee upon my bed, and meditate on thee in the night watches."*** According to this scripture, meditation would give you satisfaction and joyful lips to praise the Lord. When you meditate upon the goodness and mercies of God, you become aware and realize that it is only by His grace that you are what you are and not by your own ability. This awareness enhances praise in your life; because you become conscious of His goodness and benefits, which He has bestowed on you.

This knowledge or awareness gives you a very good reason to praise Him. Praise also becomes easier when we meditate upon the work of His hands, His power, love, and tender mercies. It is also a discipline that gives you peace that surpasses all human comprehension. The bible says that great peace have those that love the law of God and whose mind is stayed or focused on Him. When you love something or someone, you yearn to spend quality time with them, and so we spend quality time with God through meditation on His word. Meditation would also give you power to eschew sin. Psalm 119:11 says *"Thy word have I hid in mine heart, that I might not sin against thee.*

When the word of God is hidden in your heart through meditation, it becomes your point of reference and conviction of sin at all times thus helping you to eschew evil. When you meditate on the word of God, you transfer the word from your mind (conscious mind) into your heart (subconscious mind), and hide it there for future use, or when it is needed. When the word of God dwells richly in you, and you think about it all the time, you will know when it is appropriate for the application of that specific word in your life. The word of God hidden in your heart becomes a point of reference and conviction excusing or convicting you of your actions. The power of the word of God is in the application of it.

Meditation would bring profit into your life and build up your faith in the word. All these benefits can be yours if you learn how to meditate on the word of God on a daily basis. In life, whatsoever you think about a lot has the power and ability to influence your life. It doesn't matter what it is, as long as you spend time thinking about it and it becomes your dominant thought, it would affect the way you live. Thoughts trigger emotions, behaviors, utterances and create habits. The human mind is never idle. We are always thinking about something; either positive or negative; either consciously or by default. It is an endless activity. So when you think about God, the work of His hands and His manifold blessings which He has bestowed upon His children at all times, it empowers

144

you to excel in whatever you do because it (whatever you do) will be influenced by your predominant thoughts.

David was a man after God's own heart and as a result, he meditated on God and His word all the time. He had a relationship with God through meditation, which is a form of worship, and he kept his thoughts on God continually. So whatever you think about continually is what you become. Therefore, think about God and His word at all times and become as God by inculcating His ways and thoughts as your ways and thoughts. You are what you think so if you think positively, those thoughts would energize you positively to do positive things. When Jesus said in Mark 4:24 " ***be careful what you hear for the measure of thought and study (meditation) that you give to what you hear, would determine the measure of virtue and knowledge that would come back to you***". By this statement, Jesus placed premium importance on meditation of the word of God as the trump card.

The process of biblical meditation can be compared to a cow chewing its cud. A cow is a ruminant that has a four-chambered stomach that permits it to swallow food which is partially digested and then bring it up again at a later time, chew it again, swallow again, and bring it back again only to be chewed and swallowed until complete digestion has taken place. This is a perfect picture of biblical meditation. When we meditate on the word of God, we take a bite at the word of God, chew on it for a while, swallow it, bring it up again at a later time and chew some more, swallow and so forth. This is the process of spiritual digestion or biblical meditation that takes place when we meditate upon the word and promises of God. Meditating on the promises of God entails going over the truth of the word over and over in our minds, hearts and spirits. It is actually a slow and deliberate process that involves musing or chewing on the word over and over again until it becomes personal with you. This means repeating the word to yourself over and over until it sinks into the good ground of your heart which is your subconscious mind and whatever is in your heart will be reproduced.

This process would bring illumination, insight, deep revelation knowledge, comprehension, and understanding of the word through the inspiration of the Holy Spirit. By saying it over and over to yourself, you build up your faith in the specific word. As you do this, the seed of the word will sink into the good ground of your heart and take root there. As the seed of the word begins to grow in your heart, continue to water it through further meditation, prayer, praise and thanksgiving. Then, in the process of time, it becomes a habit in your life and will be able to bring forth God's intended blessing and harvest associated with the specific promise. This is the idea our Lord Jesus Christ was conveying in the three parables from Mark chapter four.

The bible says in Psalm 37:4 that *"Delight thyself also in the LORD: and he shall give thee the desires of thine heart"*. When you delight in something, you crave to spend time and enjoy it whenever you can. When you truly delight (take great pleasure in or experience a high degree of satisfaction) in the Word, you will have a desire (a craving, a longing, a hunger or thirst) to spend time in it and to meditate on it. Beloved, we (human beings) do not naturally delight in the Holy Word for we are by nature unholy. By virtue of our Adamic nature, we were born in sin. Evil and negativity comes naturally to us; but goodness and positivity is alien to our sinful nature. Therefore, we have to deliberately and consciously plant positiveness, godliness, and love in our hearts in order to reap these virtues in our life. Negative thoughts come into our minds automatically without any human effort but positive thoughts have to be consciously planted in our minds. It is said that, you cannot prevent a bird from flying over your head, but you can prevent the bird from building its nest on your head. Psychologist called this the automated negative suggestions. This is the reason why we are commanded in the bible to consciously keep our hearts or subconscious mind with all diligence, and to be the gate-keepers of our minds; because it is the fountain of all the issues of life.

When any man or woman begins to delight in the Word, they can know for certain that they are experiencing God's amazing grace, wherein they see the Holy Spirit giving them the ability to delight in the word and the dynamics to understand God's Holy Word. A close study of the book of Psalms clearly indicates that king David was a strong worshiper, who delighted so much in God that he meditated on the word of God daily.

No wonder God called him a man after His heart. David, on numerous occasions in the Psalms, made a connection between delight and adoration for the word of God with meditation on the word. It is a natural response to meditate on something when you delight in it. Let us look at a few of them starting from Psalm 1:2 *"But his*

DELIGHT is in the law of the LORD; and in his law doth he MEDITATE day and night". This scripture is making a clear connection between delight and meditation. Because he delights in the word of God, he meditates on it continually. It is impossible to delight in something but don't want to spend time with the object of your delight. *"I will MEDITATE in thy precepts, and have respect unto thy ways. I will DELIGHT myself in thy statutes: I will not forget thy word."* (Psalm 119:15-16).

Also in the verse 23-24 in the same chapter it says *"Princes also did sit and speak against me: but thy servant did MEDITATE in thy statutes. Thy testimonies also are my DELIGHT and my counselors"*. David had an intimate relationship with God through meditation on His word. This gave him a deep revelation of who God is. Since he delighted in the word of God, it was only a natural sequence for him to meditate on the word day and night. Naturally, when you love someone or delight in someone, you crave to spend time with them, and tend to adore and adapt his ways. Likewise, believers can also do the same through prayer, worship, praise, thanksgiving, and above all, meditation.

The bible also says in the same chapter of Psalm 119:47-48 *"And I will DELIGHT myself in thy commandments, which I have loved. My hands also will I lift up (in worship and surrender)unto thy commandments, which I have LOVED; and I will MEDITATE in thy statutes"* All these scriptures are clearly indicating to us that if we love God, as much as we profess we do, then we will meditate upon His word and let it become one with us. Meditation is the spiritual master-key that unlocks all the doors to our blessing, wellness, and prosperity. It is the practical way of turning each truth we learn about God into a matter for reflection before God, leading to prayer and praise to God. It is also an activity of calling to mind or recalling what is already stored in your heart, and thinking about it over and over; dwelling on, and applying to oneself, the various things that one knows about the works, ways, purposes and promises of God. It is an activity of holy thought, consciously performed in the presence of God, under the eye of God, by the help of God, as a means of communion with God.

The bible also says in Psalm 119:77-78 *"Let thy tender mercies come unto me, that I may live: for thy law is my DELIGHT. Let the proud be ashamed; for they dealt perversely with me without a cause: but I will MEDITATE in thy precepts."* If God's word is not the desire and delight of your heart, then diligently plead with Him until He grants your request, so that your soul would cultivate the appetite for the pure sincere milk of the word of God. This discipline of meditation would cause you to focus on the word of God by pondering, thinking, reflecting, musing, and contemplating continually upon it so as to discern its meaning or significance; in order to chart your course or plan of action. Meditation will cause the word of God to become a lamp unto your feet and a light unto your path. It will cause the word of God to be your guide that will order the steps you take and direct you on the right paths.

The word of God has the power to impact your life if only you believe and agree with it. Either you agree with what God has said about you in His word or disagree. You will reap the benefits of whichever stand you choose. The position you choose on the word of God would not change who God is; but it will change you. If you believe or not, the sun would still rise in the east and set in the west, irrespective of your geographical location. However, God has given us His word to frame and create our own world if we believe in it, and remember that all things are possible unto those who believe. Meditation connects and brings together the two most powerful things in life; the word of God and the subconscious mind. During biblical meditation, these two powerful spiritual forces work together to achieve the desired results. Biblical meditation renews, redirects, commands and influences the

148

subconscious mind to form a habit about whatever thought is being held in the conscious mind continually.

The ability to create your own world lies inert within your spirit or heart, waiting to be unleashed through your words. The bible says that life and death are in the power of the tongue, and whosoever loves it shall eat the fruit thereof. Whosoever loves it would meditate on it and incubate the seed of the word in their heart or subconscious mind, till it becomes one with their being whereby it will be spoken with power that generate results. This simply means that words can kill and words can give life; they are either poison or good fruit. Whichever way you choose to subscribe with your words would be the seed you will plant in your heart and reap the fruit thereof. When you come into agreement with the word of God as pertaining to a specific situation, you receive the word in its entirety and then consider what is it that you are required to do to see the manifestation of the word in your life. Seek to understand your responsibility in making the word work in your life; because God cannot lie.

Everything God has promised is yeah and amen, which we can count on. Therefore, we are the only variable factors that control what happens to the word of God in us. This is the message Jesus was conveying to the disciples, when He taught them about the three parables in Mark chapter four. Words are powerful and can change the course of our life. Through suggestions, either by ourselves or others, seeds of thoughts, ideas, concepts, and innovations are implanted in our subconscious mind, which the bible identifies as the heart. This is the divine principle Jesus taught in the parable of the sower in which He highlighted the power of the word of God. What would you do if you know that you can never fail? Imagine that whatever you put your hands to do can never fail. Will this knowledge empower you to reach for the stars? Then reach for the things above because God has promised them to His children. Just do exactly that because you can never fail if you work the system of God through His revealed word.

There are, however, certain preparations that you need to do to position yourself for deep revelation insight to come to you. Here are some preparatory activities that will position you for deep insight of the word through meditation.

Confession of your sins: Since the grace of receiving divine revelation and insight is at the heart of biblical meditation, you must prepare yourself to receive from the Holy Spirit by confessing your sins, and be cleansed by the blood of the Lamb. You must be obedient to the word and previous revelations from God; because obedience to revealed truth, guarantees guidance in matters unrevealed. Therefore, confess any sin in your life, so you are not cut off from ongoing revelation. 2 Corinthians 7:1 says *"Having therefore these promises, dearly beloved, let us cleanse ourselves from all filthiness of the flesh and spirit, perfecting holiness in the fear of God"*. Let the light of God shine and expose every hidden sin in your life, and then confess, forsake, and turn away from it.

Have a teachable and humble spirit: Revelation knowledge comes through meditation when we maintain an attitude of humility but unfortunately it is withheld from the proud and the arrogant. So keep an open, humble attitude before God, allowing Him the freedom to shed greater light on any ideas you currently hold and also to modify them as He sees fit. All illumination will proceed from the word which you have meditated on. There would be precept upon precept, line upon line, here a little and there a little. The Holy Spirit of God would reveal all truths to you. (Jas. 4:6; II Pet. 1:19). The Holy Spirit within you is your Teacher. The bible says " *But the anointing which ye have received of him abideth in you, and ye need not that any man teach you: but as the same anointing teacheth you of all things, and is truth, and is no lie, and even as it hath taught you, ye shall abide in him.*" The Holy Spirit cannot teach you if you do not humble yourself to receive His teaching.

Present your mind and heart to God: You can do nothing on your own initiative; but only what you hear and see by the Spirit. You do not have a mind to use, but a mind to present to God so He can use it and fill it with anointed reasoning and divine vision .If you use your mind yourself, it is a dead work. Lend your members onto the Lord by not having any preconceived ideas of how things

150

ought to be; but rather have an open mind. *"I beseech you therefore, brethren, by the mercies of God, that ye present your bodies a living sacrifice, holy, acceptable unto God, which is your reasonable service."* (Romans 12:1)

Pray that the eyes of your heart might be enlightened: Slow down as you read, mulling the text over and over in your heart and mind, praying constantly for God to give you a spirit of wisdom and revelation in the knowledge of Him (Eph. 1:17-18; Ps. 119:18).Do not rush through the scriptures; but take your time and study it by thinking about the wording in the whole context. Read and study the text over and over and then ask relevant questions. A good and diligent student is the one that asks relevant questions which demands answers from the teacher. Remain quite in the presence of the Holy Spirit and listen for answers to your questions.

Sometimes, an answer may come at a later time whilst doing something else, and then suddenly the Holy Spirit would drop it into your human spirit. This revelation would then be passed from your spirit into your conscious mind through the subconscious. The subconscious mind is the interface or link between your spirit and soul. It is a spiritual entity that is not visible to the naked eye. The bible says in Job 33:14-16 *"For God may speak in one way, or in another, yet man does not perceive it. In a dream, in a vision of the night, when deep sleep falls upon men (when the conscious mind is asleep), while slumbering on their beds, then He opens the ears of men, and seals their instruction."* This scripture is better understood when we acknowledge the truth that our heart or subconscious mind never sleeps. When the conscious mind is at rest or asleep, the subconscious mind is still at work to keep your heart and other vital organs of your physical body working. This is when God seals His instruction into the subconscious through dreams, bypassing the conscious mind, which is asleep.

Present the reasoning and imaginative faculties for revelation to fill and flow through into your spirit: Meditation involves presenting your faculties to God for Him to fill and use. Look for the river of God, which is the flow of the Spirit to guide and fill your members, granting you anointed reasoning, dream, and

151

vision, (Jn. 7:3739). Music can also assist you, when you are muttering, speaking, and meditating on the word of God (II Kings 3:15).Learn to experience the Lord's presence alone. Many people have various ways of experiencing the presence of God. To some, they feel his presence through fasting, some through meditation, and others through worship. Whichever way works for you is acceptable.

Lord, show me the solution to the problem I am facing: Focused attention brings additional energies of concentration of heart and mind, which helps release revelation. Take for example, for experimentation purposes, the difference between a ray of sunlight hitting a piece of paper, and sunlight going through a magnifying glass to hit a piece of paper. The focused energy creates a ray so concentrated that the paper bursts into flames. When you have a hunger and desire to master a new understanding and discipline, that hungry and searching heart will cause you to see things you would not normally see. The bible says *"**Blessed are those who hunger and thirst for righteousness, for they shall be satisfied.*** When you are totally focused on God for answers, He never fails to deliver.

Be thankful: Realize and acknowledge that the revelation came from the indwelling Holy Spirit, therefore give all the glory to God for what has been revealed. Thanksgiving is necessary; because it acknowledges God as the source of the revelation. It gives and directs all the glory and honor onto God. All good and perfect gifts come from above; from the Father of glory. Give thanks to Him for the revelation knowledge because the bible says *"**If any of you lacks wisdom, let him ask of God, who gives to all liberally and without reproach, and it will be given to him.(James 1:5)***

Keep the revealed knowledge on your lips: The words that we speak are so powerful that, they shape our lives. They either activate good or evil forces into action. The bible says that *"**Bless the LORD, ye his angels that excel in strength, that do his commandments, HEARKENING UNTO THE VOICE OF HIS WORD"***.

(Psalm 103:20). This scripture is saying that angels listen and obey the voice of His word. It does not matter, who is giving voice to His word (either God or righteous men). Angels would always respond to the word of God as long as the one making the utterance is in right standing with God.

This scripture also reinforces the truth that words are the activating forces in the spiritual realm. It means that the angels of God hear and obey the voice of God's word irrespective of who is speaking it; as long as they are in right standing with God. So you can speak or give voice to God's word in faith and His angels would hearken (hear and obey).Likewise, you can speak or give voice to evil words and it will activate evil forces. The spiritual realm is controlled by spoken words or sound. So knowing the power of your words would help you to choose them with care. Therefore strive to store the word of God in your heart by meditating on it continually, and out of that storage of God's word in your heart will come the issues of life. Your words are the overflow of your heart contents. You cannot store evil in your heart and expect to speak good tidings. A tree is known by its fruit, which is the end result of its seed. So the word of God which is the incorruptible seed is sown in our hearts by speaking it over and over to ourselves until it becomes one with our spirit and builds up our faith.

The bible says in Psalm 45:1 *"My heart is overflowing with a good theme; I recite (repeat from memory) my composition concerning the King; my tongue is the pen of a ready writer."* There is a very important spiritual truth that is embedded in the verse. The word *"overflowing"* is rendered *"inditing"* in the King James Version of the bible, and it means to compose or write. The word "recite" also means to repeat words from memory. Therefore, this scripture can be paraphrased as *"my heart is writing a new song as I speak from the storehouse of my memory and my tongue is the pen that writes on my heart"* This indicates that the tongue is used to inscribe words on the tablets of our hearts. This can be done either by yourself or by other people, when words are used through suggestion to implant ideas, concepts, and thoughts in the subconscious mind, which is also the heart. So it is very important to be careful what you are hearing; because it will end up in your heart and influence your life.

This verse is reiterating the truth that suggestions implant seeds of ideas and thoughts in our hearts. When you meditate, you recite the scriptures that you have memorized over and over until it becomes inscribed on the tablets of your heart. Just as a composer, with the help of the subconscious mind, can rehearse a song over and over again until it becomes committed to memory. This is the reason why Jesus said we should be careful what we hear; because the measure of thought and study we give to what we hear, will determine what we get out of it. The bible tells us, the righteous man Lot, who lived among sinners, vexed his spirit by constantly hearing and seeing their wicked deeds. So guard your heart with all diligence. Be the gatekeeper of your heart. Decide what goes in and what comes out. The input would definitely determine the output. You can never store evil in your heart and expect good to come out of it.

Jesus said in Luke 6:43-45 "*For there is no good (healthy) tree that bears decayed (worthless, stale) fruit, nor on the other hand does a decayed (worthless, sickly) tree bear good fruit. For each tree is known and identified by its own fruit; for figs are not gathered from thornbushes, nor is a cluster of grapes picked from a bramblebush. The upright (honorable, intrinsically good) man out of the good treasure [stored] in his heart produces what is upright (honorable and intrinsically good), and the evil man out of the evil storehouse brings forth that which is depraved (wicked and intrinsically evil); for out of the abundance (overflow) of the heart his mouth speaks.(AMP)* Whatever you store through your conscious mind into your subconscious, will be delivered back to you. Therefore, cultivate good things into your heart; because, out of your heart will proceed the issues of life.

Let us now look at the specific steps involved in meditating upon the word and promises of God.

HOW TO MEDITATE ON THE WORD (PROMISES) OF GOD

(1)First of all, find an appropriate verse in the bible that pertains to your situation or desire, and build a spiritual tabernacle on it or dwell on it. This is done by thinking, pondering, and contemplating thoroughly about it day and night at all times, until it becomes flesh or a habit with you. Also, consider the context in which it was used and how it applies to you. Then begin each day with this scripture held tightly in your thought, and eventually it will begin to permeate and dominate your whole mind, emotions and decision-making. According to the laws of the mind, contrary thoughts would seek to oppose this new way of thinking; but when you are determined with a strong desire to see this scripture manifest in your life, you will be able to cast down every negative thought, which will seek to exalt itself against the word of God. To do this successfully, you have to be very conscious of every thought that comes to your mind automatically to ensure that it lines up with the word of God. Many a time, this becomes the difficult part of meditation, since many people are not disciplined enough to hold onto a particular thought for so long; but practice always make a man perfect.

The bible says in 2 Corinthians 10:4-5 that the weapons that we use in this spiritual warfare are not physical and tangible but spiritual through the word of God and it empowers us to overcome all negative thoughts by replacing them with thoughts that highlight our knowledge of God. With time, you will be disciplined enough to hold on to every scripture you intend to meditate upon to renew your mind. Always remember that you are what you think. If you think you can, then you can; but if you think you cannot, then you cannot. You have to believe in God and also in yourself; because the bible says in Philippians 4:13 that "*I can do all things through Christ who strengthens me*". The partnership between you and Christ has strengthened you so therefore, think positive thoughts based on the word of God, and you will reap positive results. Faith is the substance of things hoped for, and so mix faith with what you believe God for and it will manifest. There are thousands of promises in the bible and a diligent search with the help of the Holy Spirit would unveil a

155

word, which will be quickened to have a special meaning and significance to you. This word would leap out of the pages of the bible and bring excitement to you.

(2)Memorize the passage so that you can keep it in your mouth at all times, when it is needed. You can never meditate on the word effectively if it is not memorized in the first place, unless you carry a bible with you at all times. Write down the scripture and review over and over again until it is fully memorized. Consciously hide the scripture in your heart through memorization, so that you can ponder over it and contemplate the meaning of each word carefully. This discipline arms you with spiritual power when you meditate on memorized scriptures; because they become incubated in your spirit man. When these words are spoken out with conviction, it comes with power and removes every obstacle in your way, thoughts and emotions. When Jesus was tempted by the devil, He quoted scripture from His memory; because He did not open a scroll to read; but instead He spoke the word. This exercise of memorization can be achieved through these four steps.

Repetition: repeat the word to yourself over and over until you can recite it verbatim. Repetition inscribes the word in your heart or subconscious mind; because your tongue is the pen of a ready writer that inscribes on your heart.

Concentration: concentrate and focus on the word day and night by checking for the meanings of the words in the phrase; cross referencing them with other bible versions to ensure complete understanding of how they were used. The singleness of purpose converges all your attention on that very scripture until it becomes absorbed. When you are totally engrossed in this scriptural verse, all your attention, focus and concentration will be directed towards the absorption of that particular passage. In most instances, revelation knowledge becomes available at this juncture.

Comprehension: rewrite the scriptural verse in your own words to the best of yourunderstanding, or how you have comprehended it.

If you can rewrite them in your own words, it will help you to understand the scripture and the context in which it was used. Understanding or clarity is the first law of learning in every area of our life, so strive to attain understanding and it will bring with it knowledge and wisdom. (Proverb 4:7). You can never know or apply a principle unless you understand it.

Application: determine the appropriate condition or situation in which this word would be suitable to apply. The end result of meditation is the ability to apply the word at the right time, in the right condition, and in the right frame of mind, and also in prayer. Memorized scriptures enhance your prayer language and power.

(3) Repeat and review over and over the scripture that has been memorized through concentration, which gives you complete comprehension. This discipline is one of the surest ways to plant the word in your heart or subconscious mind and renew it. It is scientifically proven that, repetition impresses information on the subconscious mind so repeat the word over and over until it becomes one with you like a habit that you do without thinking about. Do this until the object of your desire is imprinted in your mind, and imagination. You see, it's all in your mind. How many times have you heard that old saying? It's true. When it comes to meditation it is all in your mind with the intent to impregnate the heart.

There is no doubt that the mind of man is the greatest single force in the history of mankind. Our problem as humans is that we don't always believe what our mind is telling us. This is when our belief systems have to go to work. When your conscious mind tells you something long enough, your heart or subconscious mind will follow by accepting it as truth, and whatever is accepted in the heart will be reproduced; because the heart is the spiritual womb, ground or soil where ideas, concepts and scriptures are planted.

Acknowledge the power of the spoken word that has been incubated in the heart. The Bible even gives us direction on how to achieve great things. Proverbs 18:21, "The tongue has the power of life or death, and those who love it will eat its fruit." This simply means to be careful of what you say, it just might come true. Want

157

to persuade yourself that something you want can be accomplished? Keep saying out loud that something great is going to happen and the more you say it, eventually you will believe it. Whatever you believe, you achieve. Think positive. Keep doing that over and over until you succeed. It works the same way if you voice something negative time after time, so watch what you say. While this is a simple truth, it is not always easy to achieve; but as history has shown that it can be done. Nothing worthy ever comes easy; no. Therefore strive for the precious word of God to be planted inside you. Speak the word to yourself during meditation and edify yourself in the word. Your voice to you, is more powerful than any other voice. No matter what others may say, until you agree with it and repeat it verbally or in your heart, it will never be accepted by your subconscious mind.

The test is whether you want what your mind is telling you so badly enough to keep going, when it seems that you're going to fail. Most people give up on their desires just before success. It takes perseverance. We don't always know what we want, but we want it now. We don't want to fail. Thomas Edison, after he had invented the light bulb, admitted that he had tried over a thousand times to make the product functional. When asked how he could have kept going after failing that many times, he replied that he hadn't failed, but had found a thousand ways why it didn't work. He kept going until the bulb burned! **In repeating your goal over and over again to yourself, you're telling your heart or subconscious mind that you are going to succeed. Soon your subconscious will be telling you in your sleep that you're going to have success**. Remember, one necessary ingredient in communicating to your subconscious mind is perseverance through repetition! Think about your desire day and night. Also verbalize your thoughts day and night. This does not mean that you should not sleep; but your subconscious mind takes over the last thought that was in your mind before you fell asleep. Since the subconscious mind does not sleep, it will take over the last thought and dwell on it till the following morning. The bible confirms this truth by saying; *"I sleep, but my heart (subconscious mind) waketh"* **(Song of Solomon 5:2)**

158

Winston Churchill, one of the greatest statesmen the world has ever known, was asked to give a commencement address to the graduating class at Harrow, the boy's school he had attended many years before. This was at the beginning of World War II when Churchill was Prime Minister of England. On the morning of his address the small auditorium was filled with some of the brightest young men of the school. All were anxiously waiting patiently for Churchill's speech. They all wanted to know what wisdom this great man would have to share.

That day as he looked out over the classroom filled with young men, no doubt remembering the days when he was sitting behind those very desks, he said these lasting words, "Never give in--- never, never, never, never, in nothing great or small, large or petty, never give in except to convictions of honor and good sense. Never yield to force; never yield to the apparently overwhelming might of the enemy." **Tell yourself that you can do something, and then keep at it until you do it**! You see, repetition and perseverance are very important in the meditation of the word, and in everything that we do.

The Lord told Joshua to meditate on the word day and night, which means continually and endlessly. The ultimate goal of meditation is the ability to apply what you are thinking. Action crowns our thoughts and without actions that correspond with our thoughts, our desires would not be achieved. The blessed man in Psalm one also meditated on the word day and night. All these scriptures that talked about the blessedness of meditation pointed out the importance of perseverance and repetition as an indispensable ingredient of meditation. These same disciplines are also very vital in communicating information to the heart or subconscious mind.

Personalize each thought of the passage by replacing names and places in the verse with your name and city. Speak in the first person pronoun by using words like; me, myself and I. Bring it home by personalizing the word to suit your need. Change the names of the Old and New Testament saints to your name, their cities into yours, and personalize the scripture to make it specifically applicable to you. Let the scripture tell your story by believing that God never changes. He is the same yesterday, today, and forever. What He did in the past, He can and will do for you.

Picture and imagine the concept that the verse is describing. Form a mental pictureof it, and consider it as already done. Visualization is also another way to impress information on the subconscious mind. In Genesis 13:14-18, the bible says that *"After Lot had gone, the Lord said to Abram, "LOOK as far as you can SEE in every direction—north and south, east and west. I am giving all this land, as far as you can SEE, to you and your descendants as a permanent possession. And I will give you so many descendants that, like the dust of the earth, they cannot be counted! Go and walk through the land in every direction (exercise your faith), for I am giving it to you. So Abram moved his camp to Hebron and settled near the oak grove belonging to Mamre. There he built another altar to the Lord"* So what was the Lord telling Abraham to look and see? God wanted Abraham to see the land as his permanent possession for his descendants. He wanted Abraham to look with his spiritual eyes and see into the future. God, therefore, taught Abraham that if he could not SEE it in his mind's eye before he physically SEES it, he could never SEE it.

Also in this scripture, the Lord was teaching Abraham the principle of visualization or imagination as a form of meditation, to impress information on the subconscious mind. Then Abraham, being convinced of the promise of God, built a dwelling place on the promise land and solidified his belief with a memorial altar unto the Lord. He imagined himself already in possession of the promise. So likewise imagine yourself already in possession of the promise as you use your imagination. Abraham afterward, bought a burial ground on the promise land, where all the patriarchs were buried hundreds of years before their children possessed it.

Also, throughout the ministry of Jesus Christ, He spoke parables to teach the masses about the kingdom of God. These parables engaged the imagination of His listeners. They were stories and all stories engage the imaginative faculty of the listener or the reader in order to understand. Moreover, the biblical definition of meditation involves the act of imagination and visualization; therefore, apply it to enhance your meditation. The discipline of scriptural meditation involves memorization, visualization and personalization of the word of God.

Turn each part of the passages into a prayer to God through the Son Jesus Christ. This practice would empower and enrich your prayer life. Meditation enhances your prayer life; because the word that is stored in you becomes your prayer language. As we all know, prayers that are infused with the word; or prayers that are word-based are very powerful. Jesus said in John 15:7 *"If ye abide in me, and my words abide in you, ye shall ask what ye will, and it shall be done unto you."* The ability to have a successful prayer life, demands a good working knowledge of the word of God; which is attainable through meditation. The ability to ask what you desire and have it done onto you, depends on the measure of the word that abides in you. So whatever you ask in prayer should always align with the word; which abides in you.

Apply the truth to your life by living according to the principles outlined in the bible. The power of the word of God is manifested in the application of the word. Jesus said in Mathew 7:24 *"Therefore whosoever heareth these sayings of mine, and doeth them, I will liken him unto a wise man, which built his house upon a rock (teachings of Jesus): And the rain descended, and the floods came, and the winds blew, and beat upon that house; and it fell not: for it was founded upon a rock."* Strive to be that wise man that hears and lives according to the word of God he has heard. Apply the word to your life, because it has the ability to transform your life. Build your house upon the rock. This entails a lot of hard work; because it is not easy to lay the foundation of a building on a rock. You have to cut into the rock to lay the foundation.

There are no short cuts in building upon a rock. It is simply hard work. It takes a lot of hard work to build upon a rock! Just imagine yourself laying the foundation of your building upon a rock! It is absolutely extreme hard work. But the bible says in Galatians 6:9 *"And let us not be weary in well doing: for in due season we shall reap, if we faint not."* It is obvious from this scriptural verse that to do "good" is cumbersome and wearisome. It simply means it is tiresome to do "good"; but if you do not faint, you will reap good fruit in the long run. Meditation would empower you to apply the word as God told Joshua in the book of Joshua1:8 *"This book of the law shall not depart out of thy mouth; but thou shalt meditate therein day and night, that thou mayest OBSERVE TO DO according to all that is written therein...*

WHEN AND WHERE TO MEDITATE

When the word of God is memorized and written on the tablets of your heart through your words, you can think, reflect, ponder and talk to yourself about it wherever you go, because you become a walking carrier of the word of God or the bible. You carry the word of God with you wherever you go; on the inside of you. *"You shall love the Lord your God with all your heart, with all your soul, and with all your strength. And these words which I command you today SHALL BE IN YOUR HEART. You shall teach them diligently to your children, AND SHALL TALK OF*

THEM WHEN YOU SIT IN YOUR HOUSE, WHEN YOU WALK BY THE WAY, WHEN YOU LIE DOWN, AND WHEN YOU RISE UP." (Deuteronomy 6:5-7)

When the word is memorized, it makes it easier to share and communicate to your children and other people at various places without carrying a bible with you. When the word is in your heart or subconscious mind, you can talk about it in your house, on the street, in the field when working or you can think and meditate on it when you lay on your bed at night. This is how you meditate on the word of God at all times. The word becomes imprinted in your subconscious mind and whilst it (subconscious mind) is regulating your respiration, your blood circulation in your vessels, your digestion and the rest of your organs; it will also bring to pass everything that the word of God has promised. You will not know how but in some mysterious way, it will come to pass. Your body has been programmed by God to function automatically through your subconscious mind, and it will unconsciously bring to pass also the word of promise. Just as your body heals itself through the subconscious mind when you cut yourself, so likewise, it will bring to pass the new information programed into it. This is how you frame your own world by the word of God. The heart or subconscious mind is very creative and brings to pass the thought impulses we dwell on constantly.

HOW TO MEDITATE DAY AND NIGHT

One of the greatest promises in the Bible is found in Psalms 1:2-3. This passage teaches that if we meditate on God's Word day and night we will be *"like a tree firmly planted by streams of water"* meaning we are planted and rooted in the Spirit of God.

This is the secret to the consistent Christian life.

How does a person meditate day and night? One obvious way is to stay awake all day and all night, or meditate without ceasing. However, there is a less strenuous way to accomplish this. Have you ever awakened in the night feeling rigid and tense? Have you ever gone to bed with a problem on your mind, and awakened the next morning exhausted-as though you had worked through the night? Have you ever noticed that your last thought of the day is usually your first thought of the next morning? This phenomenon indicates that our subconscious minds keep on working while we are asleep. King Solomon knew about this phenomena and he wrote about it. He said in Ecclesiastes 2:23 "...*yea, his heart taketh not rest in the night*". He also said in the Song of Solomon 5:2, *"I sleep, but my heart waketh."*

When a person sleeps, his conscious mind rests while his subconscious mind continues to function in order to keep the body's organ's working. The conscious and the subconscious are in a closed-circuit relationship, so whatever the conscious was working on prior to his falling asleep will be transmitted to the subconscious.

Too often we will be wrestling with a problem just before we go to sleep. So rather than allowing the subconscious to work on our problems and worries, we can meditate on the Word of God while we sleep.

One of the ways of simply applying this theory is to read a passage or the one intended for the next morning's quiet time just before

163

you go to sleep. Take about three minutes to scan through, and go over the passage and ask God to give you a thought that will help you live for Him the next day. Take this thought with you to bed.

Your heart or subconscious mind will work on the thought while you sleep, and you will probably have the same thought in your mind the next morning. King Solomon was probably referring to this truth when he wrote, *"My son, keep your father's command (which is to love the Lord with all your heart), and do not forsake the law of your mother. Bind them continually upon your heart (through memorization and continuous meditation); tie them around your neck (adorn yourself with it like a*

necklace and also as a means of easy accessibility and reference). When you roam, they will lead you; WHEN YOU SLEEP, THEY WILL KEEP YOU; and when you awake, they will speak with you. For the commandment is a lamp (onto your feet), and the law a light (onto your path);" (Proverbs 6:22, NKJV). (Emphasis mine)

Make God's Word your last word every night, and with the help of the Holy Spirit through your subconscious mind you will be able to meditate on the Word "day and night." Meditation is simply engaging the heart or subconscious mind day and night to form habits that you will eventually do without thinking. This is an activity that engages your heart or subconscious mind. The psalmist said *"Let the words of my mouth, and the meditation of my heart, be acceptable in thy sight, O Lord, my strength, and my redeemer".*

CHAPTER 11

THE BENEFITS AND REWARDS OF MEDITATION

People say that Christianity is full of promises that are out of reach to many professed Christians; but I am here to tell you frankly, there is one activity that guarantees success in Christianity, and it is called meditation. This is not eastern meditation whereby a person endeavors to empty their minds of all thoughts so as to attain a desired state. I believe that an idle mind is the workshop of the devil, so when you seek to empty your mind, you become vulnerable for demonic manipulations. Biblical meditation, however, is a discipline whereby one keeps his mind and thoughts focused and fixed on God's word continually, day and night. If you do this activity, whatsoever you will put your hands to do shall always prosper. Knowledge of this principle in the bible is more important than any other knowledge in this universe. This is the reason why all religions have a form of meditation.

There is a great connection between biblical meditation and spiritual transformation.

The almighty God works through meditation to change the human heart and renew the human mind. Meditation will cause you to acquire the knowledge that God wants you to possess; because when you meditate, you give the Holy Spirit the raw materials needed to work with and bring deeper revelation to you, in order to teach and empower you. God's way of success is attained only by practicing this spiritual principle. Biblical meditation is a spiritual exercise that gives us prosperity, success, understanding, peace, joy, stability, satisfaction, significance, and also builds up our faith. It is the only means that God's kind of success and prosperity can be attained.

The bible says in Psalm 1:1-3 "***Blessed is the man who walks not in the counsel of the ungodly, nor stands in the path of sinners, nor sits in the seat of the scornful; but his delight is in the law of the Lord, and in His law he meditates day and night. He shall be like a tree planted by the rivers of water, that brings forth its fruit in its season, whose leaf also shall not wither; and whatever he does shall prosper***" There are some powerful truths embedded in these few verses we just read. David said, blessed or empowered to prosper, is the man that walks not in the counsel of the ungodly, nor stands in the path of sinners, nor sits in the seat of the scornful; because he is very conscious of the effect and influence of the association he keeps. He therefore guards his heart with all diligence; because he is very much aware of the truth that out of the heart proceeds the issues of life; and also of the truth that iron sharpens iron and so does a man sharpens the countenance of a friend. The blessed man is the man who lives according to the law of God, which he meditates on day and night.

The blessed man is very much aware of the importance of association and therefore doesn't associate with the ungodly, sinners, and the scornful or mockers. On the contrary, he associates, fellowships and spends time with God by meditating on His word day and night. As a result of his meditation and application of the word of God continually, he shall be like a tree planted (which denotes STABILITY) by the rivers of water (where he is constantly and continually nourished or SATISFIED). Since the tree is planted by the rivers of water with constant supply of water, it brings forth its fruit in its season (which means SIGNIFICANCE or producing when expected). During autumn or fall when the leaves of other trees are falling, his leaves shall not wither (because he is planted by the rivers of water where he gets continuous supply of water thereby manifesting his SUPERIORITY over the trees whose leaves are falling), and whatsoever he does shall prosper (PROSPERITY AND SUCCESS). The blessed man spends day and night meditating on the word of the Lord.

166

Meditation, according to this scripture, gives you stability; because if the object of your meditation is God, who is like mount Zion which can never be moved, then you too would never be moved; but become like Him. The bible says in Psalm 125:1 "*They that trust in the Lord shall be as mount Zion, which cannot be removed, but abideth forever*". The bible also says "*...as a man thinks in his heart, so is he*", so whatsoever you think about when you meditate on God, it will manifest in your life and give you peace and stability. It will also bring about satisfaction; because of the abundant supply of EL SHADDAI. This, in turn, makes us significant; because we are able to produce whenever it is needed since our need is continually supplied.

As long as our mind and heart is set on God and His word, whatever we do is constantly guided and influenced by the principles of God, which causes us to excel even in adverse conditions; thus bringing about success in all our endeavors. When you become aware of these benefits, it will empower you to know that you operate under a higher law which can never fail. When other people are failing because of recession, you will prosper; because God is your source. As a blessed person, you have a constant supply of all your needs according to His glorious riches in Christ Jesus. Therefore, you are not moved by what the economists say about the national economy. Look at all the precious benefits that we get out of meditation. There is nothing in the world that can guarantee you success than meditation on the word of God.

Scientifically, it has been proven that, what a person thinks about continually, has the power to transform him either for good or bad. Meditating on the word of God therefore, brings prosperity, success, understanding, wisdom, and many more benefits into a person's life. When you meditate on the word of God, you put God literally on the inside of you, and He comes with all the good things that you desire. The word of God has the power to transform you and move you from glory to glory. Therefore, it is highly imperative for believers to take the word of God, plant it in their hearts through self-talk, and water it by meditating, pondering, reflecting, and thinking about it continually. As you do this, the heart, which is your spiritual womb or matrix would reproduce exactly what you planted.

The bible is full of promises and one of them was given by Jesus Christ, saying He came so that we might have life abundantly. This abundant life can only be attained when we meditate or think about the word of God continually in an effort to renew our minds. The bible is the word of God, and this very word was the creative medium or agent in the creation of the universe. Everything that God created was done through His word, and this same creative agent has been given to us (humans) also to create our own world. Jesus said that the word of God is a spiritual seed. Apostle Peter also called it the incorruptible seed. Moreover, when God created man in the beginning, the first physical object He gave to man was a seed. The bible says in Genesis 1:29 *"And God said, Behold, I have given you every herb-bearing SEED, which is upon the face of ALL THE EARTH, and every tree, in the which is the fruit of a tree yielding seed; to you it shall be for meat"*.

God gave unto man the seed as his physical nutritional provision and for his spiritual sustenance. Symbolically, this seed is the word of God, which is upon the face of all the earth, and it has a specific ground where it can be sown or planted called the heart (subconscious mind). So we have been given the ability, power and authority to determine our own increase according to what we do with the seed that God has given to us; but until we put the word or seed inside our heart for it to be incubated and transformed into that creative power, it cannot create anything. Likewise, unless you put an orange seed in a fertile ground with favorable conditions, it would not give you an orange tree. This is when meditation on the word of God comes into prominence; because it is through memorization that we plant the word of God in our hearts.

Meditation on the word gives unto us many benefits that need to be noted. As mentioned earlier, meditation would bring prosperity into our life to the extent that everything we do would prosper. It is mentioned in Psalm 1:1-3 that the blessed man is the one who spends most of his time musing and speaking the word of God to himself. We also noticed the numerous benefits that came alongside prosperity into his life. He became stable and continuously nourished spiritually; because he fed on the word of God all the time. Meditation waters the seed that is planted in our hearts which is our spiritual matrix or womb.

Biblical meditation would also give you peace and stability; because you will come to know intimately the One who holds the key of David. When He opens, no one can close, and when He closes, no one can open. The One who holds the whole universe in the palm of His hands. This is what David meant when he said in Psalm 23:1 that "The Lord is my Shepherd and therefore, I shall not want". If God, who created the heavens and the earth and owns all things including the gold, the silver, and the cattle upon a thousand hills, is your Shepherd (Guide, Provider and Protector); then you will lack nothing; because a shepherd provides all the needs of his sheep. He guides them to greener pastures and not dried-up pastures. He also leads them by the quiet and not troubled waters. Everything a sheep needs is provided by the shepherd. This situation would give the sheep a peaceful mind with nothing to worry about.

Moreover, if the Lord is your Shepherd then you have to know His voice, which is synonymous with His word. When you know His word, you will also know His voice. The blessed man was very significant; because he bore fruit in his season when it was needed. Since he meditates on the word all the time, he operates not according to the worldly system; but according to the principles of the kingdom of God; because meditation empowers you to apply the word of God in your life.

Therefore, when people of the world are experiencing recession, inflation, and adverse economic crisis, he continues to blossom because he operates in a higher dimensional law. He is elevated above human law and is seated with Christ Jesus in heavenly places, and as a result, everything that he does shall prosper. The bible says that the ways and thoughts of God are higher than our ways and thoughts. Just as the heavens are high above the earth, so also the ways and thoughts of God are higher than ours. Meditation, therefore, is basically exchanging our ways and thoughts for God's. Thinking continually on the thoughts of God, would impregnate your heart, and eventually God's thoughts would become your thoughts.

Meditation also gives us success. When Moses died and Joshua took over, God gave Joshua a foundational principle to success, which was stated in Joshua 1:8. God told him to keep the book of the law (bible) in his mouth at all times by self-talking, muttering, pondering and thinking about it day and night so that he would be able to obey its commandments. Then, he (Joshua) will make his way prosperous and have good success. Did you know that, this is the only time the word success was used in the bible, and it was used in connection to the discipline of meditation.

Take note that the prosperity and success of Joshua depend on God and on what Joshua did with the book of the law. God guaranteed Joshua's prosperity and success only through the meditation on the book of the law by Joshua. This servant of God; became successful because he accomplished the task that was given to him by the Lord through Moses. The bible says in Deuteronomy 31:7 *"And Moses called unto Joshua, and said unto him in the sight of all Israel, Be strong and of a good courage: for thou must go with this people unto the land which the LORD hath sworn unto their fathers to give them; and thou shalt cause them to inherit it."* After this charge, God spoke to Joshua in the book of Joshua 1:8 to keep the book of the law in his mouth at all times to ensure his success in his assignment. By the time of Joshua's death, he accomplished and completed his assignment successfully.

Meditation also gives us wisdom and understanding, as it is stated in Psalm 119:97-100. The blessed man has wisdom through meditation on the word of God, and delights in the things of God. The scripture says *"Oh, how I love Your law! It is my meditation all the day. You, through Your commandments, make me WISER than my enemies; For they (your words) are ever with me. I have more UNDERSTANDING than all my teachers, For Your testimonies are my MEDITATION"*. According to these verses, meditation would make you wise and give you a deeper understanding, insight, illumination and comprehension of the mysteries of the kingdom of God. It will make you wiser than your enemies and give you more understanding than your teachers.

Meditation would also give you joy. The bible says in Psalm 63:5-6 that *"My soul shall be satisfied as with marrow and fatness, And my mouth shall praise you with joyful lips. When I remember You on my bed, I meditate on you in the night watches"*. Thinking about God empowers you to praise the Lord with all your heart, soul, and mind. It gives you the reasons, explanations and grounds why you should exalt and magnify His wonderful name above all names. The more you meditate on the word, the more you begin to appreciate His goodness, His kindness, His tender mercies, which are new every morning; His loving-kindness and His unconditional love, which propelled Him to give His only begotten Son that whosoever believes in Him would not perish but have everlasting life. It also humbles you to know of a God who is so powerful and yet so mindful of your well-being, and has made His power available to you.

Meditation would also give you progress beyond your human comprehension. *"Meditate on these things; give yourself entirely to them, that your progress may be evident to all."* (1 Timothy 4:15) When you meditate on the law of the Lord continually, His desires becomes your desires and His blessing upon your life becomes evident to all men. Finally meditation would build up your faith. The bible says that, faith comes by hearing, and hearing the word of God. So when you meditate on the word, you build up your faith in that particular word. Even though, you are muttering or speaking to yourself, it will still build faith in your spirit; because faith comes by hearing the word of God. As you are muttering the word or speaking the word to yourself, it builds up your faith.

The bible did not say that faith comes by hearing someone speak to you, but rather it comes by hearing irrespective of who is speaking. So you can speak the word of God to yourself and build up your faith. The people of the world know about this principle, and therefore some mega-restaurants, mega-companies and organizations spend billions of dollars to advertise their food and products on the television; because they know that, the more you hear and see their foods and products, it builds your faith in them, and becomes imprinted subliminally in your subconscious mind.

Then you will go out there just to indulge in unbelievable shopping sprees or consumption of some unhealthy foods; all because it is embedded in your mind through the advertisements you have been seeing on the television, billboards, and also in newspapers. Likewise, when you meditate on the word of God, it becomes imprinted in your subconscious mind and whatever you were meditating upon, would manifest in your life; because the subconscious mind or your heart works entirely by suggestions, irrespective of its source. This is the reason why you are admonished to keep, guard and consciously protect your heart or subconscious mind so that these negative suggestions would not sneak in. Therefore, it is very important to meditate on the word of God in order to enjoy all these blessings in your life.

One thing I want you to take note of is the instruction that God gave to Joshua after the death of Moses. In Joshua 1:8, the bible says that God said to Joshua

"This book of the law shall not depart out of thy mouth; but thou shalt meditate therein day and night, that thou mayest OBSERVE TO DO according to all that is written therein: for then thou shalt make thy way prosperous, and then thou shalt have good success" He said this book of the law shall not depart out of thy mouth but thou shall mutter, ponder and meditate on it daily and nightly. God was giving Joshua the key to success. This is right after the death of Moses and Joshua had taken over the leadership of Israel, leading them into the Promised Land.

And this is what God said to him: He said, if you're going to be successful, there is one thing that you should do. I want you to pay close attention, so you can relate it to what we're talking about. God said to Joshua, this book of the law shall not depart out of your mouth; but you shall meditate therein day and night. That you may observe to do according to all that is written therein for then you shall make your way prosperous and then you shall have good success. You shall have good success. So the object of Joshua's meditation should be the book of the law or what we know now as the bible.

172

There are three things that God told Joshua to do in this scripture and I want you to pay close attention to them. First of all, Joshua should memorize the book of the law so that he could keep it in his mouth at all times. A man cannot keep a word in his mouth at all times unless it is coming from the inside of him. Out of the abundance of the heart the mouth speaks. Secondly, he should meditate on what he has memorized all day and night until the precepts and principles of God become his second nature or habit engraved in his subconscious mind. Until the word becomes a habit in your life that you practice or live accordingly without thinking about, you will never see its manifestation. Finally, due to the fact that he has memorized and meditated upon the book of the law and it has become a habit or his second nature, he will do or apply the book of the law, in his everyday life which, will cause him to prosper and bring him good success. Obedience to the word of God, always leads to divine blessings.

This is the godly and divine way to good success. It entails *memorization*, *meditation* and *application* of the word of God. There are other ways which are not godly. So, in a nutshell, we are to, first of all, memorize scriptures in such a way that we can think about it when we sleep, when we are walking or going about our business, and in whatever that we do. Basically, we have to become a "*walking bible*". Then, we have to ponder over what we have memorized until it becomes easy to apply or live it out. This is your way to success and this is the key that Jesus was giving to you in the parable of the sower. When you think about the book of the law day and night, it will produce a positive effect on you; but if you think about the book of the law periodically or sporadically, every now and then, it will not benefit you.

All throughout scriptures, prosperity was always linked to obedience, keeping the word of the Lord and living by it. The bible says "*Keep (memorize, hide in the heart) therefore the words of this covenant, and DO them, that ye may PROSPER in all that ye do*". So obeying and keeping the law, always empowers you to prosper in whatever you do. When you live according to the commandments of God, you set yourself up to prosper beyond your control. Just as planting seed in a good ground will definitely bear fruit, so also living by the word of God would bring you guaranteed prosperity. This is a spiritual principle that is laced throughout the bible. There are so many scriptures that support this principle. A principle is an accepted or professed rule of action or conduct that works all the time. The bible says in Joshua 1:7 *"...that thou mayest observe to DO according to all the law, which Moses my servant commanded thee: turn not from it to the right hand or to the left, that thou mayest PROSPER withersoever thou goest".* God spoke in various parts of the bible about the way to prosperity and it always pointed to the application of the word, which is a secondary and inevitable effect of meditation. When you memorize the scriptures and keep meditating upon it, you become empowered to apply and live it. King David said *"Thy word have I hid in my heart that I may not sin against thee"* When the word of God is hidden in your heart, it (the hidden word in the heart) becomes a point of reference for your conduct and a point of conviction against evil. As we obey the word of God and live by it, the commanded blessing that is associated with obedience becomes inevitable. The Lord said to Abraham in Genesis 22:17-18 *"That in blessing I will bless thee...because thou hast obeyed my voice".* The blessing that comes with obedience to the word would be your portion, when you obey the voice of God, and the blessing will cause you to prosper.

When king David was well stricken in age and was about to die, he charged his son

Solomon thus *"keep the charge of the Lord thy God, to walk in his ways, to keep (obey) his statutes, and his commandments, and his judgments, and his testimonies, as it is written in the law of Moses, that thou mayest PROSPER in all that thou doest, and whithersoever thou turnest thyself"* Again, we see the same principle being repeated in this admonition from an aged and experienced father, to a young and newly enthroned successor of the throne in the person of King Solomon. David charged his son, Solomon, to keep the statutes, commandments, judgments and testimonies of God as commanded by Moses at all times so as to PROSPER in all his ways. So you see, biblical prosperity is the direct result of obedience to the word of God; but one cannot effectively obey the word of God unless the word has been memorized and meditated upon till the word becomes second nature or habit. Obviously, King David was passing on the principle, which he talked about in Psalm 1:1-3 about the blessed man being the one that meditates on the word day and night. One of the benefits of meditation is that, it empowers you to apply the word of God as you hide it in your heart.

On the other hand, disobedience to the voice of God will hinder a persons' prosperity. The bible said in 2 Chronicles 24:20 " ***And the Spirit of God came upon Zechariah the son of Jehoiada the priest, which stood above the people, and said unto them,***

Thus saith God, WHY TRANSGRESS YE THE COMMANDMENTS OF THE LORD, THAT YE CANNOT PROSPER? because ye have forsaken the Lord, he hath also forsaken you" Here is a contrast to the principle or the other side of the same principle; disobedience to the word of God by the people of God, hindered their prosperity just as much as their obedience to the word of God triggered blessings, which produced prosperity.

Prosperity is the end result of the blessing. All throughout the bible, whenever the children of Israel disobeyed God, calamity came upon them till they repented of their wicked ways. On the other hand, the blessing of the Lord God always causes people to prosper in all their ways and it is conditional. The bible says in Deuteronomy 28:12, " ***… if thou shalt hearken diligently unto the voice of the Lord thy God, to***

***OBSERVE and TO DO all his commandments which I command thee this day, that the Lord thy God will set thee on high above all nations of the earth: and all these blessings shall come on thee, and overtake thee, if thou shalt hearken unto the voice of the Lord thy God ***". All the blessings enumerated in this great chapter hinges on the obedience of the people of God to bring it to pass. Therefore, disobedience hinders our prosperity, which is a by-product of the blessing. So you can program your own blessing, which will cause you to prosper by simply obeying the word of the

Lord. And the good news is this; God has given us the blueprint through which we can empower ourselves to observe to do the words of His mouth. Meditation on the word empowers us to observe the law thereby bringing success and prosperity into our life.

Did you know that, Joshua 1:8 was the only verse in the bible whereby the word success was used? And the formula to achieve that success was stated right there.

What was it? Memorization and meditation on the word of God which will ultimately lead to its application; thus keeping the word of God in your mouth by speaking it and thinking about it all the time. So, as you meditate on the word so shall you become because as a man thinks in his heart, so shall he receive. As you think about the word more and more so shall you be. When you think positively because the word of God is positive, it will give you positive energy which will produce positive results. God wants you to prosper and because of that, He has given you the principle that will empower you to prosper. The spiritual discipline of meditation is very powerful because it gives you the power to control your thoughts and words.

Memorization of the word of God and its accompanying meditation is likened to putting a nail through a wall. The first tap on the nail only fastens it to the wall but the subsequent continuous tapping, drives the nail into the wall. Likewise, when we memorized the word, we only put it in our minds but the continual meditation on the memorized word sinks or drives it deep into our heart. In other words, memorization places the word in our conscious mind but meditation on the memorized word sinks it into out subconscious mind through some kind of spiritual osmosis.

Everything you see around you was created from the imaginations of the heart and also by the word, the spoken word of God. So, in this same way, you can also keep His word inside your heart and meditate upon it diligently until the word takes form and shape within you and when you speak it out, it will come out with power to create the intended purpose. You cannot do all these things if the word is not in you. This is what Jesus called the mustard seed faith.

176

The bible says in Colossians 3:16 "Let the word of Christ dwell in you richly in all wisdom" ... Firstly, you have to memorize the word so that you can think about it all the time irrespective of what you are doing.

This is the key. So, Jesus was telling us that, this book of the law, shall not depart out of our mouth; but we should meditate therein day and night. The more you are meditating upon the word, the more success will come your way. That is the reason why in the parable of the sower, some of the seed that fell on the good ground yielded thirty-fold, others yielded sixty-fold and others hundredfold. The measure of thought and meditation they gave to what they heard, determined the measure of virtue (harvest) that came back to them.

The more you meditate on the word, the more empowerment you receive to obey or apply it in your life, and as you apply the word, it triggers divine blessing. To some of them, the measure of meditation they gave to the word which they heard yielded only thirty-fold return. Others meditated more on the word of God and received sixty-fold return, and finally, others meditated yet the more and received hundredfold return. That means, how you receive the word and the degree of attention you give to the word, will determine what you will get out of it. If you don't give it enough attention it's like you don't regard it, you have no value for it; but if you diligently meditate on the word day and night (continually), you will be like a tree planted by the Lord by the rivers of water, where you will be nourished at all times.

Moreover, what you do continually will become perfected in your life. An adept musician may not be able to describe how he can play some type of music so well and with such speed; though the learning process started with slow movements and progressed through repetition, repetition, and more repetition. Through continued perseverance and discipline, slow clumsy notes became a beautiful wonder. The continual practice and rehearsal of the musical notes and keys, created a habitual groove in his subconscious mind. Once the habit was created, it became easy for him to play even when talking to someone else, or without consciously thinking about every move of his fingers.

177

Likewise, someone who has memorized large portions of Scripture cannot tell us how it got into his mind. Memorization can be dry and hard at first, but the more one memorizes, the easier it becomes. Eventually it brings deep satisfaction as we recite and repeat perfectly the words of God from memory. This knowledge prepares us for a deeper relationship with Christ as we hear His voice and Word through meditation. A diligent meditation on the word that has been memorized, would create a time of intimate relationship with the Lord Jesus Christ, because we carry him along as we think about His word at all times.

As Jesus told us in numerous parables, the kingdom of God is likened to a seed that can only grow and flourish in the hearts of men. According to the Parable of the Sower, the seed is God's Word. Once planted and nurtured, God has guaranteed a harvest of fruit from His Word. Memorization is likened to planting the seed through suggestion, and meditation is likened to nurturing and watering the seed through sustained thought patterns diligently based on the memorized scripture. The fruit of a deeper and intimate walk with God, which comes through the process of meditation, is a powerful motivation that should encourage us to cultivate the discipline of memorization of Scriptures.

When you do not make a conscious effort to memorize the word, you cannot have an effective lifestyle of meditation. Also, the devil will come and steal whatever you do not understand from you; because what you don't value, you are likely to abuse. You don't even know the use of it, so the enemy comes and steals it from you. When you don't meditate upon the word of God deep enough, the least resistance would result in crop failure; because you are not nurturing the word. As it happened in the parable of the sower, the seed that fell upon the stony ground represents the one who did not meditate on the word; and so when persecution came as a result of the word or when affliction came as a result of the word, it withered. Therefore, in the parable of the sower, Jesus was telling us that it is very, very important for believers to receive the word of God with understanding; meditate upon it, and finally mix it up with faith. It is very difficult to meditate on a principle you do not understand.

Sometimes, lack of faith can cause you to disregard or disrespect even the word of God. The Bible said that our traditions have made the word of God of none effect. So at times the uncertainties in our life negate, nullify or render the word ineffective; because we do not use it the way we're supposed to do.

CHAPTER 12

FUNCTIONS OF THE SUBCONSCIOUS MIND (HEART)

Biblical meditation is a spiritual discipline that engages and impresses information on the subconscious mind. This spiritual entity is the storehouse of all our thoughts, emotions, ideas, sense impressions and concepts including the word of God, which we have memorized. The word of God, which is stored in the subconscious mind, becomes the guiding light that directs our paths and orders our steps. Out of our heart or subconscious mind proceed the issues of life. In the parable of the sower, Jesus' main message was about the different grounds upon which the seeds fell. He then interpreted the ground to be the representation of the human heart in which the word of God is ordained to be planted, nourished, and reproduced. The only variable factor in the parable was the different grounds and how they received the seed; in other words, the hearts of men, and how it receives the word of God. Jesus placed so much emphasis on the conditions of the heart of the hearers. The heart is known as the subconscious mind in our modern day language. It is a very important spiritual entity to every man, therefore, understanding and knowledge of it is extremely vital.

The bible also admonishes believers to keep their subconscious mind (heart) with all diligence (constancy and persistence); because the state of our heart is directly impacted by the state of our life. Let us now learn about the many functions that our subconscious mind carries out for us. Jesus called it the heart in the parable of the sower.

***Servant and Best Friend*--**The subconscious mind will do whatever we ask it to do. It is a servant to us. There are no limits to what our subconscious mind will do for us either good or bad, except the limitations we place upon it (by ourselves) through the beliefs we have created in the course of our lives. Since it is the seat of our belief system, if we have a belief that it's not likely that we'll ever be healed, our subconscious will do everything in its power to see that our belief comes true for us. This explains why in some of the healings that took place during Jesus' ministry, the faith of the sick people were engaged. There were times when actions were taken based on the belief of the sick person, and many of those instances caused Jesus to declare *"thy faith has made thee whole"*. The belief, which they acted upon, triggered their healing. Belief is passive but faith is active. Jesus was basically drawing our attention to the power of our belief. What you believe or accept as true is very powerful and it can impact your life either positively or otherwise; because your belief resides in your subconscious mind and it has been ordained by God to give birth to whatever has been conceived in it.

The subconscious mind does not discriminate when it comes to thoughts and emotions. It responds to fearful thoughts as well as loving thoughts. It does not matter if you are a believer in Christ or not, the subconscious mind responds to every desire and imaginative thought you choose to entertain. The bible says in Deuteronomy 11:16*"Take heed to yourselves, that your heart be not deceived, and ye turn aside, and serve other gods, and worship them;"* The subconscious mind can be deceived to do whatever the conscious mind dictates. So, practicing awareness of your thoughts (since the subconscious hears all and responds accordingly) is certainly a skill worth having, and honing with the help of the Holy Spirit. The subconscious is the good servant that will do as the master or conscious mind asks.

The subconscious mind is our friend and is always there for us and never judges any of our thoughts, or feelings, or actions. Remember, our subconscious is the noncritical, non-analytical aspect of our mind; though we often judge ourselves with our conscious mind according to the belief systems we have created for ourselves. It is not the decision maker but rather the humble, obedient servant and therefore cannot be trusted. King Solomon said, "*He that trusts in his own heart is a fool; but whoso walks wisely, he shall be delivered*" (Prov. 28: 26). As our good friend, our subconscious is also extraordinarily protective of us. It will repress painful memories until we are ready to heal them.

Whatever you present to your subconscious mind as truth would be accepted as truth. It does not determine what is true and what is not; but accepts whatever conclusion the conscious mind accepts. This is the reason why you need to have an understanding and comprehension of truth in the conscious mind before you can meditate on it, because whatever you feed your subconscious mind continually and diligently, it will receive and reproduce whether good or bad. The heart or subconscious mind is your spiritual soil, matrix or womb that conceives and gives birth to the ideas, concepts and desires we plant in it through repetition. Biblical meditation, therefore, is simply an act of communicating between the two minds, or transferring information from the conscious mind into the subconscious mind. In other words, it is the act of transferring, impregnating, or implanting seeds of thoughts, ideas, and information from your mind into your heart. This transfer takes place only through diligent and continuous repetition of thought and word.

Home of the Emotions--The realm of the subconscious is where our emotion exists.

The spectrum of emotions from love to fear are all recorded and stored within the subconscious realm. The bible says "*Thou shalt not hate thy brother in thine heart... (Lev. 19:17)*. It also says "*I also will do this unto you... and cause sorrow of heart... (Lev 26:16).* Hate and sorrow which are very strong emotions emanates from the heart. Our subconscious memorizes all our feelings about every event we experience and encodes these memories in the cellular structure of our bodies. So, whenever a similar event occurs, the feelings we have developed from past similar events is felt instantaneously in the cells of our body. Also, the thoughts and beliefs we have created regarding those "similar events" show up instantly. Most accomplished actors and actresses utilize this function of their subconscious mind to portray grief so vividly that their acting becomes so real when they recall some sorrowful past events in their lives. This sorrowful event would be replayed in the corridors of the subconscious mind and thus reproduce the same emotions that were felt in the past when the event did happen. This makes it possible for people to relive sorrowful past events. Our subconscious mind brings our thoughts and feelings to us instantly and automatically as each event in our life occurs. Now, because the subconscious is the realm of the heart, it easily overrides the rational thoughts from our conscious mind whenever a conflict arises between the two minds. Let's take a look at exactly how our subconscious mind wins the majority of these battles with our conscious mind.

Apostle Paul gave a very strong argument in Romans chapter 7:14-20 *"I know that all God's commands are spiritual, but I'm not. Isn't this also your experience?" Yes. I'm full of myself—after all, I've spent a long time in sin's prison (and have become a habitual sinner or it has become my habit to sin). What I don't understand about myself (when I became saved) is that I decide one way, but then I act another, doing things I absolutely despise. So if I can't be trusted to figure out what is best for myself and then do it, it becomes obvious that God's command is necessary. But I need something more! For if I know the law but still can't keep it, and if the power of sin within me keeps sabotaging my best intentions, I obviously need help! I realize that I don't have what it takes. I can will it, but I can't do it. I decide to do good, but I don't really do it; I decide not to do bad, but then I do it anyway. My decisions, such as they are, don't result in actions. Something has gone wrong deep within me (in my subconscious mind) and gets the better of me every time."* **(Message Bible** emphasis mine)

According to Apostle Paul, the sinful habits that he had developed over the years, kept rearing its ugly head whenever he wanted to do good. The good that he consciously decided to do, were usually overruled by the habitual sins stored in his heart or subconscious mind, thereby, making it difficult to act upon his good intentions. Paul's actions are consistent with the truth that the subconscious mind always wins whenever conflict arise between the two minds. There is a secular saying that "**The heart is not so smart.**" This simply means that when a person is in love, (which is resident in the heart) all rational and logical reasoning becomes irrelevant; because the heart always wins whenever the two minds contend with each other over an issue. She knows the truth; but does not have the power to implement it; because her rational or conscious mind is constantly being overruled by the subconscious.

Unless renewal of the mind takes place at the subconscious level, true renewal has not taken place. True change happens at the subconscious level, and it takes continual repetition of thought and confession of the very change we are seeking to achieve over a long period of time; because change is a process and not an event. The change eventually happens when the thoughts and confessions are emotionalized and crystallized. This means mixing the thoughts, and confessions with belief and faith. This is how the subconscious mind becomes impregnated, and eventually change takes place. In the parable of the sower, the seed that fell among thorns represented those who did not mix faith with the word, which they heard. They believed the word but did not act upon it. Also, the process of growth, which takes time, was emphasized in the parable of the growing seed. The bible says when the children of Israel heard the word that was preached to them by Moses in the wilderness, the word did not benefit them; because it was not mixed with faith. (*Hebrews 4:2*). This means that without mixing emotions with the word and thought, we cannot manifest it in our life.

Let us look at another scenario. Suppose a person (let's call him Jerry) makes a "conscious" decision to lose weight; but one day at the office, someone offers Jerry a cupcake. Now, let's say Jerry holds a new belief in his conscious mind that chocolate cupcakes are fattening, though he absolutely loves cupcakes, Jerry eyes the cupcakes and tells himself that cupcakes are definitely fattening and certainly cannot be found anywhere on his carefully constructed list of edibles for his diet. Not a problem. Jerry has willpower and fortitude, and he's sticking to his diet. He'll just pass on this one, no matter how good it looks. Besides, if he wants to lose weight, passing on the chocolate cupcake is the rational, logical thing to do, and Jerry's conscious mind knows it's what's best for him; but, as if the world has somehow conspired against him, the sweet, wondrous aroma arising from the cupcakes reaches his nostrils (which is one of the entry points into his conscious mind) and then triggers the memories associated with that aroma. Making matters worse, Angela from accounting, a notorious pastry lover, is crossing the room looking intently at Jerry's cupcake. Jerry, (for the fear that Angela is coming for the cupcake) snatches the cupcake and profusely thanks his thoughtful coworker. He eats the cupcake and with each bite feels the accompanying sting of guilt from having cheated on his dieting exercise.

How did this happen? The strength of Jerry's emotional desire to eat the cupcake was greater than his conscious effort and will to lose weight. In order to stop eating cupcakes, Jerry would have to strengthen his desire at the subconscious level to lose weight so that his desire to lose weight would become stronger than his desire to eat cupcakes. But how does he do that? By thinking and talking to himself continually and persistently about losing weight until the thought becomes engraved upon his heart. The emotional strength of our love (or fear) held in our subconscious minds will almost always override rational thoughts coming from our conscious minds. When it comes to the battle of the minds, the subconscious mind will almost always win out. The key to having success in creating what we desire is to convince the subconscious mind through repetition to go along with the decisions our conscious mind makes for us; and this is what the Lord told Joshua to do by thinking and speaking the word of God day and night repetitiously until it becomes engraved on the subconscious mind in Joshua chapter one, the verse of eight.

Realm of the Imagination-- The subconscious is the creative, imaginative part of our mind. And the power of imagination is limitless. Man was created in such a way that, anything he can perceive, conceive or imagine and hold on to it tenaciously, will come into manifestation. Imagination is the seed of genius, and the seeds of genius are available to all. Albert Einstein once said "Imagination is more important than knowledge". He also said

"Imagination is everything. It is the preview of life's coming attractions". All great artists, thinkers, and inventors learned to utilize their imaginative powers within the subconscious. Of course, there is, as always, another side to the coin. When we allow our imagination to be ruled by fear, doubt and unbelief, disastrous results can occur; because what we imagine continually will come into manifestation.

Our subconscious does not discriminate. The bible says Genesis 11:6 "...*NOTHING*

WILL BE RESTRAINED FROM THEM, WHICH THEY HAVE IMAGINED TO

DO". The almighty God said this about the people of Babel when they imagined and decided to build a tower that reaches into the heavens. God said that nothing will be restrained from them, which they have imagined to do. In other words, nothing can stop them from achieving whatever they imagine to do. Can you believe that? God, the creator of the whole universe said that nothing is impossible when it is imagined. God shared this truth to emphasize the power of our imaginative faculty, which is resident in our subconscious mind. The only way God could stop them from building was by confusing their language. Today, through imagination, man has made his abode on the moon. Man has advanced from building a tower that reaches into heaven, to building a vacation resort (in heaven) on the moon. The power of our imagination cannot be under-estimated. Imagination is the seed and mother of all creativity.

The subconscious mind does its best to create what we picture or imagine. It will work just as hard for us to create the negative imagery we present to it as well as positive imagery, irrespective of our belief, race, creed, and ethnicity; for the imaginative faculty, which is resident in the subconscious mind can be used in any fashion we decree. Some use their imagination to fantasize about wickedness; but the good news is that our benevolent subconscious is always ready and willing to follow our instructions. And we can always change the ways in which we use our imagination. We can choose to cultivate our imagination to create what is always in our highest good. The bible says that *"And God saw that the wickedness of man was great in the earth, and that every imagination of the thoughts of his heart (subconscious mind) was only evil continually (Gen6:5).* The bible also says in Genesis 8: 21 *"for the imagination of man's heart is evil from his youth"*.

By virtue of our Adamic nature, our imaginations are naturally evil, until we consciously and intentionally reprogram our subconscious mind diligently with the word of God. This goal is attained through biblical or positive meditation. Imagine positive things with the help of the word of God. Let the word of God form positive images in your conscious mind and then hold on to it tenaciously until it sinks into your heart or the subconscious. This will create an image in your mind about how God sees you, and as you diligently hold on to the image, it will be implanted in your heart and build a strong immovable, unshakable faith in the Lord, which reflects how God sees you.

Words create images in your minds and so let God's word create positive images in your mind. For example, if I say a big black dog, the image of a big black dog would be formed or pictured in your mind. Words always create images in our minds, so use the word of God to form positive imaginations in your heart. The Hebrew word, *"HAGAH"*, which was translated "to meditate" in English also means to *"imagine"*. Imagine yourself through meditation to be in possession of your desired results even before it manifests, and hold on tenaciously.

The Higher Wisdom Within--The subconscious is also the gateway to higher wisdom. It is the medium, connector or interface between the spirit and soul of a man. When you became born again, the fellowship between your human spirit and the Spirit of God becomes activated. The Spirit of God then downloads information into your human spirit from God the Father. This information is taken from your spirit to your soul by the subconscious, and then to your conscious mind. This makes all wisdom available to us from God the Father through the Holy Spirit. It is available, because our subconscious is always in communion (through the spirit of man) with the Holy Spirit who is the Source of all creation and is often thought of as a kind of intermediary between man and his Creator. The bible says that *"The Spirit (of God) Himself bears witness with our (human) spirit"*... It also says that *"Eye has not seen, nor ear heard, nor have entered into the heart (subconscious) of man, the things which God has prepared for those who love Him. But God has revealed them to us through His Spirit"*.

Spiritual information is decoded into the natural through the subconscious mind. This is known as intuition, a hunch, or gut feeling by the secular world, and it is available to all men; but to the Christian, it is called revelation knowledge. The human spirit possesses three faculties, namely: intuition, conscience and communion or fellowship.

When a person becomes born-again, his spirit becomes re-united with the Spirit of God and communion (fellowship) with God is re-established. This enhances the other components of his spirit, namely: intuition and conscience. The only part of the human spirit that became separated, dormant, or "dead" at the fall of man, was the faculty of communion or the faculty that fellowships with God. The faculty of intuition and conscience were still present in the human spirit after the fall of man; but there was separation or lack of fellowship between God and man.

Those that are not born-again can still receive hunches; but they normally attribute it to an unknown source by saying, "something told me". However, born-again believers know that it is the Holy Spirit that is bearing witness with their human spirit and causing them to cry Abba Father. The subconscious mind plays a very important role in the believer who is conscious of its influence. It is the interface or connector between the human spirit and the soul. The bible says in Job 33:14-17, *"For God speaketh once, yea twice, yet man perceiveth it not. In a dream, in a vision of the night, when deep sleep falleth upon men, in slumberings upon the bed; Then he openeth the (spiritual) ears of men, and sealeth their instruction, That he may withdraw man from his purpose, and hide pride from man"*.

This passage of scripture is enlightening us about how God seals instruction into our subconscious mind when the conscious mind is asleep. There are times when God would speak to man; but due to the congestion of issues in their lives, man perceives not what God is saying. So, God then employs the medium of dreams and visions of the night when men are sleeping and the conscious mind is at rest, to seal His instruction into the subconscious mind. This instruction is then passed on to the conscious mind for implementation. God, who created man, also knows the make-up of man and how to get the attention of man, when all attempts fail.

Through dreams and visions of the night, God speaks to man and seals His instruction in the heart of man. This passage of scripture is better understood when you consider the truth that the subconscious mind never sleeps and it is the medium through which men have dreams, imaginations, and visions. God used dreams to speak to a heathen King known as Nebuchadnezzar, and revealed to him some future prophetic events starting from his era. When men are sleeping, the conscious mind, which is the gate to the subconscious mind becomes inactive, and therefore access to the subconscious mind is readily available for any suggestion. When the reasoning mind, which scrutinizes and analyzes all sense impressions is asleep, then God seals His instruction in the hearts of men. The subconscious mind is the pathway to higher wisdom in the life of every Christian.

The Super memory bank--Our subconscious mind records all events that occur within the field of our awareness; all thoughts and feelings about those events; all memories; records and meanings our conscious mind assigns to those events. The meanings we give to our experiences in life make up our belief systems. The subconscious stores our belief systems, organizes them, and brings them to us in any relevant situation or event. Our subconscious mind has a library filled with all our thoughts; feelings; memories; and belief systems from our life experiences, and they are neatly categorized. It will retrieve any memory we choose to recall.

If we desire to discover or remember an event that is at the core of one of our belief systems, all we need do is ask. This super memory banker can easily locate anything within the vast library of our mind. Nothing is ever forgotten by the subconscious mind;

but there are times that information becomes "missing" in it, when we try to remember using our conscious mind. Have you ever tried to remember a person's name and no matter how hard you try, the name alludes you until later, when you are no longer trying to remember, then all of a sudden, it pops back into your conscious mind. The subconscious mind cannot be forced to produce information; but it responds in a timely liberated manner and atmosphere.

The Editor--Our subconscious or heart is also an editor who happens to be available all the time. That's right!! Twenty-four hours a day, seven days a week, 365 days a year. Your subconscious mind never sleeps. So, whenever you decide to change your mind about who you are by renewing your mind, your subconscious mind is at your service. All that is required is desire, perseverance, and faith. It is the agent that edits the contents of our minds through diligent and persistent thought habits that aligns with the word of God. Since the subconscious mind is very habitual, it takes repetition of confessions and thoughts to renew our subconscious mind. The renewal of our minds only becomes possible when we consciously get in touch with the subconscious through constant repetition of thought and confession until that information becomes accepted in the subconscious mind.

These thoughts and confessions have to be mixed with emotions before it will be accepted as truth. No matter how long you confess and think about an issue, unless it is mixed with faith or any other emotion like desire, fear, or love, it will not be registered at the subconscious level. This was what Apostle Paul was alluding to when he talked about his inability to do the things he decides to do (Romans 7:14-20); because change had not taken place at the subconscious level or the "editor" has not edited the contents of the mind. The only way information would be received by the subconscious mind, is when it is presented through repetition and with emotions like faith, desire, etc.

Paul then went on to beseech us in Romans 12:2-3 to be transformed through the renewal of our minds by THINKING soberly. The dilemma he presented in Romans 7, was resolved in Romans 12:2-3. This is how you renew your mind, and also, this is

190

the reason why God told Joshua to meditate (think) on the law day and night continually. The children of Israel, after being in bondage in Egypt for four hundred years had a slave mentality, and so in order for them to renew the mind they had to meditate on the word of God day and night, to first of all, deprogram their minds from their old way of thinking as slaves, and then reprogram their minds with God's thoughts, principles, and laws. Biblical meditation was the medium God chose to bring this renewal of the mind to the children of Israel. Until the "editor" is put to work, true change can never happen.

Director of Energy-- The subconscious mind controls our energy levels. Loving and positive energy attracts loving and positive energy from people we interact with in our lives. Likewise fearful energy attracts fearful energy. We can be happy; peaceful; joyous; angry; hateful; loving; creative; lazy; hyper; and on and on. We draw people and events to us based on the energy we emit. Attitudes, therefore, are very important when it comes to our relationships. The bible says "***A man that hath friends must shew himself friendly***" This is the only way we can have a friendly disposition towards others, which will draw them to us.

On the other hand, our negative persona would repel people from us. Whatever happens to us is not as important as the way we react to what has happened. Our reaction to what happens is more important than what has actually happened. This means our attitude is very important. Therefore, our attitude will determine how high we can climb up in life. Your attitude determines your altitude in life. All these mood swings are controlled by the subconscious mind and are usually triggered by our thought patterns. The man, who thinks everybody at the workplace hate him, would isolate himself from others, and be resentful simply because he erroneously thinks that people do not like him. Our energy level is in direct proportion to our thought pattern.

Automation Department--The subconscious mind automatically carries out for us all the habitual behavior of our mind and body. We don't even have to think about the way we walk, eat or stand. It's all automatic. We have trained our subconscious well. A man spent twenty years of his life in prison for hitting a pedestrian with his vehicle which resulted in the death of the victim. It was later discovered that he was under the influence of alcohol and imprisoned. When he was released, as he was being picked up from the penitentiary, he asked the person who came to pick him up if he could drive. Without hesitation, the driver vacated his seat and the ex-convict took over and drove more than two hundred miles back home.

Even though he spent twenty years in prison without driving, yet he did not lose the ability to drive; because the habit that had been created from all the years of driving was embedded in his subconscious mind. It is the creator and keeper of all habits in our life. It is the auto-pilot of your life, which controls all habitual activities both mentally and physically. Some people even daydream whilst driving, and yet never crashes; because they are in auto-pilot. Ever found yourself suddenly asking, "Who's been driving the car the last ten minutes?" because you've been off somewhere fantasizing?

The subconscious will learn and carry out any automatic behavior we choose to teach it. The bible says " ***And besides they LEARN to be idle, wandering about from house to house, and not only idle but also gossips and busybodies, saying things which they ought not*** " (1 Timothy 5:13 NKJV). The bible used the word "learn" in this verse to mean "habit" in other translations like the New International Version. For example, when you began to learn how to drive, initially, you employed your conscious mind whereby you could not drive and hold a conversation simultaneously; but after driving for a while and through repetition and practice, your subconscious mind takes over and it becomes a habit or auto-pilot of your body in activities, which you do without even thinking about it. Now you can drive and do other things at the same time like talking on the phone, eating some potato chips, and having an intelligent conversation with passengers in the car. Our subconscious also automates our reactions to simple day-to-day events including our interactions with people.

We all have automated reactions to people. This is the way it is with most of the people in our lives. When we see a friend or loved one, the feeling that automatically arises in the cells of our body is usually a good feeling; we may even smile. When we see someone we have difficulty getting along with, the feelings aren't always so good; but what's important to understand is that these feelings arise automatically. We don't really think about having the feelings, they're there instantaneously. They are there instantaneously and automatically; because the vast majority of people are going around on auto pilot, and our subconscious is simply carrying out our mentally programmed reactions to the events life presents to us.

Likewise, you can create new thought patterns by continually thinking and holding on to a new idea or habit you are seeking to program your mind with, and the subconscious mind will eventually make a habit of it. As long as you keep that thought in your conscious mind continually and repetitiously, it will sink into your subconscious mind and eventually manifest its physical equivalent when the habit is created. This is one of the reasons why biblical meditation is very important in every believer's walk with Jesus Christ. Biblical meditation which is done continually builds positive habits in our life, whilst worrying builds negative habits in our life. (Joshua 1:8)

Body Regulator--Our subconscious mind regulates all involuntary functions of the body. It controls your breathing; circulates blood throughout your body; heals you when you are sick or injured; and is in charge of digestion and elimination of waste from the body. It has kept your heart beating from the day you were conceived in your mother's womb until now even as you reading this book. All throughout your life, it has controlled the organs in your body with no effort from you. It is also amazing to know that there is a connection between what we think consciously and its' effect on the physical body.

What you think and believe can have a physical effect on your body. Negative thoughts can actually have devastating effects on your physical body. What the mind cannot contain, it passes it over to the body. Stress, anxiety and depression are all effects of our thoughts. This condition is known in the medical field as Psychosomatic disorder. A Psychosomatic disorder is a disease which involves both mind and body. They are diseases that originate from the mind and thoughts. Thoughts that the mind cannot handle, the mind passes the effects of these thoughts to the body and releases endo-toxins into the body.

According to an article published on the Mayo Clinics' website, Positive thinking helps with stress management and can even improve your health. The article also said that some studies show that personality traits like optimism and pessimism can affect many areas of your health and well-being. The positive thinking that typically comes with optimism is a key part of effective stress management, and effective stress management is associated with many health benefits. If you tend to be pessimistic, don't despair — you can learn positive thinking skills. Positive thinking doesn't mean that you keep your head in the sand and ignore life's less pleasant situations. Positive thinking just means that you approach the unpleasantness in a more positive and productive way. You think the best is going to happen, not the worst. Researchers continue to explore the effects of positive thinking and optimism on health. Health benefits that positive thinking may provide include:

- Increased life span
- Lower rates of depression
- Lower levels of distress
- Greater resistance to the common cold
- Better psychological and physical well-being
- Reduced risk of death from cardiovascular disease
- Better coping skills during hardships and times of stress

It's unclear why people who engage in positive thinking experience these health benefits. One theory is that having a positive outlook enables you to cope better with stressful situations, which reduces the harmful health effects of stress on your body. It's also thought that positive and optimistic people tend to live healthier lifestyles, they get more physical activity, follow a healthier diet, and don't smoke or drink alcohol in excess.

You see, the human body is created in such a way that, it is the servant of the mind. It obeys the operations of the mind, whether they be deliberately chosen consciously or automatically expressed subconsciously. At the bidding of unlawful thoughts the body sinks rapidly into disease and decay; at the command of glad and beautiful thoughts it becomes clothed with youthfulness and beauty. Disease and health, like circumstances, are rooted in thought.

Sickly thoughts will express themselves through a sickly body. Thoughts of fear have been known to kill a man as speedily as a bullet and they are continually killing thousands of people just as surely though less rapidly. The people who live in fear of disease are the people who get it. The people who live in constant fear of something evil happening to them, usually experience their fears. Job said in Job 3:25 that *"For the thing which I greatly feared is come upon me and that which I was afraid of is come unto me "* Anxiety quickly demoralizes the whole body, and lays it open to the entrance of disease; while impure thoughts, even if not physically indulged, will sooner shatter the nervous system. The subconscious mind is the underlying factor in all these situations; because when thoughts are held continually in the conscious mind, they automatically sink into the subconscious and its' effects on the body becomes inevitable.

The placebo effect is also an example of the power of your belief system or thought over your body. It's the effect or what happens when a person takes a medication that he or she perceives will help, although it actually has no proven therapeutic effect for his or her particular condition. For example, when a patient is told by a doctor that a particular medication is the only substance that is going to heal his ailment, and the patient believes in the potency of the medication, even though it is a hoax, he will be healed. It was not the medication but rather the patients' own belief that brought about the healing. The subconscious mind accepted the information about the hoax as truth and brought about the desired healing.

So it was not the fake medication that healed the patient but rather his or her belief. Though the subconscious mind regulates our body organs without any input from us, yet we can deceive it into acting in our favor. When allograft bones are infused into the body, it is used to deceive the body to accept the allograft as its own broken bones and therefore trigger the healing process. The success of all the surgical procedures that involve organ transplants, sometimes, depends on the mental attitude of the organ recipient. We observe a parallel in the scriptures when the bible says that *"Let the weak say I am strong"*. It is simply implying that we should call those things that be not as though they are. The bible is not telling you to lie; but to speak to your body to align with the word of God. This belief will eventually manifest in our life when the subconscious mind finally accepts this confession as truth. So, let your words regulate your body because **what you think, you speak. What you speak, you believe, and what you believe, you receive.**

This is an infallible spiritual law that works all the time irrespective of creed, race, gender, educational background and belief system. I pray that, your life would never be the same after reading this book. Many people do not know the functions of the heart or subconscious mind and therefore do not know how to renew it. I am going to teach you how to renew the subconscious mind to achieve success God's way.

RENEWING YOUR SUBCONSCIOUS MIND

The only power given to man by his Creator is the ability to control his own mind and thoughts. Therefore, when you desire to make a change in your belief system, it can be effectively done at the subconscious level. The real key to making changes in our life is through the renewal of the subconscious mind by diligently convincing it that we really want to make a change. Renewing the subconscious mind successfully is dependent on our ability to convince the subconscious to accept the change based on how God ordained it to function. The bible says in Romans 12:2 *"Do not be conformed to this world (this age), [fashioned after and adapted to its external, superficial customs], but be transformed (changed) by the [ENTIRE] renewal of your mind [by its new ideals and its new attitude], so that you may prove [for*

196

yourselves] what is the good and acceptable and perfect will of God, even the thing
which is good and acceptable and perfect [in His sight for you]."AMP (Emphasis mine*).* The New King James Version renders this scripture as " *And do not be*
conformed to this world, but be transformed by the renewing of your mind, that you may prove what is that good and acceptable and perfect will of God"

Transformation only occurs when we change our subconscious mind about who we are. In order for successful transformation to occur, the change must be done at the subconscious level of your mind. The word of God can be in your conscious mind without being in your subconscious mind. But it can never be in your subconscious mind without first being in your conscious mind. Jesus said in the gospels *"these people honor me their mouths but their hearts are far from me"*. This verse clearly depicts that information can be in the mind but not necessarily in the heart. The people could not fool Jesus; because He knew the contents of their hearts. What you think about momentarily is only in your mind; but what you think about continually is resident in your heart. Changing your mind at the conscious level is relatively easy and temporal; however, renewing the subconscious mind requires a bit more: a higher level of desire; a stronger commitment to make a change; and an understanding of how to renew your subconscious mind permanently.

The continual repetition of words to yourself as a result of sustained thoughts would eventually renew your subconscious mind and build up your faith in that word. This can be achieved through biblical meditation whereby we utter, mutter, ponder, and imagine the desired result continually and persistently as being done already and believing it. We must train our subconscious to believe that we are serious about making a change and turn the desired result into a habit through continuous sustained thought patterns… Christianity is basically exchanging our ways and thoughts for God's ways and thoughts. God's ways and thoughts would not be automatically engraved in us when we think momentarily about it; but rather when we make a conscious effort through repetition of thought and self-talk to put them in our minds. Let us now take a look at the different ways whereby we create beliefs in our life, and some methods we can use to train our inner man within to renew it or make changes to instill new beliefs.

Repetition of confessions (self-talk) --Repeating the same confession over and over again and believing it in your heart can instill or change beliefs at the subconscious level. The bible says that "***faith comes by hearing and hearing the word of God***". This means that whatever we hear over and over continually breeds belief. As we grow up, repetitive confessions we hear and accept become the basis for the belief systems we carry with us as adults. The bible says that "***This Book of the Law shall not depart from your mouth, but you shall meditate in it DAY AND NIGHT***". Spending days and nights, thinking or meditating on the word of God, would form a belief system in your life that would become a guiding light all through your life. As an adult, confessions with heart-felt conviction can be used to change some of the old belief systems that we have decided are no longer in our highest interest. Biblical meditation requires a higher level of commitment and self-discipline to stick with the new confession, and it takes a great deal of time to take effect.

This demands full concentration on the object of your desire and not entertaining any destructive thought. Keeping our minds and thoughts focused is very vital in renewing our subconscious mind because it directs our confession. **What you think, you speak**. It is only at this level that true renewal of mind takes place. If you renew your mind at the conscious level without the renewal of the subconscious, it will not last. Biblical meditation, through positive confessions and thoughts, is much more effective if they are repeated day and night in a powerful, faithful and imaginative atmosphere. The subconscious mind always prevail over the conscious whenever there is a conflict between the two minds. Therefore, true renewal of mind only takes place in the subconscious mind. The objective is to repeat the confession continuously until the mind accepts it as truth and whatever the mind accepts as truth, will be transferred through spiritual osmosis into the heart. Once that happens the heart or subconscious mind then begins to create and shape your life based on the confession or the new thought that you have planted in your mind. Confessions also empowers you to change your thought process and the goal is to be transformed from having a negative thought process that looks at all the wrong things to having a positive thought process, where you see all the good in people, things and circumstances.

Repetitions of thought and study—repeating and constantly keeping the same thought over and over for a long period of time, imprints the thought upon the subconscious mind where it takes root. When you consciously think about something long enough without entertaining all kinds of distractions, the thought will be transferred into your subconscious mind where it will take root and become one with your flesh or it becomes a habit which you will do without thinking about it. When this thought is mixed with belief and faith continually, it is easily received in the fertile ground of your subconscious mind. Napoleon Hill mentioned in his bestselling book Think and Grow Rich, about Edwin C Barnes who thought his way into business partnership with Thomas Edison. Mr. Barnes held on to his thought of going into partnership with Mr. Edison for so long that, he did not entertain any setback as denial of his goal. He eventually acted upon his thought by backing his belief with action.

In the long run, he achieved his long-kept desire of business partnership with Thomas Edison. You see, when you think about something long enough and you mix it with belief and back it up with action, the thought takes form in the subconscious mind. What you think about continually, you will end up believing it or in other words, your predominant thoughts will form your beliefs in the subconscious mind. Whatever you think about continually will manifest in your life so when you think about or meditate on the word of God, it will manifest in your life. This is what Jesus was teaching about in the parable of the sower. How to plant the seed which is the word of God in your life and see it manifested. He said in Mark 4:24 "*Be careful what you are hearing. The measure [of thought and study] you give [to the truth you hear] will be the measure [of virtue and knowledge] that comes back to you—and more [besides] will be given to you who hear (AMP).*

The measure of thought and study you give to what you hear and understand, would determine the measure of virtue and knowledge that comes back to you. This is the reason why the seeds that grew on the good grounds did not yield equal harvest for all but to some, it yielded thirty-fold, sixty-fold and then hundred-fold. The level of harvest was based on the measure of thought, attention and study they gave to the truth they heard and understood.

Mental picturing, Imagination and Visualization—One of the ways of renewing your mind is by creating mental images or imagining yourself in possession of your desired result. The subconscious mind does not know the difference between reality and fantasy. Whatever is presented to it, would be accepted as true even if it is imagined. This truth becomes irrefutable when you consider the fact that, a person can be frightened beyond measure when watching a horror movie in the comfort of his home. This person can become so horrified that he starts closing the windows and doors to his house even though his life is not in any physical danger but his subconscious mind is telling him otherwise. The subconscious mind is non-analytical and non-judgmental and therefore does not have the ability to differentiate between fiction and reality. It does not make moral judgments and whatever is presented to it, would be accepted as truth whether good or bad. It will then reproduce the response associated with that event in your memory.

Actors and actresses use this same knowledge to portray grief-stricken scenes by thinking back into the past and recalling an experience that caused them grief. When they attain this state or when this event is recalled into memory, it becomes easy to weep, lament and cry by reviving the pain, the hurt and the emotions which had been associated with that sad experience. The subconscious mind, therefore, can be renewed by imagining positive things continually based on the word of God. Use the power of the word of God to form new positive imagery about who you are in Christ and tenaciously hold on to that positive image until it manifests in your life. According to the Strong's Concordance the word meditate in the English language was translated from the Hebrew word "HAGAH" which means to ponder, *imagine,* speak or mutter. Imagination therefore, is a form of biblical meditation according to biblical principles to renew the subconscious mind to achieve our desires because it is a very creative spiritual entity given to all men to profit withal.

***Group and Parental Influence*--**Identifying strongly with ethnic or cultural groups, religious organizations or parents can have a strong impact on the subconscious. We often accept the belief systems of groups we associate with and take on those belief systems as our own. Tribal, customary and superstitious beliefs can be entrenched in us and affect our perception of life. Sometimes we grow up to be very much like our parents or just the opposite— depending upon whether we choose to accept our parents beliefs or reject them. The bible says that *"train up a child in a way that he should go, when he grows up, he will not depart from it"* The training of the child develops habits in the child that becomes very difficult to break even when they are grown. The building of positive habits in our children is very vital when we understand the dynamics and workings of the subconscious mind. This is the reason why God through Moses admonished the children of Israel saying in Deuteronomy 6:6-7 that " *these words, which I command thee this day, shall be in thine heart: and thou shalt TEACH them DILIGENTLY unto thy CHILDREN, and shalt talk of them when thou sittest in thine house, and when thou walkest by the way, and when thou liest down, and when thou risest up.*

Parents can tremendously bless or curse their children from an early age by the words they say to them. A friend of mine complained to me that she hates being under the spotlight at gatherings and events where she becomes the center of attraction; because she has a very low self-esteem. She hates standing before large group of people to speak. She attributed it to the fact that, all her life, she had been hearing that she looks like her father. This was said to her over and over again by family members, friends and others. Although they meant well, it caused her to believe that she looks like a man. As a result of this, she did not consider herself beautiful even though she is extremely beautiful. She held this belief all her life and it had been deeply entrenched in her subconscious mind thus affecting her self-esteem. I thank God that after a long series of counseling, she had been able to get rid of this stronghold.

Sometimes, parents can tell their children all sorts of lies and the children would believe it until it becomes proven that it was a lie. A typical example is how parents tell their children during Christmas seasons that Santa Claus will bring the children gifts from the North Pole. In actuality, there is no such person or being as Santa Claus. Parents deceive their children into believing in Santa Claus who is an imaginary character. Children normally believe what their parents tell them without questioning or any ambiguity. This is the reason why Jesus entreats us to have a child-like faith in the word of God without questioning or doubting. Believing with your heart, as the bible entreats, is having a child-like faith.

In his book, Think and Grow Rich, Napoleon Hill spoke about how he faced adversity with the birth of his second son Blair. Blair Hill was born without any visible sign of ears and an inability to hear. Mr. Hill was determined that his son would not grow and view himself as handicapped. Right from the beginning, Hill and his wife worked with Blair to encourage him to subconsciously condition himself to consider his handicap as a "benefit" that he acquired at birth. Mr. and Mrs. Hill never spoke of Blair's condition as a handicap or disadvantage. They did not allow Blair to be placed in a specialized school but rather he attended regular school like all normal children. To the Hills' credit, Blair went on to graduate from college and became a successful merchant and civic leader. He began using a hearing aid only during his last year in college and this device was said to enable him to have near normal hearing. The parental influence exerted by the Hills paid off greatly when Blair became a very successful spokesman for the company that manufactured the hearing aids Blair was using. Mr. Hill, who believed in the power of the mind and of thought, trained, deceived or brainwashed his son from an early age to believe that his adverse congenital condition is rather a beneficial one. This is a very important principle that parents should adopt so that they do not speak evil or negative words to their children because they grow up carrying excess baggage from their childhood in their subconscious mind. The bible places the responsibility of training children on the parents especially during the formative years of the child. (Deuteronomy 11:19)

Emotionally Charged Events-- An emotionally charged event can have great impact on our belief systems at the subconscious level either positively or negatively. These events are easily remembered because of the heightened emotions that were involved at the time of the event. For instance, you will probably remember where you were and what you were doing when you heard the news of the event that happened in New York City on September 11th 2001. But you may not remember where you were the day or two before that fateful day. In life, we see things that are emotionally arousing with greater clarity than those that are not and we tend to retain more effectively the emotionally charged information we receive. For example, a child winning a science contest and being lauded by parents and teachers may develop a strong belief in his own intelligence.

On the other side, another child involved in the same contest who didn't win and whose parents displayed great disappointment in him, may develop a belief that he is not good enough or smart enough and this belief can influence the child's life until he decides to change it by renewing his mind about it. Likewise, when the word of God is magnified in a child's life, it would serve as a measuring rod by which he/she can morally judge good behavior. Emotionally charged events can have a positive or negative effect on all parties involved. These events become the catalyst that triggers either positive or negative response from the subconscious mind. The realm of our emotions is in the subconscious mind or the heart.

Authority Figures--Authority figures are people to whom we give the power to have great influence upon our subconscious beliefs. They can be doctors; parents; spiritual leaders; athletes; professors; politicians; or anyone to whom we give the power of unquestioned authority. At some point, we make a choice to accept without question whatever our "designated" authority figure(s) may say is true. When some people are told by a doctor that they have a terminal illness, they accept what they are told by their authority figure (the doctor) and pass on. Yet, others may refuse to accept what the doctor says and end up surviving and living a long, healthy life.

You see, in life your voice to you is more powerful than any other voice, even the voice of God. Therefore, no matter what anybody says, unless you consciously accept as truth, it will not be registered in your subconscious mind as truth. When God is the final authority in your life, you will accept the bible as your final authority and renew your mind according to the laws of God. So make every effort to magnify God as your final authority and not the media, the doctor or your peers. Let the word of God permeate your whole being and it will bring manifold blessings to you. Who is the authority figure in your life? Who reigns in your members? Is it Jesus Christ? He is the only One who holds all authority in heaven and on earth. Enthrone Him King in your life.

These are the ways that we can renew our subconscious mind or heart to conform to the word of God. You are what the bible says you are. You can do what it says you can do; *"I can do all things through Christ who strengthens me"* You can possess what the bible says you can possess; because you have the mind of Christ. These are some of the ways how you can renew your subconscious mind and achieve lasting results; because these biblical principles impact the subconscious mind to achieve the desired end.

CHAPTER 13

MOON WALKERS

Many Christians are so spiritual that, they are not physically good. Others are so carnal that, they are not spiritually good. Some are so heavenly-minded that, they are not earthly good. All of these extremes the Lord hates. The bible says that "*A false balance is an abomination to the Lord*". When our spirituality does not fairly balance our physicality, it displeases the Lord. Christians are supposed to live a balanced life in this world. Even though we are in the world, we are not of the world. This means we are citizens of heaven; but transiting on this earth. In the meantime whilst we are here on earth, we are supposed to impact the world for Christ through the word of God. We have to live the abundant life so that we can attract others to follow Jesus.

We are the ambassadors of Christ here on earth and we have to represent Him and exhibit His love to a dying world. Many people need deliverance from demonic oppression and the church is their only hope. Unfortunately, many believers are leading defeated lives which are so unattractive to the world. Instead of using all our God-given abilities and gifts, we have settled for a life of mediocrity. Beloved, use the power within you and be a blessing to the world. This is what Jesus meant when He compared the kingdom of God to the mustard seed. It is a kind of faith that gives birth to utterances which minister grace to our audience and brings them into salvation. Mustard seed faith speaks and declares the power of God and His kingdom which can grow in a person and transform his life.

Christians have to acknowledge the power of their minds which needs to be transformed to conform to the mind of Christ. The mind of Christ can do all things and nothing is impossible to the one that possesses it. God created man in His image and gave onto man the same creative ability which is in Hm. He breathed into man and he became a living soul which means a mental being. The power of the human mind cannot be understated. It is through its' power that we are to have dominion over all creation. Adam demonstrated this power when he named all the millions of animals and all living creatures in the beginning. Unfortunately, some Christians think that employing the powers of the mind is demonic or not biblical. The mind, which is part of the soul, can be influenced by our physical or spiritual desires. The bible says that the flesh of man is in constant battle with the spirit of man and the winner of this battle, controls or dictates to the mind or soul. The soul comprises the intellect, emotions and volition. Whatever thought and emotion you hold on to will affect your decisions.

The soul functions in two distinct ways namely; consciousness and unconsciousness. There are some functions of our being that are under our total control whilst the rest of the body functions automatically or by itself. The functions that are involuntary outnumber the voluntary ones. The involuntary actions are controlled by the subconscious mind through the autonomous nervous system and the voluntary actions by the conscious mind. However, man can control the subconscious mind to some degree through the conscious mind. Psychologically, it has been proven and confirmed (what is already in the bible) that the subconscious mind or heart is the seat of our emotions, memories, imaginations, habits and automatic activities of our body. It does not know the difference between reality, fantasy, morals and ethics. Whatever task or assignment that would be given to it either by ourselves or others would be accepted. Therefore, the input determines the output. God created the soul of man to be the core of our being. This is the reason why the soul is the only part of man that would face judgment. The physical body will return to dust from whence it came and the spirit will return to God who gave it.

It is about time that Christians wake up and apply all the principles that the bible teaches about by taking charge of our minds. The mind is like a garden. If you allow weeds to grow in it by default, disaster becomes inevitable. But if you consciously plant good seeds in it, the garden of your mind will reproduce whatever you planted in it. For your information, the subconscious mind is the garden and the conscious mind is the gardener who plants seeds of thoughts, goals and ideas in the subconscious mind. Jesus said in Mark 4:26 *"So is the kingdom of God, as if a man should cast seed into the ground"* This is the principle that Jesus was teaching in the parable of the sower. He said that if we plant the word of God in our hearts and diligently care and nurture it, it will bear fruit because your subconscious mind is the womb of your spirit man where ideas, concepts and innovations are planted, nurtured and brought forth.

He also emphasized how lack of favorable conditions can prevent the seed from yielding fruit in its season. Jesus taught, in the parable of the sower, how persistent thought and study of the word of God would yield tremendous blessing in our life. God also taught this principle to Abraham, Moses, Joshua, David, Solomon and many others in the bible. These men knew the importance of meditating on the word of God which is a means of imprinting, impressing, and creating grooves in the subconscious mind thus resulting in the power to observe, implement and do great things.

They were taught by the Holy Spirit. When you read the wisdom books of the bible, it becomes very obvious the importance these men placed on spiritually eating and digesting the word of God. So brethren, yearn to cultivate this principle of memorizing and meditating the word of God in your life and it will tremendously bless you. The battle is always in the mind. The devil knows that if he can get you to think and believe falsehood, you will act accordingly. This is the reason why believers are admonished to keep guard at the entrance of their minds. The bible says in 2 Corinthians 10:4-6 *"For the weapons of our warfare are not carnal, but mighty through God to the pulling down of strong holds; casting down imaginations, and every high thing that exalts itself against the knowledge of God, and bringing into captivity every thought to the obedience of Christ; and having in a readiness to revenge all disobedience, when your obedience is fulfilled*. Do you notice that strongholds (believing falsehood and acting accordingly), imaginations and wrong thought patterns are all embedded in the subconscious mind? Paul, through this scripture, is telling us that we should fight to keep our subconscious mind for God by keeping guard of our mind through readiness to avenge any disobedience or anything that is contrary to the word of God.

Ever since man (not Christians) realized the power of the mind, they have conquered territories which were thought impossible in times past. All through the years of man's history and existence, the advancements that man has achieved in the last one hundred years are mind blowing. All these achievements started when man came to the realization of the power of his mind and how to utilize it. This mental revolution started in the late nineteenth century. When men started harnessing the power of their mind, they have accomplished many great impossible feats. Some thousands of years ago, the thought of man walking on the moon was absurd and only attributed to the gods but now it is no more a mystery. Man has gone past the moon to establish contact with other planets like Mars and who knows where the imagination of man is going to take him next. These space explorations had brought many advantages to mankind by improving the standard of living and also the way the gospel is preached.

They have changed our way of communication to the extent that the whole world has become a global village. This has helped and improved tremendously how the gospel is preached. The word of God can now be preached in America or some part of the world but *webcasted* all over the world instantly to millions of beneficiaries scattered across the globe. Hallelujah!!! The mind is the most precious gift that God has given to man beside His Son and His Spirit. These are meant to work together in harmony to bring the will of God into the earth. Our minds are to be transformed by its continual renewal to conform to the image of Christ. When a man's mind is totally submitted to God, He infuses His thoughts and intents into him so that he can implement the plans of God on earth. I believe that all these technological advancements are in the plans and purposes of God to expedite the coming of our Lord Jesus Christ.

Through the satellite, internet and webcasting, the whole world would see Jesus, simultaneously and instantly, descending among the clouds from heaven as the bible has promised. The bible says that *"Wisdom and knowledge shall be the stability of thy times..."* Most of these awareness and acknowledgment of the power of the mind were written in the bible thousands of years ago, but in the fullness of time, man came to the knowledge of them. The people of Babel did not have God as their source and motivator when they tried to build a tower that reaches into the heavens. Their motivation was self-gratification and therefore God confused their language to sabotage their efforts.

The bible says in Genesis that these people decided to build a tower which reaches into the heavens and when God saw their intention He realized that He could stop them from building because "... *nothing will be restrained from them, which they have imagined to do.* God said that through the imagination of man, nothing would be impossible to attain and so in order to stop them from building, He confused their language. The imagination of man is a powerful phenomenon that when it is properly applied, man can achieve whatever he imagines. The imagination of man is a function of the subconscious mind as we learned earlier. So when the knowledge of men conformed to the knowledge of Christ, all things that were conceivable became achievable; because man realized that, he can do all things through Christ which strengthens him. Things that were considered impossible in times past were dreamed about and achieved; because God is able to do exceeding abundantly above all that we ask or imagine.

When Marconi started talking about how sound waves can be captured in the air and transmitted into homes and offices, his family initially committed him into a mental institution because they thought that he was losing his mind. Today, based on his invention of the wireless radio, the face of communication has been transformed beyond measure. He dared to dream and then he put his dreams into action. Many great men of old achieved great things by harnessing the power of their minds. When you read some classical books like "AS A MAN THINKETH" by James Allen, you realized that man is literally what he thinks or meditates and his character is the complete totality of all his thoughts.

Man's environment has been transformed through his thoughts and imaginations. Mr. Allen said in this book "**As the plant springs from, and could not be without, the seed, so every act of man springs from the hidden seeds of thought, and could not have appeared without them**". This book was written in the late nineteenth century and was among the books about the power of the mind that triggered what I call the "**mental revolution**" which has transformed the lives of many great men with principles derived from the bible.

The principles taught in these books were biblical principles which can be summarized as; whatever the mind of man can perceive and conceive it can achieve. Jesus used to say to people after they acted on their faith to access their miracle, healing or deliverance that "*your faith has made you whole*" or "*be it onto you according to your faith*". Even though, the power of the Holy Spirit was present to heal, those that tapped into the anointing through their belief were the ones Jesus was referring to. Nothing can happen to you in your life except you believe. As you have believed, so shall it be onto you. This is a spiritual principle that unlocks the doors into the supernatural and it emanates from the subconscious mind or heart which is the seat of our belief system.

The bible says "*For with the heart man believes...*" What you believe in your heart or subconscious mind will eventually manifest in your life either good or bad. When the subconscious mind is under the influence of the word of God, great things are conceived and achieved because the subconscious mind is the link between the spirit and soul of a man. Whatever we are hearing can tremendously transform our lives; because the subconscious mind is non-analytical and does not know the difference between right and wrong. It accepts whatever you think about continually, which you have mixed with strong emotions like faith, desire, belief, and fear.

210

CHAPTER 14

THE POWER OF TWO

So far, we have learned that God uses His word through biblical meditation to transform a persons' life and also we have learned that real change and transformation takes place in the heart or subconscious mind. Therefore, we can conclude that, biblical meditation is a spiritual discipline which engages two of the most powerful gifts that God has given to man namely; the word of God and the human mind. The human mind is such a complex machine and most achievers in life really knew the secret of employing its power. Christians, therefore, need also to employ the power of their minds in order to prosper in this life. Prosperity begins in the mind as stated in 3 John 2 *"**Beloved, I wish above all things that thou mayest prosper and be in health, even as thy soul prospereth".** When harnessed properly, the human mind can attain the impossible. Through the innovations of the mind, man has been able to fly to heights unknown to birds. When it comes to flying, birds are no match for man; for no bird has ever flown to the moon. Through the knowledge of the bible, God has gradually unveiled to man things that were hidden to the physical eyes in times past. Man has been able to explore and extract gold, diamond, crude oil and many minerals, which God hid in the earth from the beginning of time.

God knew from the beginning that there would be a time in the history of men that we would have need of these things. So, in the fullness of time, He unveiled hidden treasures to men. He gave to man the ability to recognize and utilize natural resources, which were already deposited in the depths of the earth so that man could continue with the creation which God started. Today, men have used these natural resources to improve upon the way and manner they go about their day to day activities. Transportation, communication, commercialization, and urbanization had all been influenced by the fruits of man's imagination and creativity.

However, it is scientifically proven that, only ten percent (10%) of our mind's capacity is utilized in our lifetime. The remaining ninety percent (90%) lies inert. The majority of the mind's capacity is controlled by the subconscious, which controls many of the involuntary actions and activities in the human body. Many people are unaware of the existence of the subconscious mind, and therefore, do not know how to utilize the manifold functions of this immortal part of their being. Many are unaware that the subconscious mind can be influenced by biblical meditation which stimulate, impacts and influences the subconscious mind through persistence, consistency, and repetition of thought, confessions and visualization to hand over assignments, tasks and goals to it.

Biblical meditation is simply dwelling and pondering continually on positive thoughts based on the promises, omnipotence, goodness and faithfulness of the Almighty God. Whatever goal that you give to your subconscious mind, it will miraculously achieve it and bring it to pass because it is the seat of your creativity. It is your spiritual soil or womb which you were designed to impregnate with ideas, concepts, thoughts and innovations through repetition.

Any thought, either biblical or otherwise, that is passed on to the subconscious often enough and convincingly enough is finally accepted and once received, the subconscious mind will work tirelessly to create and manifest it. It is like your built-in computer, which comes with hardware but can be programmed with any software of your choice. Based on the software that you program into this computer, it will provide a response to every query presented to it. It means that your input into the computer determines the output of the computer. Although, this divine computer came with some already loaded software, we are at liberty to also load additional information. Whatever software you decide to program into your computer will be accepted by it regardless of your relationship with the manufacturer who created it; because it was created to work in that order.

The software is likened to the thought and information that you feed into your subconscious mind (computer) through your conscious mind, which is likened to the programmer. These thoughts are suggestive impulses that reach and influences the subconscious mind or heart especially when they are mixed with emotions such as faith, desire and belief. This is a universal principle that magnifies the power of thought. When thought is based on the incorruptible word of God through faith, it brings nothing but positivity and goodness in our lives.

The bible says that without faith, it is impossible to please God. This is how God created man; whatever we think and believe, would shape our life. Our belief system shapes our lives and directs our destiny. This was the message of Jesus Christ in the three parables He taught in Mark chapter four namely; the parable of the sower, the growing seed and the mustard seed. The parable of the sower dealt with how the heart or subconscious mind receives suggested word of God from the conscious mind irrespective of the source either by yourself or others.

It is very important to remember what Jesus said in the context that the measure of thought, study, attention or meditation we give to what we hear determines what comes back to us. This truth was evident in the parable because the good grounds did not bear equal fruit to all. Some yielded thirty-fold, some sixty and others hundredfold. The parable of the growing seed dealt with how words, thoughts and seeds of ideas are incubated in the heart or subconscious mind through a divine act from God and finally the parable of the mustard seed dealt with the power of the word of God when it is incubated in the heart and spoken out of the mouth. Also, it is very important to know from these parables that words were likened to seeds of ideas and thoughts that were planted in the fertile ground of the subconscious mind or the heart.

Moreover, we saw earlier when Jesus was teaching about the parable of the sower, how He spoke about understanding the word of God with our heart which is our subconscious mind and meditating continually on what we have understood. This means you can never meditate on what you do not understand. He went on further to explain in that parable how faith should be mixed with meditation to ensure the manifestation of our desires. Understanding with your heart is simply believing and accepting something as truth without any logical, analytical, deducible, inferential or reasoning process. This is a characteristic of the subconscious mind since it is nonjudgmental and non-analytical. Whatever you present to your subconscious mind as truth would be accepted as truth without argument as long it is believed by your conscious mind. This is the reason why **understanding or clarity is the first law of learning**.

If you believe you cannot do your assignment, your subconscious mind will work tirelessly against you to ensure that you cannot do your assignment. However, you can do it if you think you can. This is how God created man to have the freewill to think and choose whatever he wants in order to shape his destiny. But when the word of God becomes our focus continually, it brings good things into our life because God is good and have given onto man His word to be used to create our own worlds. This means, whatever you accept as truth and think about continually in the conscious mind will be transferred to the subconscious mind where conception would take place and eventually birthed out.

This truth explains the reason why a person can watch a movie which is make-believe, and be grief-stricken or terrified based on the events in the movie. Some people even cry when watching a movie because their subconscious mind has associated certain emotional response with certain events in their life. So when watching a movie, the subconscious mind would align the events in the movie with the things that had happened in their life in the past and induce the emotions that were associated with the past experience. It does not know the difference between what we imagine and what is real therefore whatever is presented will be accepted as truth.

Remember, the subconscious mind is the seat of your emotions, imagination and memory. So when watching a movie, all these faculties come into action and receive the scenes in the movie as real and therefore trigger a reaction. Likewise when you feed your subconscious mind with the word of God and imagine yourself as already in possession of the desired result through meditation, it will reproduce exactly the desired results. Jesus said *"**Therefore I say unto you, what things soever ye desire, when ye pray, believe (accept, think, assume and imagine) that ye receive them, and ye shall have them**"* Jesus said that we have to believe first before we see the manifestation of our desires in prayer. Whatever is believed in the heart will be reproduced and manifested. The bible says *"**For with the heart man believeth...**"* According to this scripture, belief is the function of the heart or subconscious mind.

Whatever you plant into your subconscious mind through your conscious mind, would only be received when it is mixed with emotion. This explains why it is important to have faith in the word of God. The subconscious mind or the heart does not make moral judgments and doesn't arrive at analyzed conclusions but rather accepts whatever you present to it regardless of its nature, either good or bad as long as it is mixed with emotion. Jesus said *"**Those who are good have good things (consciously) saved in their hearts (subconscious mind). That's why they say good things. But those who are evil have hearts full of evil, and that's why they say things that are evil**"* (Mathew 12:35 ERV, emphasis mine) This scripture is rendered in the New King James Version as *"**A good man out of the good treasure of his heart (subconscious mind) brings forth good things, and an evil man out of the evil treasure brings forth evil things**"*.

Jesus was simply saying that a man's input into his subconscious mind, always determines the output of his subconscious mind through his words. What you consciously store in your heart will eventually come out of your mouth which is the outlet of your heart. In other words, your thoughts determine what you say; **what you think you speak; what you speak you believe; and what you believe you receive**. This is the spiritual progression of the word from seed to manifestation.

Therefore, meditating on the word of God is a conscious effort to store the thoughts from the mind of God in your subconscious mind through repetition, imagination and persistence mixed with emotions. Words create images and when you meditate on the word of God continually, the images that these words create in your conscious mind are received as truth in your subconscious mind. For example, when I say "a black dog", you see with your mind's eye a black dog; but when I say "a big black dog", the image changes in your mental picture.

Likewise, biblical meditation creates positive images or mental pictures in our minds based on the words that we are meditating on. Thinking on the word of God continually (day and night) denotes repetition of thought which is one of the methods used to send thought impulse to the subconscious mind to renew it. Thoughts are powerful. They can make you feel inspired or they can make you feel dejected. Thoughts can lift you up or push you down. Thoughts can weaken you or strengthen you. It can make you happy or sad. It is your thoughts that shape your belief system and create your reality. So use biblical meditation to form positive beliefs and images about yourself to align with the way God sees you. Exchange your thoughts for the thoughts of God by meditating on His word.

Claude M. Bristol once said in one of his books that repetitive words and phrases (meditation) are merely methods of convincing the subconscious mind. Bristol had learned the truth of the bible that belief creates its verification in fact. There are many scriptures in the bible that points to this truth. Just as fearful thoughts and beliefs set you up to experience the situation you can't stop thinking about, likewise thinking optimistically and expecting the best will inevitably bring favorable circumstances. Job said in Job 3:25*"What I feared most had come upon me"*. The very thing that Job was afraid of eventually came upon him. This righteous man lived in constant fear that maybe his children were sinning against God. As a result of this fear, he offered sacrifices all the time. Though it was not true but his fears somehow manifested.

The seed of negative thought that he sowed and nurtured through worry (negative meditation), eventually manifested irrespective of the circumstances that brought about the manifestation. In life any thought that is mixed with emotion and dwelt upon continually will be accepted, incubated and manifested by the subconscious mind. Job's emotion of fear which he entertained constantly solidified his thought and brought it to pass. It is very unfortunate that many believers do not know the power of the word of God when stored

216

in the subconscious mind/heart and therefore are not using it in every area of their life. The bible says *"For as he thinks in his heart, so is he"*. What you think about continually, you become. Take note that in the preceding scripture, the verb *"thinks"* denotes continuity. Therefore think of all the good things that God has said about you in the bible at all times and become what He has said.

The word of God does not become the powerful spiritual force it is in a believer's life until it has been incubated in the heart/subconscious mind for so long to become the powerful sword of the Spirit through meditation. When such words are spoken out of the mouth, they come with spiritual power and conviction because it has been incubated in the heart or has been dwelt upon continually. Jesus said in Mark 11: 23 that *"For verily I say unto you, That whosoever shall say unto this mountain, Be thou removed, and be thou cast into the sea; and shall not DOUBT IN HIS HEART, but shall BELIEVE that those things which he saith shall COME TO*

PASS; he shall have whatsoever he saith (Emphasis mine). In this scripture, Jesus basically said in this scripture that, the word of God can be in your mind without being in your heart; but it can never be in your heart without being first in your mind. In order for the word to have mountain-removing power in your life, there has to be an agreement between your heart and mind. A double-minded person cannot receive anything from the Lord.

The word of God would first enter into your conscious mind through your senses and when you dwell or think about it continually, it is then transferred, through some kind of mental osmosis, into your subconscious mind where gestation or incubation takes place. These are the words, according to Jesus, that moves mountains and obstacles in our lives; because it has fused into our spirit and has become flesh. It has become a spiritual power and force ready to demolish every obstacle.

Words that are spoken in doubt cannot create or undo anything; but words that are spoken with conviction are words that we absolutely believe in its ability and power to achieve whatever it has been sent to accomplish. When words are spoken without belief, it only comes out of our mouth without power; but words that have been meditated upon for so long, builds up your faith and proceeds from within or from your heart with spiritual power. These are words with creative power; because it emanates from the heart/subconscious mind which is the seat of creativity.

CHAPTER 15

HISTORICAL EVIDENCE OF THE POWER OF THE SUBCONSCIOUS MIND

(A) The application of visualization and imagination

Throughout the bible, God taught many great men in the Old Testament principles that engaged the services and workings of their hearts or subconscious mind. He taught great men of old to employ the use of their subconscious mind to bring His intended purposes into their lives. God taught Abraham how to visualize, imagine and have a mental picture of the future so as to influence the subconscious mind. Who else knows about the power of the subconscious mind except the One who created it. When a person finally accept the existence of this precious gift and the power that God has given to man through the subconscious mind and begins employing its' services, many things that he desires become accessible.

In Genesis 13:14-17, God said to Abraham "***Lift your eyes now and LOOK from the place where you are—northward, southward, eastward, and westward; for all the land which you SEE I give to you and your descendants forever. And I will make your descendants as the dust of the earth; so that if a man could number the dust of the earth, then your descendants also could be numbered. Arise, walk (exercise your faith or put your belief into action) in the land through its length and its width, for I give it to you.***"(Emphasis mine). This was the second time God introduced the promised land to Abraham after leaving his whole family to follow the commands of the Almighty God.

In this scripture, God caused Abraham to see with his mind's eye or in his imagination a land which He is going to give to his descendants in the future. It takes an eye of faith through imagination and vision to see into the future. Abraham imagined his descendants running around and going about their day to day activities in a land where he sojourned as a stranger. He saw, in his imagination, the manifold blessings God would pour upon his posterity which will overflow to all humanity. The bible says in Hebrew 11:10 *"For he (Abraham) looked (in his imagination) for a city which hath foundations, whose builder and maker is God".* Earlier on in the New Testament, Jesus said in John 8:56 *"Your father Abraham rejoiced to see my day: and he SAW it*

(in his imagination), and was glad". You may ask, how did Abraham see the days of Jesus since they lived in different dispensations? He saw it through his imagination or his mind's eye. He believed God and His word by thinking about the promise all the time and dwelling on that land until he was buried on the same land. Living on that land was a constant reminder of the promise of God to him. He even taught his children to do the same.

God taught Abraham that if only he could perceive and conceive the promise in his heart through his imagination, he could achieve it. Nothing can be restrained from the person who can use his imagination to conceive a dream. Jesus taught many of his doctrines through parables, which are picture stories and thus encouraging His listeners to use their imagination or form mental images (which is a function of the subconscious mind) in order to comprehend His teachings. It is therefore, very important to visualize or use your imagination when you read the bible.

Whenever Abraham walked on the land of Canaan, it reminded him of the promise of God and also it was an act of obedience as he was admonished to *"walk in the land through its length and its width."* As long as Abraham sojourned on this foreign land, he held on to the promise of God and moreover his obedience to sojourn in the land as commanded by God, triggered the blessing of God upon him. The continual visualization of the land before his eyes enforced his belief that someday his children would possess the land.

The birth of Isaac reinforced his belief in the promise of God. This enabled Abraham to hold on to the promise all through his days because there was a tangible reminder before his eyes continually and it became registered and imprinted in his subconscious mind. Abraham thought that, if God kept His promise concerning Isaac, then He is faithful also to keep His promise about giving the land of Canaan to his descendants. The constant and determined faith of Abraham broke down all forms of resistance of unbelief, and gradually pulled down all strongholds in his thinking.

Let us look at another man in our modern day who greatly utilized his imaginative faculty of his mind. Walt Disney had a very acute imagination, which produced many animated motion picture characters like Mickey Mouse and others. When Walt Disney envisioned building a theme park in Orlando Florida, he had sketches made of how it should be built from his imagination. He started constructing and bringing from the abstract what he had imagined but unfortunately, he did not live to see the opening of the theme park in Florida. During the inauguration of the theme park, one of the speakers said, it was very unfortunate that Walt Disney did not live to see the project he had conceived but when his wife (Mrs. Disney) mounted the podium she corrected the former speaker by saying that, Walt Disney saw the theme park in his mind's eye or imagination before anybody else could see it physically. It originated from his subconscious mind before it became tangible. This truth can be said about all the physical landmarks ranging from the pyramids in Egypt to the most sophisticated bridges spanning across rivers all throughout the world. The world we live in now is filled with various products of man's imagination.

From the automobiles, aircraft, electronic appliances and the array of products rolling out of manufacturing plants all over the world, to the consumable products we all so much enjoy, reiterates the truth that the dawn of the human mind have tremendously achieve great feats from man's imagination. This story of Walt Disney and numerous others points to the truth that, the heart or subconscious mind is the creative force that God has given to everyone, but unfortunately, majority of the people do not know how to engage it's services. This was the message Jesus was conveying when He spoke about the spiritual photosynthesis which we all know as the parable of the sower.

Likewise, Abraham saw his descendants possessing the promise land in his mind's eye or imagination long before Joshua and his men possessed it. The ability to form a clear mental picture of what we believe in the word of God as true, is one of the most powerful tools that any child of God possesses. So when we imagine positive things based on the bible, we are meditating on the word of God. This is one of the ways to meditate. On the other hand, we can wrongly or negatively meditate on the things that would make us sad, depress, stressed out and dejected all because we chose to dwell permanently on negative thoughts.

We learned earlier that, imagination is a function of the subconscious mind, which deals with events, things and ideas in pictures. Therefore God, the Father of all creation, taught Abraham, the father of faith, how to use the power of his subconscious mind to bring good things into his life through imagination and meditation. According to Strong's concordance, the word "meditate" is translated from the Hebrew word *"HAGAH"*, which means to mutter, *imagine*, speak, ponder, think, study or utter. All these words are deeds or actions that somehow demand an interaction with the subconscious mind during biblical meditation. God knew that until Abraham could perceive and conceive the vision in his heart through imagination, he could not achieve it. Therefore, visualization, imagination or formation of mental pictures in one's mind is one of the methods used in biblical meditation to influence and imprint tasks into the subconscious mind.

King David also used to visualize the Lord before him during worship in the sanctuary. David said in Psalm 63:2 "...*so as I have SEEN thee in the sanctuary.* According to Strong's concordance, the Hebrew word that was translated as *"seen"* in this scripture is *"Chazah"* which means to have a vision of or to perceive. It means that King David used to visualize the Lord in the sanctuary. Then, in the verse of 6 of the same chapter, he said, *"When I remember thee upon my bed, and meditate on thee in the night watches"*.

The visions that he had of the Lord in the sanctuary, became his thoughts and he meditated (imagined) the Lord all through the night by seeking Him early in the morning. David enjoyed intimacy with the Lord through meditation. This becomes evident when you study and go through the Psalms. Visualization therefore is an important component of biblical meditation. Jesus taught most of the time in parables which were picture stories and thereby demanded His audience to use their imagination in order to comprehend.

(B) The power of confessing the word of God

The Lord also changed Abraham's name from Abram to Abraham, which means father of many nations, to teach him another spiritual principle. After God spoke to Abraham to visualize his descendants on the promise land in Genesis 13, he (Abraham) was still speaking doubt; because at that time the promise had not been implanted in his subconscious mind. He was not fully convinced of the promises of God since there was still doubt in his heart. He, therefore, spoke unbelief to reveal what was in his heart. It takes more than just momentary beliefs to influence the subconscious mind. Instead, it takes a diligent, continuous, repetition of thought and declaration of words to one's self to impregnate the subconscious mind especially when it is mixed with emotion. Whenever there is an agreement between what you are saying and what you believe in your heart, power is released and it triggers manifestation. Abraham declared what was in his heart by his words but his words did not align nor agree with the word of God.

Abraham said in Genesis 15:2-3 "...*Lord God, what wilt thou give me, seeing I go childless, and the steward of my house is this Eliezer of Damascus? And Abram said, Behold, to me thou hast given no seed: and, lo, one born in my house is mine heir*" Abraham was speaking things which were contrary to what God had promised him. After he was told to visualize and imagine or have a mental picture of his descendants inheriting the land of Canaan, Abraham was still speaking unbelief, because he was focusing on his circumstances and not on the promise of God. Eventually, his dominant inner thoughts were articulated and verbalized. In life, whatever you think about a lot, would find its way out of your mouth and you will end up believing in it, and what you believe would be manifested. In other words, **what you think you speak; what you speak you believe, and what you believe, you will receive**. It also means that your predominant thoughts form your beliefs and your beliefs shape your destiny.

So when God saw unbelief in Abraham through his speech, He decided to change or fix the problem by changing his name. God knows the power of the spoken word so He decided to use it to the good of Abraham. The bible says that "***Death and life are in the power of the tongue…***" This simply means our words can either bring life or death to us. Jesus said that "***For by thy words thou shalt be justified (life), and by thy words thou shalt be condemned (death).***" The bible also says the tongue is the pen of a ready writer which inscribes upon the tablets of the heart or subconscious mind through repetition of our confession. The objective is to repeat a confession continuously until the mind accepts it as truth. Once that happens the subconscious mind then begins to create and shape your life based on the confession or the new thought that you have planted in your mind. The subconscious mind was made by God as the center of our creativity. It recreates new tissue and heals all our injuries that we sustain in our physical bodies irrespective of our religious beliefs.

When a knife or a sharp blade cuts you, your subconscious mind goes to work immediately to create fresh tissues and skin to heal the cut. When you lose a fingernail, it goes to work immediately to recreate a new finger-nail. God has already ordained the subconscious mind to recreate your physical body as well as the mental commands of the conscious mind. So you can renew your mind at the subconscious level, you can also imagine new things into existence through the creative power of your heart and you can create your world based upon the words you speak. This is already programmed and built in us.

Do you know that, you are renewed every seven years? Science has proven that the human body, through the subconscious mind, recreates new cells every seven years. Old body cells are replaced by new ones in every seven years. So you see, God gave you an

224

eye to see, an ear to hear, a mouth to speak and a subconscious mind to create and bring into manifestation everything thing that you imagine continually. This is the function of the subconscious mind which is called the heart in the bible.

I want you to use your subconscious mind and imagine a man who was very old and had no children and then God promised him that he was going to have many children as the scripture said in Genesis 13:14-17. Abraham waited for twenty five years without any sign of the promised child through Sarah. So there were times that unbelief crept into his mind when he looked at his circumstances. When you walk by sight; (that is when you walk by what you are seeing, hearing, feeling, smelling and touching) as opposed to walking by faith in the word of God, wavering and instability becomes your lifestyle. Abraham was focusing on his circumstances and not on the promise of God. So God then decided to change his thinking by changing his name. This is another principle that reinforces the importance that God places on the power of our words. Repetition of words which are filled with faith influences our subconscious mind because the tongue is the pen of a ready writer which inscribes our words on our heart or subconscious mind (Psalm 45:1).What we confess continually will eventually be accepted by the mind as truth even if it is a lie.

Then God appeared to him again and said in Genesis 17:5-6 *"No longer shall your name be called Abram, but your name shall be Abraham; for I HAVE MADE you (past tense) a father of many nations. I will make you exceedingly fruitful; and I will make nations of you, and kings shall come from you."* What was God teaching Abraham and what was the significance of the name change? God was simply teaching Abraham how to use his words to shape his world. Moreover, it was meant to change his mindset, his way of thinking and build his faith because the more he kept calling himself, Abraham (which means father of many nations) he was building up his faith in the word of God and also influencing his subconscious mind.

Remember that repetition, persistence and consistency are some of the ways by which one can access and influence the subconscious mind to assign goals to it during biblical meditation. Since the subconscious mind or the heart is the center of our belief system, what we say continually can change our beliefs even if it is a lie. Have you ever heard of the saying that a person tells so much lies that he even believes in his own lies? It is because of this same principle. So whatever you keep repeating day and night, you will eventually believe and belief is one of the strong emotions that stimulate and influence the subconscious mind. The bible says, "*If you can believe, all things are possible to him who believes*".

This also explains why when the angel from the Lord appeared to Zacharias in the gospel of Luke, he (Zacharias) was stricken with dumbness by angel Gabriel because Zacharias did not believe in the word of God concerning the conception and birth of John the Baptist. So in order not to confess or speak unbelief that could have hindered the manifestation of the promise, God supernaturally shut his mouth to prevent him from speaking unbelief. The bible says in Luke 1:20 "*And, behold, thou shalt be dumb, and not able to speak, until the day that these things shall be performed, because thou BELIEVEST not my words, which shall be fulfilled in their season.*" This is the reason why God shut the mouth of Zacharias to prevent him from speaking unbelief. This principle was first used on Abraham to highlight the importance God places on our words. In biblical meditation, we adopt God's words, ways and thoughts as our own and allow them to impregnate our subconscious mind which will eventually shape and frame our world. The very God, who created man and gave him the subconscious mind, also knows how it operates. God gave absolute control of man's own soul to man but there are times He would make us to do what He wills. You see, God engages the will of man to accomplish in time what He had ordained in eternity. God also, sometimes, partners with man in the affairs of men to accomplish His purpose. But God does not allow man to circumvent what He had ordained from eternity.

As Abraham kept on calling out his name, it built up his faith and edified his beliefs. The bible says that faith comes by hearing and hearing (continually) the word of God; so the more he called out his name, the more faith was generated in his heart. It has also been proven psychologically that faith is one of the emotions that influence the subconscious mind. So we can safely say that God taught Abraham how to build up faith and strong belief at the subconscious level through his words of confession by changing his name.

The more Abraham mentioned his name to others, saying "my name is father of many nations", and the more others called him by that name, his faith became grounded on the promise of God. He used his tongue to inscribe faith upon the tablets of his heart or subconscious mind (Psalm 45:1). This is the reason why the bible says "l*et the weak say I am strong*" because God calls those things, which be not as though they are. Even the secular world calls this act of influencing the subconscious mind with our words as AFFIRMATION. It is rather a biblical principle which God taught His children in the Old Testament. Biblical meditation involves speaking to yourself continually faith-based statements until it becomes a habit that you say and do without even thinking about it. It became a habit with Abraham to call himself "father of many nations" without thinking about it anymore.

So you see the progression of how God moved Abraham from unbelief to total dependence on the word of God. In Genesis 13, God appeared to Abraham when Lot departed from him and introduced to him the land which his offspring would inherit. Then, Abraham started speaking unbelief in Genesis 15 about how God have not given him seed to inherit his wealth. Finally, God appeared to Abraham again in chapter 17 and changed his name from Abram to Abraham which means "father of many nations". God changed his name so as to change his faith at the subconscious level because as Abraham continually called out his name, or when others continually called out his name to his hearing it built up his faith. In both instances, he was hearing something, and what he was hearing built up his faith; because faith comes by hearing and hearing the word of God.

So what is the subconscious mind? Is it biblical or is it mentioned in the bible? Just like the word *trinity*, the subconscious mind is not mentioned in the bible; but it is implied and you can see it all through the bible. The bible calls it the *heart,* and there are many references that points to it. There are about 900 references made in the bible about the heart. In some instances, it referred to the subconscious mind. There are some references that points to the human spirit, others point to the conscious mind whilst others points to the soul which comprises the conscious and the unconscious mind. The subconscious mind is the part of the human mind where all information including thought impulses, sensory perceptions and emotions that reaches the conscious mind through the five senses are classified, recorded and stored irrespective of their nature either good or bad.

These thoughts and information may later be recalled and withdrawn when needed like withdrawing letters from a file cabinet. Think of the subconscious mind as the inbuilt computer of the human mind where your thoughts, memories, emotions, beliefs and imaginations are recorded and stored. It is in your subconscious mind that you have the memory and imaginative faculties of the mind. Everything that is in the past or in the future involves the unconscious mind whilst the conscious mind deals with the present through reasoning, choice and decision making.

A man cannot entirely control the subconscious mind but can to some extent, voluntarily and deliberately through the conscious mind, hand over some vital and pertinent information such as plans, ideas, purposes, goals and desires to it. This is accomplished through repetition of thought, imagination and declarations of words through self-talk. Another way of achieving this goal is by writing your desires on paper to be read continually. Many great men of God in the bible knew in principle how to appropriate the power of the subconscious mind in various ways and manners. The almighty God taught these men about these principles. You see, **the ways of God are very diverse but His principles are always the same.**

(C) Obedience to the word of God always triggers the blessing of God

God taught Moses and then later Joshua to meditate on the word of God on a daily basis. He said to Joshua *"This Book of the Law shall not depart from your mouth, but you shall meditate in it day and night (repetitively), that you may OBSERVE TO TO according to all that is WRITTEN in it. For then YOU will make YOUR way prosperous, and then YOU will have good success".* God, the creator of man, told Joshua that, in order to succeed in whatever he does, he should meditate or think on the word of God continually by putting it in the inside of him through repetition so that it will control and direct everything he will ever do. God told Joshua to meditate on the book of the law continuously so that he would be able to observe to do or conduct his life according to all that is written in it. Then he (Joshua) would make his way prosperous and have good success.

This scripture also reveals another principle, which is that obedience to the word of God, always leads to prosperity which is a product of the blessing. This means your prosperity and success depends on your obedience or ability to observe to do the word of God. Biblical meditation empowers you to observe to do the word of God. God has also given you the ability to determine your own increase by what you do with His word. All throughout scripture, obedience to the word of God always triggered the blessing which produces prosperity. The bible said in Deuteronomy 28:1-2 *"Now, IF you will be careful to obey the Lord your God and follow all his commands that I tell you today, the Lord your God will put you high above all the nations on earth. IF you will obey the Lord your God, all these blessings will come to you and be yours"* As per this scripture, the blessing of God is conditional based upon your obedience to the word of God.

This is a principle that was later mentioned by Moses in Deuteronomy 30:11-16 *"For this commandment which I command you this day is not too difficult for you, nor is it far off. It is not [a secret laid up] in heaven, that you should say, who shall go up for us to heaven and bring it to us, that we may hear and do it? Neither is it beyond the sea, that you should say, who shall go over the sea for us and bring it to us, that we may hear and do it? But the word is very near you, in your mouth and in your mind and in your heart, so that you can do it. See, I have set before you this day life and good, and death and evil. If you obey the commandments of the Lord your God which] I command you today, to love the Lord your God, to walk in His ways, and to keep His commandments and His statutes and His ordinances, then you shall live and multiply, and the Lord your God will BLESS you in the land into which you go to possess."* According to this scripture also, we determine our own increase based upon what we choose to do with the word of God. If we obey it, blessing and prosperity becomes our portion. He who decides to be on the side of God through obedience to the word of God, would be tremendously blessed.

The Lord told Joshua that, by meditating on the book of the law he would be empowered to observe the law (being obedient), then he will prosper and be successful in all his endeavors. This is God, (the creator of the heavens, the earth and the fullness thereof), giving a divine principle to His servant as to how to be successful in all that he does. The potency, power and magnitude of this divine truth is astronomical; because whatever you think about continually day and night, will become your words and influence your actions which would lead into forming habitual character to shape your destiny. God was teaching Joshua how to influence his subconscious mind with continuous meditation on the book of the law which is the bible. You see, what you think in the inside of you, influences what you do on the outside. What you think about continually will form your beliefs. The late author James Allen said in one of his books that "The outer conditions of a person's life would always be found to reflect their inner beliefs". All these disciplines are methods or ways that impregnate the subconscious mind through biblical meditation and give it goals to achieve.

(D) The principle of writing information down on paper

Another principle that God taught His children in the past that engaged the heart or subconscious mind was the practice of writing vital information down and making it plain on paper which would be read continually. Information, ideas and concepts must be written down so that it can be reviewed at a later time. God taught this principle all through the Old Testament to His children. Today, many motivational speakers are touting this principle as one of the ways to influence the subconscious mind and achieve all important and specific goals. The bible says in the book of Habakkuk 2:2-3 *"WRITE the vision and make it plain on tablets, that he may run who READS it. For the vision is yet for an appointed time (in the future); but at the end it will speak, and it will not lie. Though it tarries, WAIT (patiently or persevere) for it; because it will surely come, it will not tarry."* (Emphasis mine)

This was an instruction that the Lord gave to the prophet Habakkuk. He was told to write a vision down so that whosoever shall read it would be inspired by the vision, embrace it and follow through with it. Even though, it was something for the future, Habakkuk was entreated to be patient and wait for its manifestation. Though it will take time, patiently wait for it; because it will surely come to pass. Whatever is written down is perpetuated and can be handed down from generation to generation without losing its core message or information.

Writing is a great tool that helps people to know more about the way they think, and it also crystallizes ideas and thoughts, and allows the author to ponder, think, and reflect on it better than if they were to remain in their minds. When a thought is written down, it is preserved so that it can be reflected upon at a later time for modification, adjustment and revision. Many great documents in life were written down in times past and they are still relevant today. All over the world, national constitutions had been preserved to be the final authority of the people to whom it was written.

This had been a principle intended to perpetuate ideas, concepts, beliefs, perceptions and constitutional laws that needs to be preserved; but it all began with God. The bible says that, God told Moses in Exodus when Israel defeated the Amalekites in a war that *"Write this for a memorial in a book, and rehearse (recite, read) it in the ears of Joshua (next generation): for I will utterly put out the remembrance of Amalek from under heaven (Exodus 17:14 emphasis mine).* The Lord told Moses to write down in a book, the victory over the Amalekites as a memorial or something to be remembered by future generations. So the writing of the victory was meant to be memorialized, perpetuated and conserved. This victory over Amalek was to be remembered together with God's promise to wipe them all out from the face of the earth. By writing that historical information in a book, it perpetuated it and it was handed over to future generations. Writing is a principle that God Himself used to perpetuate, preserve and guard the Ten Commandments.

By God's own hand, these laws were monumentalized on tablets of stone and handed over onto the present generation. The bible says in Exodus 34:1*"And the Lord said unto Moses, Hew thee two tables of stone like unto the first: and I WILL WRITE upon these tables the words that were in the first tables, which thou brakest"*. The Lord used this principle to turn His thoughts into something tangible so that when it is read over and over, the impression on the mind become deeper and stronger. Words that possess the power to transform a person's life were handed down from ancient generations to the present because it was written. The bible also says in Exodus 31:18 *"And HE gave unto Moses, when he had made an end of communing with him upon Mount Sinai, two tables of testimony, tables of stone, WRITTEN WITH THE FINGER OF GOD."*

These scriptures clearly reveals that God, who created man in His own image, is a writer of information He desires to preserve (meditated upon), and expects us also to be writers of information we desire to preserve, meditate upon and remember. Do not keep vital information you wish to retain in your mind; because it is very easy to forget. The reason why God wrote down the Ten Commandments on tablets of stone was to create a set of positive moral instructions for our subconscious mind to assimilate and carry out.

The subconscious mind or heart is a very efficient tool, but it cannot determine right from wrong and it does not make moral judgment. One of its functions is to carry out instructions given to it by the conscious mind. The bible says the heart is deceitfully wicked above all things therefore it cannot be trusted. So when given positive information and instruction to follow through faith, the subconscious mind will carry it out. On the other hand, when

232

given negative information and instruction through fear, the heart will also carry it out.

To enforce this principle of remembering the word of God, Moses told the children of Israel to *"Always remember these commands that I give you today. Be sure to teach them to your children (parental influence to the subconscious mind). Talk about these commands when you sit in your house and when you walk on the road. Talk about them when you lie down and when you get up (Let them not depart from your mouth at all times). Tie them on your hands (let the commandments influence whatever you do) and wear them on your foreheads (adorn yourself with it to ensure easy access by carrying with you) to HELP YOU REMEMBER MY TEACHINGS. WRITE them on the doorposts of your houses and on your gates (as a constant reminder to you when you are going out or coming in). (Deuteronomy 6:6-9 ERV emphasis mine)* All these instructions was meant to impress the law on the subconscious mind but because they did not mix faith to these instructions, they were unable to honor and abide by it.

The message that Moses was sending to them was to have the law memorized so that they can talk about it wherever they go and thereby influence whatever they do. A similar command was given to the Jews a few chapters later in Deuteronomy chapter 11 where God explained how they should treat His words in order to enjoy the benefits from it. In order to remember, the children of Israel were told to keep the law in their heart (subconscious mind) which is the seat of our memory by writing them on their doorposts where they would constantly see it as a reminder.

It says in Deuteronomy 11:18-21 *"Remember these commands I give you. Keep them in your hearts. (How?) WRITE them down and tie them on your hands and wear them on your foreheads (for accessibility) as a way to remember my laws. Teach these laws to your children. Talk about these things when you sit in your houses, when you walk along the road, when you lie down, and when you get up (teach them all the time). WRITE these commands on the doorposts of your houses and on your gates. Then both you and your children will live a long time in the land that the Lord promised to give to your ancestors. You will live there as long as the skies are above the earth*" (ERV). This scripture can be paraphrased as "remember these commands I give you by keeping them in your heart or subconscious mind when you write them down for continual future references.

Let the law influence everything your hand touches to do as you adorn or wear it on your forehead for easy access and reference. Talk about the law all the time to your children in all situations and at all times so that it would be imprinted in your subconscious mind as well as theirs through continuous hearing by repetition". This is a principle that works at all times. Whatever you desire, simply write it down and read it continually day and night with passion until it is achieved. Visualize yourself already in possession of it and it will surely come to pass.

We learned in a previous chapter how the subconscious mind can be impacted by what parents teach to their children since children believes everything their parents tell them. This principle was also taught by Moses to the children of Israel. Moreover, he told them to write them (law) on their doorposts where they will see them all the time when they are leaving the house or when they are coming into the house. This was meant to be a constant reminder; because what they see continually will eventually be imprinted and influence their subconscious mind. So God taught the children of Israel to memorize the law so that they could recite from memory all the time in all places, and teach it to their children. Parental influence on a child's subconscious mind is very powerful and God taught the children of Israel to employ this principle in teaching their children about the word of God.

Children believe mostly what their parents tell them especially religious beliefs. Therefore, God taught them the importance of shaping the belief system of their children so that it will shape their future. The bible says "*Train up a child in the way he should go: and when he is old, he will not depart from it* ". Whatever is memorized is also stored in the subconscious mind and whatever we repeat continually with faith becomes engraved on the subconscious mind. Therefore God was teaching the children of Israel how to utilize the power of the subconscious mind by these instructions. They were supposed to write the law down on their doorposts as constant reminders to create new habits of thinking to replace their old way of thinking. Today, people write affirmations on sticky notepads and paste them all over their house as constant reminders to impress it upon the subconscious mind. The only missing link is that, affirmation does not involve the emotions of the individual and without emotions, you cannot impress new information on the subconscious mind. All these things were supposed to be done repetitively to create new habits in the subconscious mind which will be very difficult to break.

All habits of all kinds are created by man through repetition of thought and action either voluntarily or by default. However, these habits are enforced by the subconscious mind. Meditation helps to create positive spiritual habits in our life which are then enforced by the subconscious mind. Since the subconscious mind is habitual by design, it takes the formation of new habits over a long period of time to eradicate and change the old ones. Many of our daily activities are done out of habit. WE walk, talk, eat and breathe without thinking consciously about it.

No one thinks about walking; but walks automatically based upon a habit which started when he took his first step as a baby. How we talk is also controlled by the subconscious mind. There are people who stammers in their speech. To stammer is to speak with involuntary breaks and pauses or spasmodic repetitions of sounds and syllables. These speech impairment happens involuntarily. Some even speaks so fast that it becomes difficult sometimes to understand anything they say. All these physical activities are controlled by the subconscious mind according to the ordinances of the Almighty God and they are done involuntarily. Likewise, we can voluntarily, form or create new habits which would be embraced by the subconscious mind since it does not know the difference between voluntary and involuntary habits. This is the reason why biblical meditation is extremely vital to our success and prosperity because, it helps us to form new spiritual habits over time.

So you see, all that God was telling the children of Israel was to create new forms of habits of thinking that would be engraved on their subconscious. All the old habits which they picked up during the days of slavery were still holding them captive mentally. **A slave mentality is normally influenced by ways of thinking and patterns of behavior that promotes inferiority complex and low self-esteem**. God knew that the children of Israel needed renewal of their minds so as to possess the blessings that HE was showering on them. Therefore, HE taught them how to renew their minds. A critical look at these principles corresponds and agrees with scientifically proven truths about the subconscious mind, which is referred to as the heart in the bible. It is becoming obviously clear that science is continually proving, validating and supporting the bible in many ways but unfortunately, when it comes to the subconscious mind, Christians' knowledge about it is very limited.

Many believers do not believe that the subconscious mind is their godly ally that can work in their favor. It is one of the most important gifts that God gave to man. It was meant to positively serve us but when our forefather Adam ate the fruit of the tree of the knowledge of good and evil, it planted a two sided seed of good and evil in all humanity and it manifests itself in our ability to do good and evil. I believe that men were created to be led by the subconscious mind whereby we will be in constant fellowship with God; but when Adam ate the fruit, the conscious mind became the leader. This double-mindedness has plagued mankind all through the ages because we live in a physical three-dimensional world, which feeds all kinds of information into our conscious mind. The physical or conscious mind only believes whatever is tangible, visible, audible and tasty. It is very difficult for the conscious mind to believe what is not tangible to the senses. This is the reason why some people find it very difficult to believe in a God whom they do not see.

This also is the reason why even when you are born-again, you still have to constantly renew your mind to conform to the image of Christ Jesus because of the Adamic nature in us. Sin comes naturally with us as descendants of Adam; we do not teach our children to do evil or to be sinful but they do bad things naturally. We were all born in sin and we thank God for the sacrificial death of Jesus in our stead. But it takes biblical meditation to renew our minds to conform to the image of Jesus Christ who is the second Adam.

You see, the subconscious mind is not demonic or new age; but just like all things, the devil always seek to pervert the creation of God. The things that mean so much to God, the enemy always seeks to pervert them. Remember that the devil did not and cannot create anything. Therefore the subconscious mind is not demonic or devilish; does not belong to or magnify the devil, and it is not new age; but rather, the devil wants to turn man's dependency from God onto the power of the created subconscious mind so as to highlight its power. Jesus was referring to it as the creative fertile soil where the seed is sown in the parable of the sower. That parables' teachings is to highlight the importance of the heart in relation to the word of God.

Just like all creation, it can be used for good or for evil regardless if you believe in God or not. This is where believers are missing it; because we are supposed to renew our minds through biblical meditation; but many believers think that meditation is demonic or not biblical. By so doing, the enemy has neutralized many Christians and has made them ineffective. Know that, as your heart has been beating since conception and all your organs functioning in synchronization, the subconscious mind is at work within you. Put it to good use; because it was given to you for your own good. Whether you accept it or not, your subconscious mind is at work right now even as you reading this book.

Biblical meditation, therefore, engages the subconscious mind in order to be effective but if you think that it is demonic to meditate, then you are being robbed by the enemy. The daily activity of a believer is influenced by the subconscious mind constantly. When you are going about your normal chores of the day, the subconscious mind keeps your heart beating and pumping blood to all parts of the body. You walk by the subconscious mind and drive by the subconscious mind through habits that had been developed over the years.

You are basically operating on auto-pilot. There are many involuntary functions of your body that are controlled by the subconscious mind. By the grace of God, biblical meditation is God's way of teaching us how to use our subconscious mind to activate the promises of God in our lives. On the other hand, worrying is a negative form of meditation when you think of all the things that can go wrong. This kind of thinking robs you of positive energy, positive drive and motivation because you throw in the towel or give up easily whenever you encounter obstacles.

The bible says in Mathew 6:31-34 *"Don't worry and say, 'What will we eat?' or 'What will we drink?' or 'What will we wear?' That's what those people who don't know God are always thinking about. Don't worry, because your Father in heaven knows that you need all these things. What you should want most is God's kingdom and doing what he wants you to do. Then he will give you all these other things you need. So don't worry about tomorrow. Each day has enough trouble of its own. Tomorrow will have its own worries.* Worrying is the negative form of meditating on our fears instead of thinking about the good things in the bible that would build our faith. Meditate on the word of God day and night so that you will make your way prosperous and have good success. The creative power, which is encoded in the word of God manifests when it is planted in the hearts of men. The only place ordained by God for the seed of the word to bear fruit is in the hearts of men. The combined power of your subconscious mind and the word of God are tremendously marvelous and capable of removing every obstacle and giving birth to new creative innovations. Whatsoever you desire, when you pray believe that you already have it and it shall be done because that is how God created man. Whatsoever we believe and accept as true, and nourish continually through repetition would be attained in a very mysterious way unknown to man. It's the repetition of your confessions that leads to belief. And once that belief becomes a deep conviction, things begin to happen.

238

CHAPTER 16

THINK ON THESE THINGS

"And God said, Let us make man in our IMAGE, after our LIKENESS: and let them have dominion over the fish of the sea, and over the fowl of the air, and over the cattle, and over all the earth, and over every creeping thing that creepeth upon the earth" (Genesis 1:26).

When God created man in the beginning, He created him in His own image. God created man in a way which ensured compatibility between God and man. He created man for fellowship and worship. He created man to be compatible with Himself so there is a part of God in every man. God is self-sufficient but the only thing that God cannot do is to worship Himself. Therefore, God created man to worship Him and also to be His representative on earth.

He shared with man some communicable attributes that equipped man with the ability to execute the purpose for which he was created and these attributes made man compatible with God. However, HE did not share some of HIS attributes with man. God did not share HIS OMNIPOTENCE, OMNIPRESENCE and OMNISCIENCE

with man. As a result, man is not all-knowing like God even though he was created in the image of God. Man cannot be everywhere simultaneously and finally man is not all-powerful. The bible says in Psalm 139:1-4 *"O LORD, You have searched me and known me. You know my sitting down and my rising up; you understand my thought afar off. You comprehend my path and my lying down, and are acquainted with ALL my ways. For there is not a word on my tongue, but behold, O LORD, You know it altogether"*.

According to the preceding scripture, God is all-knowing and there is nothing hidden from Him. He knows what we are thinking even before we speak and moreover, the thoughts of our innermost being is known to Him. Also, it is written in Psalm 139:712 that *"Where can I go from Your Spirit? Or where can I flee from your presence? If I ascend into heaven, you are there; if I make my bed in hell, behold, you are there. If I take the wings of the morning, and dwell in the uttermost parts of the sea, even there your hand shall lead me, and your right hand shall hold me. If I say, "Surely the darkness shall fall on me," Even the night shall be light about me; Indeed, the darkness shall not hide from You, But the night shines as the day; the darkness and the light are both alike to you"* According to this verse, God is everywhere. He is, even, in hell. His presence is everywhere but He only manifests His presence where He is acknowledged. Then the verse of 13 to 16 of Psalm 139 also declares the omnipotence of God. So man was created in the image of God after His likeness and endowed with some God-like characteristics and attributes. Let this truth be retained in you that you were created in the image of God and after His likeness.

So what is the image that man received from God? Well, according to the Strong's' Concordance the word "image" was translated from the Hebrew word "**Tselem**" which means *a phantom, illusion, resemblance and representative* figure. Upon careful analysis of this word and its' definition, you will notice that there are two words in the definition of the Hebrew word for image that gives us a clue as to the image that God shared with man.

Since God is a Spirit and therefore invisible to the human eye, He gave this same attribute to man so that man also was created primarily as a spiritual being in the image of God. The words *"phantom"* and *"illusion"* in the definition of the Hebrew word for image speaks of objects that are invisible and not tangible. So the image that God gave to man was invisible, immaterial and intangible. In view of this, I can safely say that the image of God is the spiritual nature that God breathed into man; the immortal part of man or the inner man.

Then God also created man after His likeness. Notice, it did not say that God created man "*in His likeness*" but rather "*after His likeness*". This means that the image of God is different from the likeness of God. According to the Strong's Concordance, the word "*likeness*" was translated from the Hebrew word "**dmuwth**" which is pronounced as "**demooth**". This word means *resemblance; concretely, model, shape, fashion* or *similitude*. All these words denote something visible and tangible with form or shape. When you compare the meanings of the two words, it becomes obvious that the words "**Tselem**" and "**Dmuwth**" do not mean the same. "**Tselem**" is referring to the invisibility of a Deity with no physical or material substance and the "**Dmuwth**" is referring to the shape and form of a Deity which was the template by which another being was fashioned after the similitude of an original Deity. However, both definitions used the word "*resemblance*" which was used in two different ways. The word "*image*" refers to the spiritual resemblance between God and man whilst

"*likeness*" refers to the resemblance in shape, form and anatomy. Although, God is a Spirit yet He has a spiritual body. The bible tells us in 1 Corinthians 15:44 "*...There is a natural body, and there is a spiritual body.*"

All throughout scripture, the bible describes God as having eyes, ears, nose, mouth, hands and feet. The bible says in Psalm 34:15 "*The EYES of the Lord are upon the righteous, and his EARS are open unto their cry*" This verse is saying that God has eyes and ears. It is also written in 2 Samuel 22:9-10 "*There went up a smoke out of his NOSTRILS, and fire out of his MOUTH devoured: coals were kindled by it. He bowed the heavens also, and came down; and darkness was under his FEET*". From this verse also, we are informed that the Almighty God has a nose, mouth and feet.

Even though God is a Spirit and therefore invisible, yet He has a spiritual body. This truth becomes very evident when we look at the creation account of man in the beginning. In Genesis 1:26, God created the spirit of man and then in chapter 2:7, He formed, shaped and fashioned the physical body of man out of the dust of the ground after his likeness. You will agree with me that the spirit of man which was in the image of God, was not derived from the dust of the ground but rather the physical body of man was fashioned from the dust of the ground after the likeness and similitude of God. He then, breathed the spirit that was created in Genesis1:26 into the formed body of man and man became a living soul. The bible says *"And the Lord God... breathed into his nostrils the BREATH of life"*(Gen 2:7) The Hebrew word translated as *"Breath"* in this verse is *"Nshamah"* and in English it is the same as the word "spirit". So God breathed into the nostrils of man the spirit of life and man became a living soul. This means that every spiritual being has a soul. These were the two separate accounts about the creation of man. One dealt with the spiritual aspect of man and the other the physical aspect or the body of man.

So God created man in His image as a spiritual being but gave him a physical body that was formed out of the dust of the ground and concretely fashioned like the spiritual body of God. God has hands so He gave man hands; He has eyes so He gave man eyes; He has ears so He gave man ears. He created man after His likeness, shape and form. The image of God is His spiritual nature which He shared with man. The Lord God said in Genesis 6:3 that *"My Spirit shall not always strive with man (man's spirit), for that he also is flesh "* According to this verse, The Lord God acknowledged the complex nature of man as a being that operates on three unique levels of existence namely; spiritual, mental and physical.

Since man is a spirit just like God, he can relate and strive with God in the spirit. He can also function in the physical realm and relate to his environment whilst simultaneously interacting with his fellow man. This characteristic of man was evident in the beginning when Adam and Eve were able to communicate with one another and at the same time relate to God and the devil. He also related to his environment by keeping the garden and naming all the animals. Indeed, we are fearfully and wonderfully made.

Now, let us look closely at the image of God in man and some of the communicable attributes HE shared with man in the spirit.

There are several attributes but I have selected only five to briefly discuss in this chapter. The attributes of God in man are:

THE POWER TO THINK AND REASON

The mental power given by God to men to form judgments, draw conclusions, and make inferences is a typical attribute of God, which He shared with man. Our ability to think, understand, and form judgments is God-given and it is part of His image and characteristic He shared with man. These are spiritual, intangible attributes and through these abilities, God can reason with man and man with God. The bible says in Job 13:3 *"...and I desire to reason with God"* In this scripture, Job desired to reason with God just like he would reason with his fellow man. He desired to have an intelligent conversation with God. You can only reason with your kind. Also in the book of Isaiah 1:18, God invited Isaiah to come so that they can reason together. It says *"Come now, and let us reason together, saith the Lord"*.

Our ability to reason, ponder, contemplate and think is a gift from God. Man can copy and imitate the divine thoughts of God to guide and guard him in all his ways. *"For my thoughts are not your thoughts, neither are your ways my ways, saith the LORD...For as the heavens are higher than the earth, so are my ways higher than your ways, and my thoughts than your thoughts.* According to this scripture, the thoughts of God are higher in wisdom than the thoughts of men. So God is the original Thinker and He has given onto man the ability to also think.

The human mind is so powerful that it plays an important role in achieving all kinds of success in our daily endeavors. Human intelligence is unequal to none of the created beings found in the animal kingdom. We ponder curiously the meaning of our existence, the sheer significance of our actions and the prospects of our destiny. The ability to think sets humans apart from all living creatures on earth. God created man in such a way that a man's thought is the steering wheel, which determines the direction of his life.

God gave this power to man so that he can rule over his environment and all living creatures on the face of the earth. HE created man in such a way that his thought shapes his life. A man is the sum total of what he thinks. Whatsoever the human mind can imagine and conceive, it can achieve. If a man thinks he cannot succeed, he can't but if he thinks he can, then he can. God, the creator of the heavens and the earth, said in Genesis 11:6 *"nothing will be restrained from them (men), which they have IMAGINED to do"*. Did you hear that! Anything that you can imagine, you can achieve.

Whatsoever the mind can imagine, it can achieve without any restraints from anybody except himself. God created the human mind in such a way that it can achieve whatever it can imagine and conceive. In the Darby translation of the bible, the same verse (Genesis 11:6) is rendered as *"and now will they be hindered in nothing that they meditate doing"*. God said anything that a man thinks about and imagine or meditate continually can be achieved and no one can prevent him from doing so, not even God can prevent it. This is a God-given power to every man which is the ability to manifest his own reality. Whatever you envision to accomplish and think about continually, can never be restrained from you as long as you back up your imagination, thought and desire with action.

A man can be whatever he chooses to be without any restraints except the ones that he places upon himself. Other people can restrain you temporarily but you are the only one who can restrain yourself permanently. This is how God created man. Reality is basically the reflection of our thoughts. The bible says in proverbs 23:7 *"As a man thinks in his heart, so is he"*. Through the thoughts in our minds, we determine our own increase by the choices we make.

Many great men in past generations had profound understanding of the power of their thoughts. Albert Einstein once said *"The world we have created is a product of our thinking; and it cannot be changed without changing our thinking"*. The mind is the decisive factor in your life. What you think affects your emotions, your choices, your behavior and your total well-being. Your dominant thoughts also forms your belief system. Belief is a thought, which has been accepted as true in the mind. Belief simply means accepting something as true. The thought accepted as truth and held consciously in the mind continually, will mysteriously execute itself automatically without any input from you. Belief is very powerful indeed. The thoughts you hold as true are mighty and strong in their effect. The power of thoughts that had been believed or accepted as truth is virtually unlimited.

We give power to the thoughts we believe. Jesus said in Mark 9:23 *"If thou canst believe, all things are possible to him that believeth"* This means, we give life to our beliefs and we cause them to have effect in our life. We experience our beliefs through manifestation. We, spiritual beings, have innate power through the mind and a Godgiven ability to literally create physical reality with our thoughts. Jesus again said in Mathew 9:29 *"...According to your faith be it unto you"*. According to this verse, we create what we truly and deeply believe. One of the greatest abilities God has given to man is the ability to believe. So where do beliefs come from?

Basically, they come from indoctrination which took place when we were children. Beliefs are passed on through parents, family members, school teachers, peer groups and other sources. Some of these beliefs were accepted as truths initially when we heard them even though there were no proofs to support them. Some of our beliefs were acquired through experiences in life. Therefore, the ability to think and accept our thoughts as truth and believe them, is one of the attributes God gave to man as part of His image. All things are possible to him that believes. The human mind is so powerful that it can create almost anything that it conceives as long as it's within our domain which God entrusted to men on earth which is to rule, dominate, subdue and replenish. Use your God-given ability and think continually on what you aspire to do and eventually it will manifest.

CREATIVITY

We were created in the image of God; and since God is creative; therefore we are also creative just like Him and we become more like God when we live and think creatively. Human beings have creative power. The way God created the earth of old have been transformed somewhat by man to suit his needs. Through man's creative ideas, many inventions have been made to enhance the living conditions of man and his environment. We have power to create, first of all, with our words. Just as God created all things with his words, so also He have given to us the ability to create our own world with our words. Our words create our world and they are the most powerful forces in our lives. In them is the power to bless, to heal, to prosper, to overcome, and in them is the power to curse, to make sick, to impoverish, or to defeat. What many people don't realize is that just as God has set in motion laws that govern the physical world we live in, He has also set into motion spiritual laws that govern the spiritual world. One of these spiritual laws is that words are the activating forces in the unseen world. Words are like spiritual containers delivering and manifesting the very things they carry and describe. Everything that is visible, originated from the invisible. So if you want to change the things which are seen, you first have to change them from the unseen world. The creative power of words is one of the most important laws that govern the spiritual realm. Words are powerful forces! They are carriers of either faith or unbelief, optimism or pessimism, life or death.

The bible says in proverbs 18:21 *"**Death and life are in the power of the tongue: and they that love it shall eat the fruit thereof.** As the above verse indicates, words have the power to produce life or death. If we want to receive the best that God has for us in this life and in the life to come, we must learn to use our words wisely. In the spiritual realm, the laws of faith and confession have been established by God and since man is primarily a spirit, he is bound to operate by these laws of faith and confession. Words are also seeds as Jesus said in the parable of the sower and they are meant to be planted in the creative ground of our hearts. When words are planted through repetition in the fertile ground of your heart or subconscious mind, and meditated upon continually with faith, it reproduces after its' kind. In fact, whatever is in a seed must produce after its own kind. For example, an apple seed will produce an apple tree with fruits, an acorn will produce an oak tree and an orange seed will produce orange tree with fruits. Likewise, the word of God will produce the kingdom of God within you. Since the kingdom of God is within you, the seed of the word of God has to be planted upon the fertile ground of your subconscious mind and nurtured continually in order for it to produce the kingdom blessings. This principle is especially true where words in general are concerned. Words are spiritual containers and manufacturers of things incubated in the heart. Jesus said; *"If ye had faith as a grain of mustard seed, ye might SAY..."* Jesus declared that words of faith spoken out of our mouths are like mustard seeds impregnated with spiritual DNA to produce mustard plants. When the creative power embedded in words come in contact with the creative medium of the heart or subconscious mind, it reproduces after its kind. Just as the encoded DNA in a seed is only released when planted in a fertile ground, so also the creative power of our words are released when they are planted in our subconscious mind through repeated declaration which is emotionalized. This is the message of Jesus in the parables in Mark chapter 4.

Words are powerful forces which can be positive or negative. The bible says *"Pleasant words are like a honeycomb, sweetness to the soul and health to the bones."* According to this scripture, a situation can worsen when you speak negatively about it. By the same token, when you speak positive words, the same situation will change for the better. This is because words are like the rudder of a ship. Once spoken, they begin to steer your life in a specific direction. The bible says in proverbs 21:23 *"He who guards his mouth and his tongue keeps himself from troubles."* The person who guards his mouth by choosing his words carefully always keeps himself from troubles.

Words are more than a means of communication, they can shape our beliefs, behaviors, feelings and ultimately our actions. Words that are filled with faith will bring you victory and words that are filled with fear will bring you defeat. It is written in Psalm 34:13

*"**Keep your tongue from evil, and your lips from speaking guile. Depart from evil, and do good; seek peace, and pursue it**"* Have you ever considered the power that God has placed in the spoken word? By them God created the whole world and the heavens. By them He created mankind; male and female. With Words He created the mountains and the waters and divided them. By His word He hanged the sun, moon and stars on nothing and sustains them by the word of His power. These celestial bodies are still suspended in space by His word. God, in His wisdom, gave this same creative ability to man to enable him to create his own world with his words. These words are meant to be planted in the hearts or subconscious minds of men to create their desires by continually repeating these words through self-talk.

When these incubated or repeatedly thought about words are spoken with deep convictions and belief, tremendous things happen. The lame walk, the blind see and the dumb speaks.

Secondly, we have creativity in our actions. Creativity is the ability to **IMAGINE** new things and bring them from the abstract into manifestation. Everything you see around you came from somebody's imagination. Creativity can be positive or negative irrespective of your religious beliefs and it is the product of your imagination. God told Adam in the beginning to name all the animals and whatever Adam called them became their name. The bible says in Genesis 2:19 " ***And out of the ground the Lord God formed every beast of the field, and every fowl of the air; and brought them unto Adam to see what he would call them: and whatsoever Adam called every living creature, that was the name thereof.*** " This was the first intelligent and creative act by man as recorded in the bible. Adam demonstrated his creative ability when he gave names to all the different species of animals on the face of the earth. This very creative ability has been given to all men to utilize in order to create our environment. The medium or agent of our creativity is the heart which is also known as the subconscious mind.

God, afterward, placed Adam in the garden and gave him work to do. The assignment of keeping the garden also involved thinking, planning and decision making, all of which are aspects of the creative process. When mankind started populating the earth, the building of cities and agricultural activities became the hallmark of man's creativity. We saw the rise of agriculture, making of tools to till the land and also invention of musical instruments as evidence of man's creativity. Genesis 4:21-22 says "*... he was the father of all those who play the lyre and pipe (musical instruments). Zillah bore Tubal-cain; he was the forger (maker) of all [cutting] instruments of bronze and iron...*".

Men created musical instruments and agricultural tools to entertain and sustain them respectively. All these activities indicated that men began to exercise the creative powers embedded within them. Since God is creative, He also gave onto man creative ability in their heart. God also gave onto Noah the blueprint to invent an ark which was borne out of sheer creativity.

Also, in Exodus 31:1-6 " *And the Lord spake unto Moses, saying, see, I have called by name Bezaleel the son of Uri, the son of Hur, of the tribe of Judah: And I have filled him with the spirit of God, in wisdom, and in understanding, and in knowledge, and in all manner of workmanship, (why?) to DEVISE cunning works, to work in gold, and in silver, and in brass, and in cutting of stones, to set them, and in carving of timber, to work in all manner of workmanship. And I, behold, I have given with him Aholiab, the son of Ahisamach, of the tribe of Dan: and in the HEARTS of all that are wise hearted I have put wisdom, that they may MAKE (CREATIVELY) all that I have commanded thee;*"

When God commanded Moses to build the tabernacle in the wilderness, He put special abilities in the hearts of certain craftsmen to create the patterns of the furniture and the physical layout of the Tabernacle, which God had given to Moses. So Moses would receive the descriptions from God and then instruct the craftsmen to make the furniture according to the specifications from Moses. This also reinforced the truth that all creativity comes from God and He freely gives to whosoever He chooses to accomplish His purpose. Every individual has been equipped with the seeds of words, which are meant to be planted in their hearts to create their own realities. This is exactly what our Lord Jesus

Christ was talking about in the parables in Mark 4. You have been given the seed and the spiritual ground where the seed is intended to be sown is within you. The creative power of your subconscious mind is within you. In other words, the kingdom of God is within you.

THE ABILITY TO COMMUNICATE THROUGH ARTICULATED SPEECH

Our ability to speak or the gift of speech is also one of the attributes of the image of God that we inherited. As creatures who have been endowed with minds and the ability to think, speech therefore becomes imperative to express our thoughts in words so that we can be understood. Without the power of speech, it would have been very difficult to communicate with God. The relationship or compatibility which He sought with man would not have been possible without the ability to speak and express ourselves. We cannot worship God without articulating our thoughts, emotions, beliefs and convictions to Him. We could not have been able to interact with God if we did not have the ability to speak. Speech has, therefore, been the key to our relationship with God and also to our fellow men.

The ability to speak promotes interpersonal relationships and creates bonds between people, families, tribes and groups. In Shakespeare's **Macbeth**, King Duncan, when he heard the report of execution of the treacherous Thane of Cawdor, said, "***There's no art to find the mind's construction in the face: He was a gentleman on whom I built an absolute trust***." By this statement, King Duncan, meant that there is no skill or craft that can enable anyone to look at a person's face and see what is going on in that person's mind. The Thane of Cawdor seemed to be so honest that King Duncan thought he could trust him absolutely; but unfortunately he was wrong in his trust. Since we cannot read a person's mind from his face, we communicate with people to know what is in their mind. Communication declares our thoughts and intentions to others.

250

All through scripture, God continually spoke at diverse times through the prophets to the children of Israel to make His intentions and plans known to them. The bible says in Hebrews chapter 1:1-2 *"In the past God SPOKE to our people through the prophets. He SPOKE to them many times and in many different ways. And now in these last days, God has SPOKEN to us again through his Son"* Through the prophets, God spoke in times past to our fathers to make His thoughts and intents known to them.

God has given this power to man so as to forge a relationship with him. Through speech, we worship God, through speech we praise and thank Him. We are able to pray to Him; because of the power of speech and it is part of the image of God, which he imparted to man so as to foster an unforced relationship between them.

A man can bless or curse his fellow man by speaking good things about them or evil things about them. The bible says proverbs 12:18 *"There are those who speak rashly, like the piercing of a sword (TO HURT OTHERS EMOTIONALLY), but the tongue of the wise brings healing (COMFORT).AMP (Emphasis mine).* There is a saying that sticks and stones can hurt me but words cannot. This saying is absolutely untrue, because words have the power to hurt you deeper and leave a permanent scar with lingering effects than physical objects, if you permit it.

SELF-CONSCIOUSNESS

This simply means that man has the ability to recognize the sum total of his physical, mental, emotional, and social characteristics of himself. Man was created to be aware of his Creator, his environment, his feelings, his thoughts and was also endowed with the ability to interact with other human beings. We were designed to be distinguishably unique in our own special way and every man strives to attain their own unique identity. Nobody wants to be like somebody else; but themselves. There are no two people alike among all the people in the world. Everyman is completely different from his fellow man; because we all have unique DNA molecules which are different from one another.

God created man to be conscious of himself. Just as God is tri-une and self-conscious, so also was man created as a tri-une being. Man is originally an eternal spiritual being, who possesses a soul and dwells in a physical body. 1 Thessalonians 5:23 says "… *and I pray God your whole SPIRIT and SOUL and BODY be preserved blameless unto the coming of our Lord Jesus Christ*" .This scripture confirms the truth about the tri-une nature of man. So, by the faculty of his spirit, man communicates and relates to God who is also a Spirit. By the faculty of his soul, man is aware of his own personality which enables him to interact with other men like himself and finally, by the faculty of his physical body, he relates to his physical environment through his five senses.

The spirit of man also has three faculties namely; communion, conscience and intuition. It is only through the faculty of communion that man communes with God in prayer, praise and worship. Then the faculty of the conscience is the "inner policeman" or moral checker which approves, accuses or excuses man in every deed or action of his life. The bible says in the book of Romans 2:15 " …*Which shew the work of the law written in their hearts, their conscience also bearing witness, and their thoughts the mean while ACCUSING or else EXCUSING one another;)* . The conscience comprises the moral code written upon the heart of every human being upon the face of the earth. In every culture, irrespective of their religious beliefs and knowledge, there are some universal moral codes written upon their hearts that restrains them from doing certain things. For example, murder is wrong in every society whether they know about the Ten Commandments or not. By the faculty of the conscience, man knows what is right or wrong. This is an inherent quality available to every man through his human spirit.

The faculty of intuition, which the bible calls discernment, is the part of the human spirit through which we know things beyond our senses. Intuition is the pure, untaught, non-inferential knowledge which a person perceives independent of any reasoning process. When this faculty is in operation, some people usually use the expression "something told me from within" thus attributing their knowledge to an unknown source from within. Some call it the "gut feeling" and others call it "instinct" or "hunch"; but no matter what you call this innate human characteristic, it is part of the image man received from God. This is the still small voice in every man and these three faculties make up the human spirit.

The human soul is also made of three faculties namely; volition (will), intellect and emotion. The intellect comprises the conscious and the subconscious mind and in these are the three sub-compartments namely memory, reasoning and imagination. The memory deals with events in the past and the imagination deals with events and things in the future. These two are resident in the subconscious mind but the reasoning ability is the function of the conscious mind, which deals with present situations. The conscious mind is your physical mind, which receives most of its information from the five physical senses.

The subconscious mind, however, is the spiritual mind and it is the interface between God, the human spirit and his soul. When God communicates spiritual information to the human spirit (intuitively), it is the subconscious mind that first receives the information from the human spirit before it is passed on to the conscious mind. The faculty of volition (will) is also another function of the conscious mind whereby choices are made in everyday life circumstances. Finally, the faculty of emotions is also a function of the subconscious mind.

Emotions, however, are reactive secondary effects and responses of the subconscious mind to the activities of the conscious mind. This means that your thoughts and decisions always creates your emotions. The bible says in the book of Psalms 118:24 that "*This is the day which the Lord hath made; we WILL rejoice and be glad in it*" This scriptural verse clearly indicates that emotions are choices or decisions we consciously make. David said, this is the day the Lord have made and so we will rejoice and be glad in it. They chose to rejoice. David and his men chose to be glad and rejoice in the day the Lord has made regardless of the circumstances and happenings around them.

In life, whatever happens to you, is not as important as your reaction to what have happened. Your attitude towards what have happened is very crucial. Apostle James said it better in James 1:2 " *My brethren, count it all joy when ye fall into divers temptations"* Take note that, James did not say " it is all joy when you fall into diverse temptations" but rather he said to consider it, reckon it, count it or look at it as joy. This means that your attitude towards whatever happens to you is very important and it's a decision, which is absolutely in your power. This is divine truth declared throughout scripture.

My favorite one of them all is what the prophet Habakkuk proclaimed to conclude his powerful book in Habakkuk 3: 17-19 which says, *"Although the fig tree shall not blossom, neither shall fruit be in the vines; the labor of the olive shall fail, and the fields shall yield no meat; the flock shall be cut off from the fold, and there shall be no herd in the stalls: Yet I WILL rejoice in the Lord, I WILL joy in the God of my salvation. The Lord God is my strength, and he will make my feet like hinds' feet, and he will make me to walk upon mine high places"*. This man chose to rejoice in the Lord irrespective of the happenings around him. He did not allow the circumstances around him, which he consciously perceived to dictate how he feels but instead, he made a decision and chose to rejoice. Many a time, people allow their circumstances to mold them into all kinds of emotions; but if they apply the truths in the scriptures, they will always master the things that come their way.

Finally, the human body is also made of three main substances namely; flesh, bones and blood. The blood is the life-line of both the flesh and bones. Without the blood, the physical body will die. The blood is the carrier of oxygen (breath or spirit) to all parts of the physical body. A person can survive about four to five weeks without food and a few days without water; but a person cannot survive for a few minutes without oxygen. The preceding statement magnifies the importance of oxygen for our sustenance. Oxygen is the physical manifestation of life in a person and it is a byproduct of photosynthesis, which is a very vital phenomenon for the sustenance of all life on planet earth. In the physical body, these two elements (blood and oxygen) are inseparable and provide life to the body. So man's ability to know himself is also an attribute, which he received from God as part of HIS image or as part of his immortal nature. The spirit and soul are eternal beings. Even after physical death, when the spirit and soul leaves the physical body, a man's consciousness of self and environment will still be present.

This truth is evident in a story Jesus taught in the gospel according to St Luke 16:1920,22-23 " *There was a certain rich man, which was clothed in purple and fine linen, and fared sumptuously every day: And there was a certain beggar named Lazarus, which was laid at his gate, full of sores,...And it came to pass, that the beggar died, and was carried by the angels into Abraham's bosom: the rich man also died, and was buried; And in hell he lift up his eyes, being in torments, and seeth Abraham afar off, and Lazarus in his bosom"* . In this story, the rich man saw and recognized Abraham and Lazarus in the spiritual realm. He also acknowledged his environment as an unfavorable condition which is not desirable. So, man's consciousness will transcend this physical world of ours into eternity where we will recognize our family, friends, loved ones and leaders. God has placed something precious in you waiting patiently to be recognized and used. As the bible says in 2 Corinthians 4:7 "*But we have this treasure in earthen vessels*" You are a carrier of a tremendous treasure in the earthen vessel of your physical body, so appropriate it to the best of your ability.

SELF-DETERMINATION

Self-determination is also a communicable attribute of God which HE shared with man. It refers to a characteristic of a person that enables him to make choices and decisions based on his own preferences and interests, to monitor and regulate his own actions and to be goal-oriented and self-directing. It means that man has been given the power to determine his own increase based upon his decision to appropriate the resources available to him. The bible says in Genesis 1:28-29 "*And God blessed them, and God said unto them, be fruitful, and multiply, and replenish the earth, and subdue it: and have dominion over the fish of the sea, and over the fowl of the air, and over every living thing that moveth upon the earth. And God said, Behold, I have given you every herb bearing seed, which is upon the face of all the earth, and every tree, in the which is the fruit of a tree yielding seed; to you it shall be for meat"* . From this scripture, we notice that God gave onto man the ability to rule, dominate, and exercise his authoritative power over himself and over all creation.

There was a five-fold mandate given to man to exercise authority on earth. Man was commanded to be fruitful, multiply, replenish the earth, subdue the earth and have dominion over all created beings on earth. All these mandates were in direct relationship to his environment. He is supposed to be fruitful and productive by planting the physical seed and multiply numerically through procreation or childbearing. He is mandated to populate the earth through replenishment. This means that if man fails to procreate, God is not going to re-create a new set of people to populate the earth. He is also mandated to subdue the earth by harnessing its' vast resources to better improve his living conditions. For example, man has built ships to sail over the vast seas, airplanes to fly in the firmaments and dammed rivers to generate electricity to light up his surroundings.

Man has built bridges to span miles over seas and water bodies all throughout the earth. All these activities are man's methods of subduing the earth. He is supposed to dominate all living creatures to meet whatever need he may find himself to desire. Horses have been tamed and domesticated to be our means of transportation. Oxen have been employed for agricultural endeavors. Dogs have become man's best friend and companion. However, it is very important to take note of the fact that, God did not give man power over his fellow man; but over all other created beings.

In order to understand the implication of this commandment, we have to go back to the same chapter of Genesis 1 and the verse of 26 which reads *"And God said, Let us*

make man in our image, after our likeness: and LET THEM HAVE DOMINION

over the fish of the sea, and over the fowl of the air, and over the cattle, and over all the earth, and over every creeping thing that

creepeth upon the earth. This verse is simply saying that God decided to create man in HIS own image and gave the rulership of the created earth entirely onto man. So, as far as the earth is concerned, God has elected man to be the ruler. Everything that happens on earth is in the controlling hands of man.

Whatsoever man chooses to do on earth is already approved by God as long as it does not violate his fellow man. If man decides not to exercise his authority on earth, the whole earth will lay dormant, uncultivated and unfruitful. God has already given to man the seed and the earth in which he is to plant the seed in order to be fruitful and productive. He has also given to man a creative heart that will receive any seed that he may choose to plant in it to determine his own increase. It is, therefore, in the power of man to cultivate both the physical and the spiritual ground to yield fruit onto him. Everything that man needs to fulfill this mandate is already provided by God so there is no excuse.

HE has also given to man the ability to multiply and procreate through biological reproduction. By virtue of the duality of mankind, God ensured procreation through all generations until the Second Advent of Christ. The male gender is the seed carrier and the female is the recipient of the seed, which will eventually produce the fruit of the womb. Moreover, every human being has been endowed with a duality of inherent powers that enables them to create their own world from within based upon their preferences. Man is free to determine his own increase by the choices he makes concerning the word of God. When He chooses to consciously plant the word of God in the subconscious mind, it will reproduce based on the kind of seed sown. This means the subconscious mind is a powerful creative medium that creates our reality either by our own design willingly or by default. It also means therefore that, the conscious mind is the gardener and the subconscious mind is the ground, which needs to be cultivated to produce whatever a man needs. When these two work in harmony and in agreement, all things become possible. The bible says "*if two shall agree here on earth…*" When the mind and the heart are in agreement, great things are given birth to.

Every seed that God created has a specific ground where it is ordained to grow. The seed of a man can only grow in the womb of a woman. The natural seed can only grow in a fertile soil and also the word of God which is an incorruptible seed can only grow in the hearts of men or subconscious mind. The word of God will produce the kingdom of God in the hearts of men and cause them to be fruitful. Jesus said in the gospel according to St John 15:5 *"Abide in me, and I in you. As the branch cannot bear fruit of itself, except it abide in the vine; no more can ye, except ye abide in me. I am the vine, ye are the branches: He that abideth in me, and I in him, the same bringeth forth much fruit: for without me ye can do nothing.* The partnership between God and man also equips us for greater works. This is the message of Jesus when He spoke about the three parables in Mark chapter four. The spiritual photosynthesis of the incorruptible seed coupled with the creative medium of the heart or subconscious mind was the theme of His address.

There is a God-given power in the inside of you waiting to be awakened. Those that have discovered this power have achieved great things in their various fields of life. Discovery of this power would not give you instant success; but through diligent adherence to its laws of operation, you will eventually reap the benefits of this powerful medium within you. The universal law of cause and effect or seedtime and harvest, as the bible calls it, is at work in all of creation and it starts from within you. There is an effect to every cause, and every cause is the root of its effect.

By understanding through meditation backed by faith with action, every desire of your heart can be achieved when you put into practice what Jesus taught us. Finally remember that, what you think, you speak; what you speak, you believe; what you believe, you receive. Until you believe the truth in your heart, it is just information in your mind. Therefore, plant the seed of truth in your conscious mind through memorization and meditate on it continually until the truth sinks into your subconscious mind, where it will take root and bear fruit in your life. This principle can be applied to every desire of your heart. The kingdom of God is within   you.

Made in the USA
Lexington, KY
19 January 2018